THE
FAT MAN
AND
INFINITY

And Other Writings

THE
FAT MAN
AND
INFINITY

And Other Writings

António Lobo Antunes

Translated with an Introduction by
MARGARET JULL COSTA

W. W. NORTON & COMPANY
New York | *London*

Selections originally published in Portuguese in *Livro de Crónicas*
and *Segundo Livro de Crónicas*

The Portuguese Institute for Book and Libraries supported this book.

For information about permission to reproduce selections from this book,
write to Permissions, W. W. Norton & Company, Inc.,
500 Fifth Avenue, New York, NY 10110

For information about special discounts for bulk purchases, please contact
W. W. Norton Special Sales at specialsales@wwnorton.com or 800-233-4830

Manufacturing by Courier Westford
Book design by JAM Design
Production manager: Devon Zahn

Library of Congress Cataloging-in-Publication Data

Antunes, António Lobo, 1942–
[Livro de crónicas. English. Selections]
The fat man and infinity and other writings / António Lobo Antunes ;
translated with an introduction by Margaret Jull Costa.—1st ed.
p. cm.
ISBN 978-0-393-06198-7 (hardcover)
I. Costa, Margaret Jull. II. Antunes, António Lobo, 1942– Segundo livro de crónicas.
English. Selections. III. Segundo livro de crónicas. English. Selections. IV. Title.
PQ9263.N77L5813 2009
869.4'42—dc22

2008041551

W. W. Norton & Company, Inc.
500 Fifth Avenue, New York, N.Y. 10110
www.wwnorton.com

W. W. Norton & Company Ltd.
Castle House, 75/76 Wells Street, London W1T 3QT

1 2 3 4 5 6 7 8 9 0

To the memory of my Grandfather
António Lobo Antunes
(1889–1960)
whom I greatly miss

———————

For Margarida da Beira Cardoso
de Melo Machado de Almeida Lima
my beloved Grandmother

CONTENTS

PART II: PORTRAIT OF THE ARTIST

PART III: *MA PETITE EXISTENCE*: **STORIES**

Map by Joe Lops and Hannah Wood.

INTRODUCTION

by the Translator

A ntónio Lobo Antunes was born in Benfica, then a suburb of
Lisbon, in 1942, the oldest of six brothers. His sole ambition,
from the age of seven, was to be a writer, but he was diverted from
this path by his father, a professor of neurology, who counseled
him to study medicine instead—hoping, perhaps, to save his eldest
son from what he imagined would be an impecunious future. The
young António took his father's advice and chose psychiatry, which,
it seemed to him, was the branch of medicine most closely allied to
literature. When he graduated in 1969, he was almost immediately
called up to do his military service in Angola, which was, at the
time, still a Portuguese colony and where the Portuguese Army
was embroiled in an increasingly hopeless war against indigenous
independence movements.

As a medical graduate, Lobo Antunes was often called on to
deliver babies (when the local midwives ran into problems) and to
perform amputations (with the aid of a quartermaster who hated
the sight of blood but was able to read the instructions in the surgi-
cal manual to the apprentice surgeon). He writes:

> The loveliest thing I've ever seen was Angola, and despite the
> poverty and the horror of the war, I still love her with a love that
> does not die. I love the smell and I love the people. The moments
> when I have perhaps been closest to what is commonly called
> happiness occurred when I was delivering a baby. . . .

. . .

HIS Angolan experiences—the horror, chaos, injustice, and camaraderie—marked him deeply and filled his early novels, *Memória de Elefante* [*Elephant Memory*] and *Os Cus de Judas* [*South of Nowhere*], for which he found a publisher in 1979, six years after his return from Africa. Working as a poorly paid intern in various Lisbon hospitals, he wrote in his spare time, usually late at night and into the early hours. Only in 1985 did he become a full-time writer, although he continued to treat psychiatric patients at the Hospital Miguel Bombarda, in order, he says, not to feel that he himself was mad. When engaged in a novel, he still spends fifteen hours a day immersed in his writing. His novels are long, seamless, and polyphonic, with many voices jockeying to have their say. Miraculously, out of what can seem at first like an incomprehensible hubbub, there emerge complex characters, a powerful sense of place, and the thread of a gripping story.

The pieces collected in this book are a selection from the weekly or biweekly columns or *crónicas* that Lobo Antunes has written over the years for various publications, notably the Portuguese newspaper *O Público*. He has always spoken of these pieces rather dismissively, as *divertissements* written purely to earn a little money and which gave him no pleasure. He did, in fact, stop writing them for a while because he felt they were a distraction from his novels, and he was earning enough from royalties and the sale of translation rights, but then he returned to them, feeling that they acted as a kind of diary, parallel to the novels. "In [the *crónicas*]," he has said, "I can say what I want, whereas in the books, I say what they want to say." There are now three Portuguese volumes of these collected *crónicas,* and they have enjoyed the kind of popular success his novels never have; his novels are seen to be—and are—difficult, whereas the constraint of writing only 600 to 800 words forces him to rein in his expansive novelistic sensibility, and the result is these intense, evocative little gems of memoir, reflection, and fiction. Part of the pleasure of reading the *crónicas* week by week, or every other week, is that one never knows what he will write about next, or how, and in making this selection, drawn from the first two *Livros de crónicas*, I have, I hope, preserved a sense of the wonderfully random and serendipitous nature of Lobo Antunes's imagination.

Just a word about the term *crónica*. It is the normal Portuguese word for such newspaper or magazine opinion pieces or columns, but it is also a word that harks back to the chroniclers appointed by the kings of fifteenth- and sixteenth-century Portugal to record the important events of their respective reigns. One of the most famous, Fernão Lopes, wrote that he was not concerned with the beauty of his writing but rather in setting down the naked truth. With Lobo Antunes we get both beauty and truth, and these *crónicas* could be seen as a modern-day chronicle of Portugal's recent past and present seen through the eyes of a master fiction writer.

He chronicles, for example, his own childhood, effortlessly (re)capturing the child's view of adults—their legs forming a palisade under the lunch table, the way they slip into French whenever there's anything they don't want him to understand, their strange worship of paintings in museums when, to him, the silver spittoons are the only real works of art. These pieces, while suffused with humor and affection, are also filled with the idea of childhood as a lost realm, and, more important, the sense of an irretrievable loss of security and love. He remembers the weight of his grandfather's hand on his shoulder and his feeling "that as long as I was with him nothing bad, nothing sad, nothing nasty could ever happen to me because my grandfather wouldn't allow it."

CHILDHOOD, he suspects, lives on in some kind of parallel universe, in which he is still a fair-haired boy racing across the yard with marbles in his pants pocket. "Having your childhood stuck in your throat," he writes, "is worse than a fishbone: you can eat as much bread as you like, but it won't go down."

This "paradise" existed, however, in the prim, hypocritical, class-riven, and priest-ridden Portugal of the dictator Salazar. Young António went to a different school from his friend Pedro because he lived in a house with six rooms and Pedro in a house with only two; Sunday mass for the maids was at 7 a.m., while mass for the masters and mistresses was at noon; when gifts were given at Christmas, the servants lined up like serfs, then returned to the "catacombs of the kitchen"; the priests who were invited into the family home would question him about his chastity (a word he didn't know) while stroking his knees; his mother tried to lure him away from the cook's physical charms by opening an account for him at a local bakery. The child-adult is not deceived.

These memoirs, passed through the filter of an adult who has known war and pain and loss, bear witness to that imperfect past and to the people whom he loved and who have gone into the dark, and who would otherwise continue to exist only as long as he and his memory exist. In the same way, the names of Lisbon's *bairros* [districts] and its streets—Benfica, Amadora, Bairro Alto, Campo de Ourique, Rossio, Laranjeiras, etc.—become a secular litany celebrating and commemorating the city in which he was born and brought up and where he still lives.

In the short stories, collected here under the title *Ma Petite Existence*, he has created an extraordinary cross section of Lisbon losers who, given a voice, speak with painful honesty, often addressing not the reader but a silent, unresponsive "other"—an absent wife, a departing lover, a dead husband. His themes, Lobo Antunes has said, have always been "loneliness, death, as well as life, of course, then love or its absence, and, more and more now, tenderness," and what is so impressive and so moving about these chronicles of modern life is the sheer variety of human experience imagined and described and the rare blend of unflinching honesty, compassion, and black humor with which they are written.

Lobo Antunes has often remarked in interviews that his original ambition was to be a poet. Feeling that he lacked the necessary talent, however, he turned to novels instead, yet his prose is infused with poetry—a colonel is described as looking like a sharp breeze that has run out of puff; the invisible sea creaks like the rusty hinge of a cradle; surprise grips someone's shoulders like a borrowed jacket; a faded beauty's eyelashes are as long as cockroach legs; a voluptuous Greek woman has amphora hips. As the best poets do, he transforms and subverts language. One of the pleasures and challenges of translating his prose lies precisely in trying to keep that quirkiness and freshness, and in allowing his idiosyncratic way with punctuation and, occasionally, grammar, to disrupt the "proper" English rules without the translation merely sounding raw and inept. There is something very exhilarating about translating a writer whose every sentence is a surprise. Indeed, it is, I think, the combination of Lobo Antunes's vivid, poetic prose and the sense of teeming life remembered, reimagined, and invented that makes these *crónicas* so very potent.

I WOULD like to thank António Lobo Antunes, Tânia Ganho (and her family and friends!), and, as ever, my husband, Ben Sherriff.

Margaret Jull Costa

PART I

BEFORE DARKNESS FALLS

IN PRAISE
OF THE SUBURBS

I grew up on the outskirts of Lisbon, in Benfica, which, at the time, was small gardens, side streets, low houses, and listening to mothers calling in the dusk

—Víííííítor

so loudly that, from Rua Ernesto da Silva, it reached the storks on the tops of the tallest trees and drowned out the peacocks in the lake beneath the poplars. I grew up next to the little castle of Portas de Benfica, which separated us from the area of Venda Nova on the one hand and the Estrada Militar on the other, in a land whose border posts were Senhor Jardim's drugstore, Careca's grocery store, Senhor Madureira's bakery and Senhor Silvino's notions store. I would linger in the afternoons as I passed the cobbler, Senhor Florindo, who hammered away at the soles of shoes in a small, dark room, surrounded by blind men seated on low benches who gave off a smell of shoe leather and poverty, which remains the only odor of sanctity I know. Dona Maria Salgado, tiny and thin and in permanent mourning, carried the Holy Family in a box from house to house, and for a period of two weeks my grandparents would welcome into their living room those three clay figures beneath the clouded glass dome that the maids would illuminate with miniature oil lamps. I grew up with Senhor Paulo who mended the wings of sparrows with string and bits of reed, and the Ferra-O-Bico family whose aunt ran off with a gypsy and ended up on the beach, reading people's fortunes and swathed in black like the widow of a sailor who never made it back to shore. My friends had resounding surnames

(Lafayette, Jaurès)

and lived in basement apartments with windows level with the sidewalk and through which one could see gigantic radio sets, pots of basil and godmothers wearing slippers. The barking of the tannery guard dog glowed phosphorescent in the July night, as the pollen from the acacias rained down on my eyelids, and I, dying of love for Sandokan's wife, discovered myself to be a unicorn while locked in the school toilet, and Brigadier Maia, wearing a Basque beret, strode down to the local bar—the Adega dos Ossos—fulminating against the regime. In the days when I was thirteen years old and first played ice hockey at the Benfica soccer club, the goalkeeper, as padded and protected as a medieval baron, pointed me out to his astonished friends

—That fair-haired guy's father is a doctor

in what proved to be both my first sporting glory and my first grim responsibility, from the moment the trainer, giving my muscles an appraising glance, said doubtfully

—Well, let's see how you shape up, blondie, because your father was a real demon with his fists.

The owner of the União drugstore practiced stick-fighting; the wife of the owner of the Marques drugstore was a sumptuous Greek woman with amphora hips and fiery eyes who, when I saw her on Sundays on her way to church, made me forget all about Sandokan's wife; the bell-ringer—whom everyone called José the Tongue and who, at the Elevation of the Host during midday mass, played the nursery tune "The Golden Parrot" instead of the reverent and obligatory "Thirteenth of May"—owned a funeral home whose brochure opened with the words: "Why go on living when for 100 *escudos* you could have a really beautiful funeral?"

When I wasn't playing hockey or smoking a clandestine cigarette, I wrote poetry—one half of me worshipping the hockey ace
Jesus Correia and the other half Camões*—and I was indecently
happy.

Now, if I go to Benfica, I can't find Benfica. The peacocks have
fallen silent and there isn't a single stork on top of the palm tree
outside the post office

(there is no palm tree outside the post office, and the house
owned by the Lobo Antunes family has been sold)

Senhor Silvino, Senhor Florindo and Senhor Jardim have died,
tall buildings have been built where the houses were, but I suspect that underneath those blocks of five and six and seven and
eight and nine stories, somewhere underneath the awnings and the
bank branches, Senhor Paulo is still mending the broken wings of
sparrows with string and bits of reed, Dona Maria Salgado is still
going from house to house with the Holy Family in their clouded
glass dome, Lafayette and Jaurès are swapping cigarette cards on
Calçada do Tojal surrounded by pots of basil and godmothers wearing slippers. There are no peacocks and no storks and yet the acacia
in what was my parents' garden stubbornly endures. Perhaps only
the acacia endures, perhaps it alone survives from those days, like
the mast of a submerged ship, sticking up above the waves. The
acacia is enough for me. The shops and the yards have been swept
away, no one plays "The Golden Parrot" on the church bells any
more, but the acacia endures. It endures. And I know that if I stand
next to it, close my eyes and press my ear to its trunk, I will hear
my mother's voice calling

—Antóóóóóóóóónio

*Luís de Camões (c. 1524–80). Portugal's national poet, whose most famous work
is The Lusiads. First published in 1572, this epic poem is widely considered to be
the Portuguese poem. It is a Homeric account of the Portuguese voyages of dis-
covery in the fifteenth and sixteenth centuries.

and a fair-haired little boy will run across the yard, with a bag of marbles in his pocket, and pass right by without even seeing me and will disappear upstairs to his room, to dream of Sandokan's wife, who would never force him to eat mashed potatoes or turnip soup during the torment of supper.

THE CHAMPION

oday, I happened upon a photograph from 1925 showing rows
of people in hats applauding three men vaulting over hurdles on a track that resembles a plowed field that a flock of sheep
has left in disgust: it is a photograph of the first athletics meeting
held between Spain and Portugal, and, more specifically, of the 110-
meter hurdles race. My Uncle Eloy won.

If, as the novelist says, it is true that
the heart has more rooms than a whorehouse
then, in my heart, Uncle Eloy occupies not a cramped back room
but a whole suite of rooms with a view of the river. I inherited his
monogrammed shirts, each with its carefully embroidered F and E,
shirts that were altered by my mother to fit my torso, that of a small
adolescent frog, an F and an E that, following surgery performed
with scissors and needle by the author of my existence, would, when
I undressed for PE at school, appear upside down on the tail or on
the back or under an armpit.

On Mondays and Thursdays, my fellow students would gather
round me in the locker room, placing bets on where the letters
would turn up this time. Cavaco collected the money. I remember
the morning when the winner was a near-albino diabetic, who had
bet ten *tostões* on the nape of my neck. Alas, it never occurred to my
mother that she could make a fortune out of this poplin lottery. And
Uncle Eloy, quite unwittingly, became the idol of Class 4A.

Eloy's mother was Grandmother Gui, who had two unique qualities: she was not my grandmother and she ate her greens with such
an elastic mouth that the spectacle of those plasticine molars still
constitutes the most astonishing act of dental contortionism I have
ever seen. Apart from that, she was a woman of great note in Pombal, so much so that the grocer, when he added up her purchases out
loud with the stub of a pencil, would announce respectfully

—Four plus five is nine plus three is twelve carry one, but since
it's you, Senhora, carry two, two plus seven is nine plus nine is eighteen plus seven is twenty-five carry two, but since it's you, Senhora,
carry three

and Grandma Gui would proudly and munificently pay for the
weight of her own importance.

Uncle Eloy dressed as no other man dressed: without a crease
to be seen, and with discreet elegance from his collar down to his
magnificent shoes, shoes capable of sending a ball

(Uncle Eloy had played left wing for Académica)

the whole length of the beach at Praia das Maçãs with just one
kick, straight over the lagoon to get lost somewhere beyond that
ruin of a bar at the top of the cliff, Alto da Vigia Seafood & Drinks.
A ball kicked by Uncle Eloy in Benfica would quite possibly be
found on the other side of Portugal, floating down the River Gua-
diana, watched by astonished fishermen. His exploits encouraged
my brother João and me to imitate him—arranging races along the
sandy paths in my grandfather's garden and going up to the attic of
the house in Calçada do Tojal to read ancient copies of *Très Sport*, in
which Georges Carpentier displayed his fists with the slightly comic
solemnity of a god in long johns.

My Uncle Eloy also smelled very good. He had a sense of humor.
He was intelligent. Manners, according to the family catechism,
revealed themselves at the supper table and the gaming table, and
Uncle Eloy was unbeatable at both: he ate with the precise gestures
of a watchmaker and if he lost at cards, he would sigh softly and say

the nonsensical phrase that I still hear in my head today whenever
I think of him

—I've been a cop all these years and I never thought it would end
in tears

On Thursdays, we, his nephews, would dine at his house. Over
dessert he would offer us a drop of anisette, Anís del Mono, served
in small blue glasses, then he would check that all his wall clocks
were telling the correct time, drop us in Travessa dos Arneiros and
set off, so he said, for the late shift at the post office. He was not, of
course, really going to join the late shift at the post office, but, in
another sense, he was. When he was already very ill

(and in illness he maintained the same affectionate dignity as he
had when he was well)

I used to visit him in the hospital, and his pajamas were more elegant and more tasteful than my brand-new jacket. He was so impec-
cably combed and shaved that it seemed more as if he had come to
visit me. One night, he was no longer there. I understood from the
look on my aunt's face that he had gone to join the late shift at the
post office. I wasn't too concerned: when I walk along Calçada do
Tojal, I'll find him there as usual, at the window, bare-chested, waving from up above like a champion of the 110-meter hurdles at the
end of a race. A race he won because the son of Grandma Gui

(carry two, but seeing as it's you, Senhora, carry three)

was not a man to lose anything.

PARADISE

When I was little, there were two bakeries in Benfica. One right by the church, frequented by the bagaço-swigging proletariat, the floor always strewn with sawdust and flattened cigarette butts, and that was called the Adega dos Ossos, where I was advised not to go for fear I might become fatally addicted to cherry brandy and cheap cigarettes and end my days playing dominoes, losing at cards and coughing into my handkerchief. It was a dark place, with lots of bottles on the walls, and in the window were more flies than custard tarts. Beyond the shelves and the spines of the bottles, a library of delirium tremens, I remember the squint-eyed bartender, his right eye furious and his left benevolently tender, and Senhor Manuel, the sacristan, who dropped by in his red surplice between masses and downed a few glasses with eucharistic unctuousness, hiding behind the fridge, afraid he might be spotted by the prior, who was all sternness and buttons from his neck to his shoes, and for whom wine, when not taken with wafers, had the devilish quality of leading the flock astray and causing them to postpone the six o'clock rosary in favor of the abominable vice of cards.

The other bakery, the Benfica Paradise, almost opposite the first, was frequented after mass by ladies whose devotion was rustproof, antimagnetic and bulletproof—for example, my grandmothers and my aunts whose intimate knowledge of the saints amazed me and who hastened to teach me the catechism after I asked, pointing my finger at the Holy Spirit

—What's that sparrow doing there?

explaining to me that God was not a sparrow, he was a dove, and I immediately imagined him in Praça de Camões eating out of the hands of pensioners, which hardly seemed to me an activity compatible with the creation of the universe.

Paradise was filled by ladies after mass and by men during it.

(When a cousin of mine indignantly asked her husband why he wasn't going to church, he replied with a small smug smile

—I don't need to: I'm in Paradise already. It's cooler and they serve beer.)

Unlike the Adega dos Ossos it smelled good, none of the employees had a squint, and dominoes was banned, Senhor Manuel's surplice did not flutter furtively behind the fridge and, most important of all, my brothers and I had an open account there for cake and ice cream. At first I was so touched by the generosity of that open account I almost wept with gratitude. I realized later that it was not really an act of generosity: it was because on Sundays we had lunch at my grandmother's house and the gift of ice cream and doughnuts was intended to distract me from the firm posterior of the cook whose charms I had recently discovered. Torn between two equally celestial Paradises, I hesitated for months on end between coconut fancies and the four rings of the stove.

I finally opted for the stove. When, sometime later, the cook married a policeman

(all the cooks married policemen)

and I tried to go back to the doughnuts, my grandmother, disillusioned with my sinful ways, had canceled the account. In desperation, I accompanied her on an excursion for widows to Fátima in an attempt to win back both her affection and the cakes: not even this heroic sacrifice moved her. And I went on to live in a painful state of double orphanhood from which no cheese pastry and no apron has yet shown any interest in rescuing me.

THE OLYMPIC SWIMMER
AND THE ALMOND

In my adolescence, when I spent my summers at the swimming pool at Praia das Maçãs, the world was presided over by two tutelary figures, one who dominated the day and the other who dominated the night. The day belonged exclusively to the Olympic Swimmer, the night was the realm of the Nightclub Pianist.

The Olympic Swimmer wore a panama hat, a whistle round his neck and rubber sandals, the kind with a strap that fits between your big toe and the toe next to it, just like the cryptoshrews who live in Olivais Sul, and he marched around the swimming pool like a brigadier, ordering the drowned to swim the crawl. More than that, he wore mirrored sunglasses, had shoulders that were beginning to soften slightly like plasticine, and had written a book with the definitive and imposing title: *Knowing How to Swim Is as Important and Useful as Knowing How to Read or Write*, which was on sale at the shop in the locker rooms where you could rent imitation tiger-skin bathing trunks. The first chapter was entitled "Camões, Portugal's First Champion Swimmer," and this intellectual side of the Olympic Swimmer filled me with a feeling of ecstatic admiration: I had finally found someone who had made the link between the diving board and the decasyllable, pondering sonnets while school-children splashed around in the waters screaming for help until the glug-glug of their final breath.

When dusk fell, the Olympic Swimmer was replaced by the Nightclub Pianist, who filled the Concha Club, a paradise of shadows and subdued lighting above the darkness of the swimming pool, with passionate laments in the form of *boleros*.

Not being old enough to be admitted into this sanctuary of slow dances, I would sit outside on the step, allowing myself to be impregnated by a melancholy full of confused desires while the Nightclub Pianist whispered into the microphone

> *Your body by my side*
> *Makes the temperature rise,*
> *Hot as a toasted almond.*

Unlike the Olympic Swimmer, the Nightclub Pianist was plump and did not wear mirrored sunglasses or a whistle round his neck and appeared unconcerned about the importance or usefulness of nautical knowledge. He would approach the microphone, lips pursed, eyelids fluttering, and announce in a passionate murmur

> *Your body by my side*
> *Makes the temperature rise,*
> *Hot as a toasted almond.*

The toasted almond must have been his wife, a Spanish woman who resembled the drawings from *Cara Alegre*, which, at the time, represented for me

(and just between you and me still do in a way)

the ideal of feminine beauty. When, at around one o'clock in the afternoon, the Toasted Almond arrived at the swimming pool, blonde, voluptuous, inaccessible, moving as slowly as a Virgin being carried in procession and wearing enormous silver hoop earrings, I felt as if my bones were smoking with passion. Time seemed to stop, the boys jumping from the high board froze in midair, a tremor of desire shook the gaping bathers, and only the Olympic Swimmer, who remained indifferent, continued to blow his whistle at the apprentice shipwreck victims who had suddenly discovered the ability to walk on water. I was astonished to learn one day that the Toasted Almond and the Olympic Swimmer had scandalously vanished from the pool and gone off to swim the crawl in some hotel in the north of Portugal. Personally, I felt as betrayed as the Nightclub Pianist. I started singing to myself at home, unaccompanied, with a spoon as microphone

Your body by my side
Makes the temperature rise

in the hope that one of the drawings in *Cara Alegre* would step out of the magazine, take me by the hand, and carry me around the day in eighty worlds in the bed where, night after night, I sighed for the Toasted Almond, meanwhile solitarily pedaling between the sheets.

THE SONNETS TO CHRIST

During interviews, which I find the most terrifying form of interrogation in the world because someone thrusts a tape recorder under my nose and orders me to have ideas and opinions, neither of which I've ever had, the conversation inevitably turns to the ominous question: How did you start writing? To which I must have given at least 300 different answers, varying from those I imagined to be intelligent to those I presumed to be ironic, but none of which was sincere. The truth is that I started writing when I was thirteen out of dire financial need, just as I might have specialized in selling overpriced Band-Aids in cafés or standing at traffic lights, displaying a medical certificate declaring that I had TB, hoping to provoke the generosity of others.

At the time, it seemed easier to provoke such feelings in my grandmother. First, out of concern that my family might look unfavorably on their firstborn going from table to table in bakeries, offering relief for ingrown toenails, and second, because I found it hard to cough convincingly over the half sheet of official paper that guaranteed that I regularly spat blood at the local sanatorium. A cough cannot be invented: it is acquired at the cost of several packs of Português Suave a day, and, at the time, I was reduced to smoking only the occasional Chesterfield filched from my mother and smoked at the bathroom window, in constant terror that I would be surprised in this sinful act, which translated into diz

ziness, watering eyes and a great deal of toothpaste afterward to cover up the smell.

That was when I had the brilliant idea of writing the Sonnets to Christ. The Sonnets to Christ saved me from poverty. To them I owe having enough money to buy chewing gum, balcony seats in the Eden cinema, coffees in the Adega dos Ossos, cakes at school recess, and secondhand books from the Editorial Minerva with their abominable translations of Maxim Gorky, whom, at the time, I considered to be a sublime writer, and whose smudgy paragraphs stuck to my fingers as they spoke of sad, wretched childhoods borne with heroic defiance around the samovar

(for ages, I presumed that the samovar was the Russian equivalent of Salgari's* scimitar, not that I knew what that was either, but the incomprehensible connection between the two sufficed for me).

The Sonnets to Christ, of which I wrote, on average, one a week, consisted of two quatrains and two triplets rhymed and metered, describing episodes from the Son of God's brief earthly existence. I soft-pedaled a bit in the quatrains but pulled out all the stops in the triplets, with the introduction of a few nasty Jews and some Romans in helmets very keen on sticking spears into people, and, generally speaking, I concluded with the agony on the cross, with a thief on either side, supporting Our Lord in the way ivory elephants supported the beautifully bound books in elegant third-floor apartments on the Rua Visconde de Valmor.

Having penned the tragedy, I would make a fair copy on pink writing paper with little doves in the corner, slip it in an envelope, ring my grandmother's doorbell with a stricken air of imminent doom, and when she ushered me into her room, concerned to learn what new misfortune had befallen me

---

*Emilio Salgari (1862–1911). Italian writer of swashbuckling novels, the most famous of which was the *Tiger of Malaysia* series, featuring the hero Sandokan.

(misfortunes were my specialty, and my grandmother devoted a large part of her life to sorting out my foolish mistakes)

I would strike a pose near the little shrine—where the heavenly court was represented in carved wood, clay, bronze and other less noble materials—take the sonnet from my pocket and read it out in as cavernous a voice as I could muster, rolling my eyes like a martyr. My grandmother, convinced that her grandson was preparing for a career as an archbishop, would immediately open her money box, which, for some reason, was always kept alongside the saints, and would reward my devotion with the equivalent of a side seat in Benfica's Stadium of Light and a clandestine glass of eau-de-vie at the Adega dos Ossos, knocked back in manly fashion with much spluttering and sneezing.

I think that everything I wrote subsequently, and which I only began to publish after her death, is still addressed to her. And whenever my publisher hands me one of the first copies of my latest novel, I think of my grandmother. I don't know if she would like my books, just as I never knew whether she liked my Sonnets to Christ, but I still hope that she'll give me twenty *escudos* for them and, above all, the kiss that accompanied the twenty-*escudo* note and which, since she left, I have never again received.

GROWN-UPS

I got to know grown-ups from the ground up as my age slowly grew in inches marked on the wall by my mother's pencil. First, they were only shoes, sometimes discovered under the bed, enormous, with no foot inside, which I then wore to walk about the house, lifting my legs like a deep-sea diver, with a tremendous clattering of soles. Then I became familiar with knees covered in cloth or thin, thin stockings, which formed an impenetrable palisade around the table beneath which I used to crawl. Afterward came the stomachs from which voice, cough and authority issued forth despite the vain constraining efforts of suspenders and belts.

When I reached the level of the tablecloth, I learned to distinguish the various adults by the medicines placed between napkin and glass: my grandmother's drops, my grandfather's cough syrups, the various colors of my aunts' tablets, my cousins' little silver pillboxes, the vaporizer for asthma that my godfather used, jaws gaping like some desperate grouper fish. It was around this time, too, that I realized their smiles could be taken apart: they would remove the jokes from their mouth after lunch and scrub them with a special brush. I chanced upon them hidden behind the alarm clock on Sunday mornings in the form of small necklaces of teeth set in a bed of rose-pink gums, mocking the faces that, without them, had aged a thousand years and become as withered as dried flowers, concentric wrinkles devouring their lips.

When I was able, given my increased size, to look them in the face, what most surprised me about them was their strange indifference to the two truly important things in the world: silkworms and chocolate umbrellas. Nor did they like collecting grasshoppers, chewing candles or snipping lumps off their own hair; on the other hand, they had an incomprehensible mania for baths and toothpaste, and when, in my presence, they talked about a certain blonde relative of ours, very nice, very painted, very perfumed, and prettier by far than the whole lot of them, they would start speaking in French, casting distrustful, apprehensive glances at me out of the corners of their eyes.

I've never quite understood when one stops being little and becomes grown up. Probably when the blonde relative starts being referred to—in Portuguese, not French—as that slut Luísa. Probably when we replace chocolate umbrellas with steak tartares. Probably when we start enjoying having a shower. Probably when we stop being afraid of the dark. Probably when we grow sad. But I'm not sure: I don't know if I have grown up.

Obviously, I've finished high school, been to college, and am now addressed by people as Doctor, and it's been ages since anyone thought to remind me to clean my teeth. I must have grown up, I think, because the blonde relative stopped sitting me on her knee and stroking my hair, provoking in me a kind of itching in the nose that filled me with languor and that I learned later to be the equivalent of what is known as pleasure. Their kind of pleasure, obviously, not to be compared with chewing candles or snipping away at my own bangs. Or tearing paper along the dotted line. Or showing a toad to the cook and watching her fall flat on her back, her eyes turned up, knocking over, as she fell, the containers labeled Beans, Chickpeas and Rice, which, in fact, contained pasta, sugar and coffee.

I must have grown up. Maybe I have grown up. But what I would really like is to invite that blonde relative to dinner at Gambrinus. I'll ask the waiter to bring us two portions of chocolate umbrellas, and while we're sucking the plastic handles, I'll show her my collection of grasshoppers in a cardboard box. I may be wrong, but from the way she used to stroke my hair, her eyes as young as mine, I'm pretty sure she'd like that.

THE EXISTENCE OF GOD

I don't need anyone to prove the existence of God to me as a priest did yesterday on television, pen at the ready, serious, accusing, definitive. I don't need anyone to prove it to me because I've known God since I was born, even before I learned the catechism, even before I had classes in ethics at school, even before I joined the choir. He's changed a bit since then, but the God of my childhood self was an elderly man, about sixty years old, with a long beard and long white hair, which, at the time he was introduced to me, was a style affected only by Walt Whitman and Dom João. Dom João

(about whom I've written in one of my novels)

used to walk in the rain through the streets of Nelas, Beira Alta,* dressed in rags and leaning on a walking stick, proclaiming that he was the emperor of all the kingdoms in the world, which seemed to me perfectly reasonable, since it was he who had created the Universe. Times have changed, and in addition to Walt Whitman and Dom João, there are loads of people who look like God in the cheap Bairro Alto bars frequented by artists

(Gide was always amazed that there were so many more artists than there were works of art)

*Beira Alta. The old designation for a province in the north of Portugal, on the border with Spain, the principal towns being Guarda and Viseu. Beira Baixa is the old designation for the province below Beira Alta; its principal town was Castelo Branco.

usually accompanied by hideously ugly women. They produce poetry in self-published volumes and become very bad losers after their second glass of wine. The God of my childhood did not frequent restaurants or write poetry: he lived in a vast house called church, always, apparently, at odds with the electric company because there was never any electric light, only candles whose flames leaned tremulously in the direction of the curtained doors. One of the first things I was told was that God loved the poor, who, when they died, shot straight up to heaven like an arrow, which did not prevent him from largely ignoring them while they were alive: the poor knelt on the stone floor or, if they were lucky, in wooden pews that bruised their bones, whereas the rich, condemned to follow to their last sigh an apprenticeship in second-degree burns on the barbecue of Purgatory, had chairs with cushions and a little plaque bearing the owner's name. Even if the rich were doomed to suffer a little on the spit-roast that preceded Paradise, I never quite understood the social segregation that God's department head, the parish priest, only emphasized by arranging to hold a mass at seven for the maids and another at noon for the masters and mistresses. I believe that at the mass for the maids, he spoke of the marvels awaiting them in a Heaven that I imagined to be full of candy and kiddie cars, and yet none of the maids seemed particularly enthusiastic when I asked them if they wanted to go for a spin in mine. Perhaps they preferred blessings, which I did not quite understand and about which the baker seemed better informed than I, because as soon as he rang the bell, the maids would rush to the door to receive him, and when my parents were out, they would stand in the backyard with him, talking about Paradise, and if I went near them, they would send me away to prevent me from knowing in detail the delights God had in store for them.

What they told me, of course, was that God basically hated three things, all of which, given their unforgivable gravity, led straight to Hell: not finishing your soup, annoying your aunts, and calling the cook names. The chauffeur did not fall into any of these abominable sins

(he ate like a horse, took off his hat and bowed to the young ladies and, far from insulting the cook, he was in the habit of running an appreciative hand over the buttocks of same)

neither was he rich, and so, for years, I envied him the pepper-mint candies he would blithely be sucking while I, transformed into a chicken in the Prego de Oiro bar, would be roasting on a spit turned by men with goat's feet, while my brothers turned and turned on neighboring spits because they had broken the living-room window while playing soccer, which was the fourth sin on the list presented to us along with a lot of threatening looks and grimly wagging index fingers. Besides, the grown-ups never sinned because they didn't break windows, they washed their hands before sitting down to eat

(God loved people who washed their hands before they sat down to eat)

and they went to mass carrying huge, fat books full of pious pictures and portraits of great-grandparents and great-great-grandparents with a cross above them. The maids only had little books with no pictures

(the poor have no grandparents)

and glass rosaries instead of ivory ones, and I don't think they put in the collection the five *escudos* they were given for that purpose, but squandered them, instead, on orange soda at the dances held at Futebol Benfica, which, according to my grandmother, was the anteroom to Hell. The only maid who never wanted to go to the dances at Futebol Benfica had already died and was in Heaven and her name was Santa Zita

(it would never have occurred to her to be so arrogant as to be an Ana, a Teresa or an Isabel)

and yet, for all her virtue, I doubt that, if she came to our house, she would be allowed to eat with us. She would more likely be granted the intermediate status of the seamstresses, who ate in the sewing room on a tray placed on top of their Singer sewing machine. A fate they would share, in fact, with the whole heavenly court, with the possible exception of Holy Queen Isabel, who might perhaps know how to hold her knife and fork properly, which made me think that Paradise was a kind of Poorhouse, full of gardeners and housemaids, all of them with toothpicks in their mouth and elbows on the table, and I never understood why my family wanted me to be a member of that vulgar crew. Especially when, by the time I got there, they would have stuffed all the cakes and candies into those plastic bags the poor always take to wedding feasts, so that these goodies can be handed round later at home while they listen to the latest radio soap. Perhaps my family thought I would feel more at ease among the doilies, photographs of firemen, and chrome Bambis and that I would like to be called Edgar. It's not entirely true, although I've never been keen on fine china soup tureens, and all the girls I was forced to play with turned out to be terrible bores. And so now, between Heaven and Hell, I hesitate as to which to choose. I'm beginning to suspect that the only solution is not to be so foolish as to die.

THE POOR

In my family, we didn't keep dogs or cats or birds as pets. In my family, the poor were our pets. Each of my aunts had her own personal and untransferrable poor person, who came to my grandparents' house once a week to collect, with a grateful smile, their ration of clothes and food.

The poor, as well as being manifestly poor

(preferably barefoot, so that they could be shod by the owners of the house, preferably ragged, so that they could be dressed in old shirts, which would thus be saved from their natural fate as dust rags, and preferably sick so that they could be given a pack of aspirin)

had to possess certain other vital characteristics: they had to go to mass, baptize their children, remain sober and, above all, be fiercely loyal to the aunt to whom they belonged. I can still remember one man, decked out in sumptuous rags, and who resembled Tolstoy right down to his beard, saying in proud, offended tones to an absentminded cousin of mine who insisted on offering him a sweater none of us wanted

—I'm not your poor person, I'm Senhora Teresinha's poor person.

The plural of poor person was not the poor, it was these people. At Christmas and at Easter, the aunts would gather together, arm themselves with slices of fruitcake, little bags of almonds, and other similar delicacies, and descend piously on the place where their pets lived, an area of wooden shacks built on the outskirts of Benfica, in Pedralvas, next to the Estrada Militar, in order to distribute, with all the pomp of Magi, woolen socks, underpants, sandals no one wore, pictures of Our Lady of Fátima, and other marvels of equal caliber. The poor rushed out of their hovels, excited and grateful, and my aunts, pushing them away with the backs of their hands, would warn me

—Don't get too close, these people have lice.

At these times, and at these times only, it was permitted to give the poor money, a dangerous gift, since it ran the risk of being spent

(—These people, poor things, have no idea about money)

in a deleterious and irresponsible manner. My Aunt Carlota's particular poor person, for example, was banned from my grandparents' house because, when she pressed ten *tostões* into his hand, urging maternally, out of concern for her pet's health

—Now, don't go spending it all on wine

the bold creature responded very rudely indeed

—No, Senhora, I was thinking of buying an Alfa Romeo.

The children of the poor did not go to school, were very thin and died a lot. When I asked the reasons behind these unusual characteristics, I was told with a shrug

—What do you expect, that's what these people are like

and I understood that being poor was not so much a destiny as a vocation, like having a talent for bridge or for playing the piano.

In my grandmother's personal shrine, two people presided over this love of the poor, one in clay and the other in the form of a photograph; these were Father Cruz and the Little Saint, who directed the charitable work being done from beneath a mahogany crucifix. Father Cruz was a hollow-cheeked fellow in a cassock, and the Little Saint was a young woman hung with holy medals and with the lewd smile of one of those movie stars who used to appear on packs of chewing gum, and these two, I was informed, had, in exemplary fashion, offered up their lives to God in exchange for the health of their parents. The actress-cum-saint kicked the bucket, and her father made a complete recovery, and from the moment they told me about this miracle, I would tremble with panic every time my mother sneezed, fearing that she would demand

—Go on, then, offer up your life, I've had enough of blowing my nose

and I would have to go straight to the cemetery just so that she wouldn't have to drink any more hot water and lemon.

In my mind, Father Cruz and the Little Saint were married, especially since in a magazine to which my family subscribed, called *The Little Saint's Almanac*, the miracles of both were spoken of as common property, miracles that consisted largely of cures for paralysis and wins in the lottery, miracles accompanied, most improbably, by the sickly smell of incense.

All those poor people, all those Little Saints, and all those smells irritated me. And I think it was around this time that I began to view with increasing affection a dusty engraving relegated to the attic, which showed a jubilant multitude of poor people standing around the guillotine where the king and queen were having their heads chopped off.

TO THE BEACH

And so, at the beginning of August, we prepared to set off for the beach at Praia das Maçãs. It all began like the flurried, final departure of Russian aristocrats during the 1917 Revolution: curtains at doors and windows were taken down, carpets rolled up, sofas draped with white sheets, paintings were removed from walls, revealing pale rectangles hanging from nails, candlesticks, cutlery, teapots and silver trays were swathed in newspaper, the house grew in size, and sounds took on the explosive amplitude of footsteps in an underground garage at night. A truck arrived to take fridge, luggage and maids, all heading off before us, first thing in the morning, into the exile of holidays, and, in the afternoon, my parents dispatched the children, who fought in the back seat for a place by the window, crying, kicking, whining, apart from my younger brother, that is, who stood on the seat, with his bib round his neck and a rubber Pluto clutched to his chest, waving good-bye, all the way from Benfica to Sintra, to the cars following us.

After Colares, the good-byes became impossible because of the mist: you could just make out the roofs of vacation homes and the vague tops of pine trees in a blur of fog, the invisible sea creaked like the rusty hinge of a cradle, and we arrived, at nightfall, at a dank, unfamiliar house, surrounded by horribly sad trees that the waves had forgotten to carry off with them; we fell asleep beneath damp blankets, with the foghorn from the lighthouse confusing our dreams. The next day, at nine o'clock in the morning, our mother, in her dressing gown, would appear on the deck of the garden to observe the mist with an admiral's arched eyebrow and declare confidently

—The mist will lift by one

and we children, wearing panama hats and submerged in concentric layers of woolen sweaters, bundled up like pioneering motorists, would set off, shivering, in single file, shepherded along by the maid—her nose purple with cold—to the beach, where you could just make out the vague igloo shapes of beach tents, as well as drifting icebergs and the penguin-children from a holiday camp, squealing like piglets and flailing around, while Eskimo-bathers grabbed them and, despite a climate worthy of some northern dawn, plunged them into the water, among ice pebbles and the skeletons of polar explorers.

Sitting on the sand, shaking as if with the onset of flu, with our spades and plastic buckets and useless baking molds, we could only recognize each other by our hacking coughs and by the sounds of our sneezes; and in the Lifeboat and Rescue Institute, on the stone slabs reserved for the drowned, people lay dying of pneumonia, wearing as many woolen sweaters and panama hats as we did.

At eleven o'clock, when, among the mountains cloaked in filmy gray, a tiny scrap of castle began gradually to grow in size, our mother would come down to the beach, place her shoes next to the pole in the middle of the beach tent, around which there was already a pile of sandals, and, opening her copy of *Paris-Match*, she would declare radiantly, pointing in triumph at that fragment of rampart

—Didn't I say it would clear up soon?

meanwhile handing out the aspirin.

I never went back to Praia das Maçãs. Some of my brothers continue to make these arctic explorations, and I'm always amazed that they use a car rather than a sleigh pulled by reindeer in order to traverse Colares. I imagine that, in September, they dine on seal oil and salted meat, with stalactites of ice hanging from their ears, and that they burn tapers soaked in whale blubber to light them at night. I meet up with them again in October, and they, having survived, embrace me, grunting, in an effusion of walrus flippers. This Christmas, you'll see us balancing balls on our noses at the circus. It'll be easy to recognize me: I'll be the one taking the fish out of my pocket at the end of each trick.

CHRISTMAS CHRONICLE

At this time of year, when Christmas comes around, I always think of my grandfather. I mean I often think of my grandfather anyway, but I think of him even more at Christmas because the period when my grandfather was alive was the happiest time of my life. I was the oldest son of his oldest son, I was named António Lobo Antunes after him

(although I would have preferred my identity card to bear a name like the Cisco Kid or Hopalong Cassidy)

he took me to Padua for my first communion, once I'd been duly confessed at his house by the prior

(on Saturdays my grandfather invited the priests to lunch, and the priest from Amadora always made the most of this opportunity to cover my face with tender kisses

—Ah, he has the face of an angel, the face of an angel

making my cheeks wet with mystical fervor, well, let's assume it was mystical fervor, and I would wriggle and squirm because I hated his spit and his hands, which were too hot and too soft)

he took me to Padua, in a Nash, to make my first communion, Spain, France, Switzerland, Italy. I spent days throwing up in the car, I was bored to death in the museums where my grandfather would stand me in front of a painting or a statue and lecture me interminably, and I was bored to death because there wasn't a single painting of the Cisco Kid, only ladies in lace, Christs in agony and stone lepers with bits missing. I was run over by a bicycle in Berne, in the Church of Santo Antonio I had problems with the host, which stuck to the roof of my mouth and I was torn between a desire to unstick it with my finger and terror that I might scratch Jesus with my fingernail. I got lost in Venice, I ate enormous ice creams, and when I came back, my brother João had broken his arm, to which my Aunt Madalena had ordered a plaster cast to be applied, and I was green with envy because I had returned unscathed and didn't have a sling hanging around my neck.

But to return to the subject of Christmases, at my grandfather's house these were real events. After the turkey and before the visit to my dusty aunts from Brazil who lived somewhere near Rua Braamcamp and whom I only saw in December

(I remember dark rooms, the glint of silver in the shadows, pianos, maids who were all called Conceição, little old ladies who smelled of medicine, Aunt Mimi, Aunt Biluca, large threatening pieces of furniture and endless corridors)

my grandmother would say to one of her daughters

—Send in the staff

the staff would line up against the wall, the housekeeper, the housekeeper's wife, the housekeeper's children, the gardener, the cook, the other *muzhiks*, and then my grandmother, as solemnly as if she were giving out medals on National Day, distributed *Croix de Guerres* in the form of soft packages containing socks, vests and so on to the grateful serfs. Once the *muzhiks* had been satisfied, they filed back down into the catacombs of the kitchen

(I loved going to the kitchen because everyone would get up and bow whereas in the living room no one took the slightest notice of me and continued to play cards or, if they did notice me, it was only to say

—Be quiet, child

between hands of canasta)

and we would move on to the Nativity scene with its cardboard mountains, moss, and bits of mirror pretending to be lakes, before which rose a Himalaya of presents. There were things to wear that pleased my mother and infuriated me because things to wear were presents for her, and I'd never noticed Hopalong Cassidy in an overcoat and short pants, and things that pleased me and infuriated my mother such as cap pistols and other marvels for making noise that would disturb the canasta

(—Fire your gun and play your pennywhistle somewhere else, I can't concentrate)

not to mention balls that would break windows and soup tureens, the candies whose sticky wrappers would stay glued to the family's clothes, and the windup cars that could make anyone who stepped on them perform a backward somersault far more spectacular than any performed by the acrobats at the Coliseu. My grandfather, cigarette holder in mouth, would preside over the chaos with a smile

(he was the only person who never told me to be quiet or to stop firing my gun and who actually enjoyed pennywhistles)

and like any good cavalry officer and war veteran, he saw nothing wrong with my killing visitors by firing my gun into their ear, visitors who jumped with fright and fell off their chairs, deathly pale, one hand pressed to their heart, looking at me as if they would like to pulverize me and smiling at him and giving a feeble little laugh

—Such a lively lad, your grandson

in which one could sense an incomprehensible desire to see me bound hand and foot and gagged.

When my grandfather died, they sold the house, the family dispersed and the Christmases came to an end. Christmases now are what I see in the store windows: the Happy Christmases from the management, the bakeries with 500-ESCUDO notes attached to the fir trees with clothespins, a sad Father Christmas at the door of a supermarket distributing advertising flyers about margarines and cell phones. Christmases now are me on the trail of the words for a novel, my notepad on my knee, with not a single *muzhik* in the kitchen, my brothers all white-haired now, nephews who have never even heard of the Cisco Kid. But maybe next year someone will give me a cap pistol and when I fire it for the first time my grandfather will reappear, place his hand on my shoulder again, and stroke my neck with his thumb the way he used to do

(—My little grandson)

and I will feel again his strength and tenderness, feel again, as I always felt, that as long as I was with him nothing bad, nothing sad, nothing nasty could ever happen to me because my grandfather wouldn't allow it.

FIX THE SOUND,
YOU IDIOT

For me the cinema continues to be a shack on the beach with, fixed to one wooden wall, a sheet that billows and ripples in the evening breeze, long wooden benches and behind the benches the little hole of the projector that shuddered like a very ancient airplane and traversed the cinema from hole to sheet in a ray of dusty light that was the Holy Spirit of my childhood. You could hear the waves while the film was running, and I could smoke there with no risk that my father would suddenly appear

(for some reason, the other members of my family and adults in general didn't enjoy spending two hours sitting on hard wooden benches with no backs)

there were a few really pretty eleven-year-old girls who didn't seem at all impressed by the cigarettes I stole from my Uncle Eloy or by my mother's perfume with which, when she wasn't looking, I drenched my armpits in the hope that this would gain me the admiration of those indifferent sirens, all whispers, giggles and bubble gum, fascinated by old men of fifteen, already decrepit, already with beards, already in long pants, and who sometimes even drank beer and were allowed to stay out until past midnight.

For me the cinema continues to be an out-of-focus image on a sheet with the audience protesting loudly

—We can't see the guy's face

it continues to be Jeff Chandler getting off his horse, now clear now fuzzy, in order, singlehanded, to demolish a whole battalion of Indians, something that I, unlike the decrepit fifteen-year-olds who were only interested in magazines with naked women in them

(what possible interest can a magazine full of naked women have compared with Donald Duck?)

felt that I could do with the greatest of ease if someone gave me a revolver just like his, and that the eleven-year-old girls gazing at the beer-swilling idlers would never understand, and at this point the sound would fail, Jeff Chandler would move his lips in a bronchitic wheeze of reels and waves on the beach, and the audience would get angry

—Fix the sound, you idiot

the green light from the lighthouse came in through the cracks between the planks, a trawler arrived sputtering diesel, Jeff Chandler fired his gun in absolute silence and with each shot the Indians fell not one by one but by the handful

(a single bullet killed at least a dozen Sioux)

without so much as a moan, the audience grew desperate

—Fix the sound, you idiot

the sound returned for a second when Jeff Chandler went over to Maureen O'Hara all feathered and flummoxed, and disappeared again for the final kiss

(Maureen O'Hara should be an example to all eleven-year-old women because I never saw her whispering or giggling, much less chewing gum)

the public roared wildly

—Fix the sound, you idiot

the words The End appeared in tremulous red on the sheet, the lights in the shack came on and I seized the opportunity to finish off all those old men of fifteen with the Colt .45 formed by my pointed index finger. The girls' parents were waiting to take them home and I stood in the midst of a multitude of defunct admirers of naked women, filled by the lofty pride of the solitary sheriff while the sea advanced and retreated on the beach, my heart suddenly terribly sad, missing those irresistible, indifferent sirens, with no breasts as yet and with their faces concealed behind pink bubbles of gum.

ANTÓNIO JOÃO PEDRO
MIGUEL NUNO MANUEL

Whenever I go to supper at my parents' house, I leave there with my childhood stuck in my throat: Benfica has changed, my mother is no longer thirty years old, I can smoke without anyone telling me off, when they bring the dish to the table, it's no longer full of sticky cakes, I don't find my brothers there in their pajamas, their fair hair still wet from the bath. My parents' house hasn't changed much: the boys' bedrooms have been made into living rooms, but the smell is the same. There are photos of the dead: my grandparents, a few uncles, some aunts, all dead, although I've never gotten used to the fact that they're dead, and who I wouldn't be surprised to see walk right in, people I miss like mad but who don't miss me one iota because they miss nothing now and certainly not me. Whenever I go to supper at my parents' house, I leave there with my childhood stuck in my throat: I don't know the people or the buildings, Paraíso has disappeared, the Havaneza has evaporated, I don't know what's happened to Dona Maria José the smuggler, I don't know what's happened to the madman with the birds, it's ages since I watched my father shave, it's ages since my mother, nail scissors in hand, said to me:

—Show me your fingers

in order to trim my nails. I trim them myself now with some nail clippers and because I'm clumsy I take forever to pick up the clippings from the floor tiles with my forefinger wet with saliva.

And I trim them in silence, without bleating like a calf, startling my mother
— I haven't even started yet
my mother who trimmed our nails, gave us injections, transformed Uncle Eloy's shirts into shirts for us and, since I'm the eldest, always seemed to be pregnant, with João Pedro Miguel Nuno Manuel. I leave there with my childhood stuck in my throat and I sit in the car looking at the garden wall, at the main door with a stone pineapple on each side, the closed windows, the top of the acacia tree dark now because it's night, the Travessa do Vintém das Escolas unchanged apart from Cabecinha whom I've never seen again, something or other da Costa Cabecinha, leaning on the windowsill of his basement apartment on a level with the sidewalk, with whom I got caught collecting money for Santo António and who had photographs of naked women, rectangles of black paper with pictures of women so blurred you couldn't see anything although he thought you could
— Look at the tits on her
and me embarrassed and willing but unable to see any tits at all and Cabecinha putting these precious items back in his pocket
— Idiot
and sharing his treasures with the Ferra-O-Bico boys who were more enlightened than we were, knew about sex and used to take gypsy girls into the woods behind the school to engage with them in mysterious operations. Having your childhood stuck in your throat is worse than a fishbone: you can eat as much bread as you like but it won't go down. Perhaps that's why I go to Benfica at most once a month and why when I go there I feel like a dog looking for a bone it thinks it buried when in fact there was no bone at all. A bone that I nevertheless look for until my eyes hurt. As I look for myself in photo albums, as I look for myself under my bed
(it's still there my bed)
as I look for myself in the garden, in the fig tree in the garden, in the place where the well was, where the chicken run was, and so

after supper I sit in the car and look at the wall, at the main door with a stone pineapple on each side, the closed windows, the top of the acacia tree dark now because it's night. Perhaps it's always night when we grow up. I sit in the car waiting for my mother to call me and knowing that she won't because she thinks I've left. And I have left. Forever.

TODAY I FEEL LIKE TALKING
ABOUT MY PARENTS

Being the oldest child of two oldest children was slightly strange because I had young grandparents and uncles who were barely out of diapers. My mother was a pretty young twenty-something

(I do not take after my mother)

who looked eighteen, strangers would mistake us for brother and sister and I remember my father turning thirty-three and me thinking that he was not only extremely ugly

(I take after my father's side of the family)

but as old as Methuselah. Methuselah inhabited the study, surrounded by pipes and books, and the pretty girl inhabited, as do all women

(it's inevitable)

the whole house. My father had dark hair and my mother didn't. My father had blue eyes

(when I think about it, perhaps he wasn't so very ugly)

and my mother green. My father slept on the same side as the alarm clock and my mother next to the baby because for ages and ages there was always a baby crying. The origin of these babies was, moreover, a mystery to me

(between you and me, I believe that, happily, it still is in a way)

and the story about Paris and storks was too riddled with inconsistencies for me to believe in it, partly because on the stork's journey from Paris to Benfica with the babies in its beak

(Paris was almost as far away as Lisbon is from Praia das Maçãs)

some hunter, annoyed by my brothers' howling, would have shot the stork. Besides, if the stork delivered them personally the way postmen do with registered mail, it seemed odd to me that my mother should have to go to the maternity hospital where I visited her in bed unless, of course, the maternity hospital was a kind of central station, like the Rossio, where the babies would be collected like merchandise marked Fragile, and the beating of the birds' wings had given my mother a cold. Anyway, the babies who were there devoted themselves alternately and unremittingly to suckling and bawling. One day when one of the babies was suckling, my father asked me

—Do you want to have a look?

he squeezed my mother's breast, milk spurted out, and I was so amazed that I haven't recovered to this day. As soon as one of my brothers was transferred to the bedroom, another howling baby would take his place in the cradle, screaming

(I felt really sorry for the storks having to do that job)

and on the bedside table there was a sugar bowl in which the pacifier would be dipped as a way of calming the monster, who exercised his lungs for months on end. I'm astonished that none of us has turned out to be a tenor, and whenever I go to the opera I have to restrain myself from going down onto the stage with a pacifier and a sugar bowl to calm the singers who are equally chubby, equally bald, equally purple with effort, equally decked out in frills, snatched from the cradle by the evil conductor. The problem with the sopranos is that they weigh too much and if I sat them on my knee to rock them to sleep, I'd be sure to put my back out.

Once we were transferred to the bedroom, my father would teach us to ice-skate

(he himself was a champion ice-skater)

my mother, who wasn't a champion anything, taught us to read, and with those two skills in our luggage we were deemed to be ready for life and packed off to Senhor André's school for a post-graduate course on the tributaries flowing into the left bank of the Tejo and the stations on the Beira Baixa line

(it's astonishing how many tributaries and stations there are, which leads me to wish that the whole world was like the Gobi Desert)

and once we were armed with this indispensable knowledge, my parents launched us upon the world where we immediately started reproducing and getting white hairs. Strange though it may seem, only a minute ago, there I was with my pacifier in my mouth, and the President of the Republic invited me to his swearing-in cere-mony to which I didn't go because I wasn't sure which pair of short pants to wear, my mother wasn't there to part my hair nor was my father there to warn me

—If you come home after eleven o'clock on Saturday, you're grounded.

It was a bad idea ever to let me leave Benfica: I miss the babies, I miss the smell of pipe tobacco, I miss my first-grade textbook, I miss having supper in my pajamas after my bath, with my bangs still damp, I miss the young twenty-something who looked eighteen. When Jünger declared

The older I get the more future I have

he was speaking like a fool. The truth is that I left part of my future behind me. On Thursday, which is when my brothers get together at my parents' house, I go there to look for it. And now I'm going to stop writing because I feel like being silent and that's of no interest to you at all.

BRAZIL

It was always a source of amazement to me that Pedro Álvares Cabral should have spent months sailing across the Atlantic to Brazil when Brazil was a mere half an hour's car ride from my grandfather's house. Every Christmas I went to Brazil with him without recourse to caravels, it was a land whose frontiers were Rua Alexandre Herculano and Rua Barata Salgueiro, and whose main geographical features were large houses and dark apartments inhabited by very ancient aunts

(Aunt Mimi, Aunt Biluca, Aunt I've-forgotten-her-name)

at the far end of long, long corridors amid the gleam of silverware, cookie tins and the shadowless objects with which the very old surround themselves. As well as aunts, Brazil was peopled by plump maids who would look at me in rapt amazement

—How he's grown

stuffing my pockets with candies while beyond the curtains passed the shadows of silent ships draped in purple silk shawls, bathtubs with rusty, rheumaticky lions' feet, prehistoric heaters in which the gas sobbed out its sorrows like some decrepit infant, a sickly cousin moaning in a bed, my aunts swaying toward me like the figures on music boxes, tremulously offering me glass jars full of coconut ice. There was a picture of them and of my great-grandmother, four long-lashed ladies in Belém do Pará, with hearts of gold and imposing bottoms

(the two feminine qualities most appreciated in the last century
by gentlemen who hastened to marry them until the bottoms finished them off, and the hearts of gold

were covered forever,

those were different times,

by widow's weeds)

a picture in which I found no resemblance at all between those
generous, dark-skinned, nicely turned young women and the ladies
with walking sticks, embalmed in faint perfumes, addressing my
grandfather

(who was to me a considerable figure in both volume and years)

with the tender smile one reserves for children and to whom my
grandfather replied from the depths of a rediscovered childhood
as if they were all still living in the Amazon jungle. Christmas was
the only time of year that aroused in me the vague suspicion that
the world had not begun when I was born and it made me a kind
of stateless person with no accent and no real home, floating about
among mythical rubber trees and genuine acacias, with one half of
me in each continent, neither of which truly belonged to me, just
as I hovered above the large houses and dark apartments, prevented
from flying off down Rua Barata Salgueiro by the ballast of candies
given to me by the adoring cooks

—Hasn't he grown and such lovely manners too

proud of my three foot six inches of mute timidity. Then gradually Brazil began to disappear: my aunts dissolved one by one into
the paths of the Prazeres cemetery, the apartments were sold, the
pianos fell silent, becoming first a memory of nothing and then
nothing, the candies ceased to bring joy to dentists, there were no
more plump maids saying to me

—Hasn't he grown

and

—Such lovely manners too

and Brazil was lost forever in the abyss of time with its heaters, its
bathtubs, silk shawls and jars of coconut ice. I still look for it in Rua

Alexandre Herculano and in Rua Barata Salgueiro because it seems to me impossible that a whole country can have been replaced by travel agents, hotels and banks. And yet it's true: Brazil has gone. Or rather it remains deep down, in one small corner of myself, with its pictures, its furniture, its crystal glasses and above all its mirrors

(I remember the mirrors)

dozens of mirrors reflecting each other, staring at each other, placed opposite each other to observe themselves in silence from their carved wood frames. More than anything and more than the death of a country, that is what still intrigues me today: when one mirror looks at itself in another mirror, what on earth does it see?

DESCRIPTION OF CHILDHOOD

Every August I would be taken to see the source of the Mondego River, a little explosion of water among moss, rocks and trees, twenty
(I think it was twenty)
miles from my grandfather's house, in a fold in the hills not visible from the verandah. My father was very young, my mother was very young, I was still so young that I knew nothing about death
(or about life)
and at seven years old I was dying of love for the gypsy girls at the Saturday markets who helped their families sell mules whose sores they disguised with black paint. I remember dark eyes, sometimes surprisingly fair hair, bare feet, dealers in gold jewelry on bicycles with an umbrella hooked in the back of their jacket collar and I would think
—They're widowers
I would think
—They're all widowers
as they pedaled off together along the Viseu road with a jewel box lashed to the saddle with belts.
(At night they would come in dreams to trouble me, cawing like crows and saying nothing. They merely looked at me.)
My mother, who could be my daughter now, cycled round

the chestnut trees, my father played tennis in Urgueiriça and painted, my grandfather read the newspaper while the bells tolled for the dead

(only other people died because we were eternal)

I saw the open coffin of a child pass by, a little white coffin, I told my brother João, my brother João said

—That's impossible

my brother Pedro leaned right over the wall

—Don't fall

the mayor was sitting smiling on the porch, there was no funeral and I felt reassured: it was the wind in Zé Rebelo's pine woods, the smell of the blackberries when we went to watch the sunset, hoping to see the green flash, the Caramulo Mountains in the distance, the curate's maid

(I can't remember her name)

—What lovely boys

giving us black grapes to eat.

The curate used to play cards with the pharmacist who was a Freemason, and I wanted to steal eggs from the chickens but was afraid they would peck me. The pharmacist was sure that God was just a load of bullshit, the curate picking up the winning hand

—You carry on sinning and I'll carry on winning

they drank tangerine liqueur from a tray with a doily on it, a liqueur made by monks and served in tiny glasses on which the sun danced

(my mother still cycling round the chestnut trees, I think her hair was light chestnut, her eyes, I'm sure, were green)

At night, a branch used to beat against the window in the table-tennis room, down below, where we slept

(António, João and Pedro, said the policeman, António, João and Pedro, like the three big feast days in June, then along came Miguel and spoiled everything, I wanted a brother called Euclides, everyone stared at me openmouthed, my uncle started to laugh and I thought

—I'll kill him

fearful of wolves, we would listen to the grown-ups' conversation but not understand the words. Senhora Dona Irene played the harp, sipped her tea very carefully, terrified of staining anything, she dyed her hair yellow, it was said that she owned some very beautiful rugs, and that many years ago she'd been rich

(how long ago was many years?)

and the lost fortune was a mystery greater than the Holy Trinity, in which I didn't believe but didn't not believe either: it was a bearded gentleman, a man with a heart surrounded by thorns, a dove, and my grandmother praying to avert the September thunderstorms. Then the sun came out, Vergílio let us take the reins of Carriça, the cook was fired, the cook trying to cling to her colleague

—Give me a kiss just one little kiss

and me frightened

—What happened?

—Nothing

before supper they gave us a shower using a bucket with holes in it, we would go to bed in pajamas and dressing gown, our cheeks as red and polished as apples. The two worst tortures in the world were brushing your teeth and eating soup, all kinds of strange things happened that were never explained, but it didn't matter as long as there were mints to eat and coloring books, lying on my stomach on the floor, getting everything dirty and no one telling me off and being taken up to the mountains to see the source of the Mondego, a lot of tiny wet pebbles in which people and animals drowned

apparently

when it reached Coimbra. Senhora Dona Irene had the face of someone who had once been in love with a boy who drowned, a second lieutenant with a mustache who smiled at her while she played the harp and he languidly smoked a cigarette. Before I was born there had been a war in Spain and another one called World, the same as the cough lozenges

(World Cough Candy will make you feel just dandy)

bought by the ounce in the grocery store owned by Senhor
Casimiro who wore glasses held together with sticky tape. Senhor
Casimiro's wife called us the Senhora's little grandsons, and the
grocery store smelled of shadows and mold. Colégio Grão Vasco,
Colégio Grão Vasco: boys the same age as me behind the railings.
Senhor Casimiro's wife was neither fat nor thin, she gave us colored
lollipops, the branch beat all night on the window of the table-tennis
room and down below the howls of the dogs and the bells ringing
wildly because of a fire they wouldn't let us see. There was a kind
of reddish glow, people running about and shouting. Right, back
to bed, im-me-di-ate-ly. We went back to bed and almost at once
we were thirty years old. Then I noticed that most of the people
had become photographs, but the little explosion of water from the
Mondego is still there, among moss, rocks and trees. One day I'll go
up to the mountains in August and find

—What lovely boys

the Senhora's little grandsons. I still know nothing about life.

OF HORSES, KINGS, PRIESTS,
AND AUNT PURITY

Calçada da Ajuda was my place of torment on Saturday mornings. Calçada da Ajuda was home to the 7th Cavalry Regiment, and in the 7th Cavalry Regiment was a riding school, in the riding school was a colonel, in the right hand of the colonel was a whip, in the left hand of the colonel was a rope, at the end of the rope was a horse and on the horse there was me walking, trotting and galloping with my grandfather shouting

—Sit up straight

shouting angrily

—Don't be such a pansy, sit up straight

while I shook with fear, on the verge of tears, perched on the very summit of the creature, an unstable thing rather like a rocking chair with no arms, dangerous at either end and uncomfortable in the middle, and that smelled of the leather chests in the dressing room at home and of rose manure, a rocking chair with no arms that snorted, jumped and bucked

—Sit up straight

until the colonel ordered that confusion of legs, mane and eyes to stop, and I staggered away, biting my lip, pursued by my grandfather's sadness

—All you inherited from me was my name

and one of my brothers took my place on that rotatory torment. It was true that all I had inherited from him was his name: I wasn't

interested in the royalist cause, which was a newspaper called *The Debate* and photographs of ugly fair-haired children wishing you Merry Christmas at Christmas time, I wasn't interested in my grandfather's grandfather who was called Bernardo and had been a viscount

(by an accident of birth the viscountship fell to me, a fact that left me completely indifferent, quite apart from not wanting to read *The Debate* or to receive pictures of ugly children at Christmas, the children of an equally ugly gentleman who didn't even wear a crown)

I wasn't interested in spending my Sundays being bored to death at horse shows at the Jockey Club while my grandfather talked to other officers, and the President of the Republic, a little old general called Carmona, patted my head when he entered the stand. The little old general had defended my grandfather after the Monsanto Uprising,* which was when my grandfather wanted to put the king on the throne, but very bad men with black beards wouldn't let him. Because of those very bad men with black beards, my grandfather had to go and live in Morocco, but fortunately, otherwise I would have been born a Moor, up jumped Salazar,† who loved Our Lady of Fátima and people like us, and my family returned to Portugal where there was a house called Casa da Santa Zita that sent us maids to bring me breakfast in bed, and, thank God, order was restored to the world because Salazar sent packing the sons of the very bad men with black beards who called themselves democrats and whose dream was to drive the priest from the church, steal our silver and force us to eat at the same table as the gardener. To the grave concern of my uncles

—Who ever do you take after?

---

*Monsanto Uprising. A monarchist rebellion against the Portuguese Republic in 1919.

†António de Oliveira Salazar (1889–1970). Founder and leader of the Estado Novo (New State), which controlled Portugal's social, economic, cultural, and political life from 1933 to 1974, he was de facto dictator of the Portuguese Republic from 1932 to 1968.

this gloomy prospect didn't bother me in the least because the gardener was much nicer than the visitors who filled our garden on Sundays and played canasta and always got my name wrong

—Are you João, Pedro or Miguel?

more than that he taught me to trap birds and didn't tell on me if he caught me smoking. Besides, the gardener's sons played better soccer than the fair-haired boys of the Christmas cards, who had mouths like the fish in the lake and who you just knew would be useless at everything, and if the priest disappeared from the church I wouldn't have to assist at mass and there would be no more lunches at home for the priests who were always whispering virtuous things to me as they stroked my knees. I never understood why, but if my grandmother suddenly came into the room the priests would immediately move away and stop pestering me with questions about my chastity, a word I didn't know but that was related to strange matters for which the democrats had no respect and so Salazar had, of course, packed them off to prison. To avoid being packed off to prison with them, I looked up *chastity* in the encyclopedia and learned that it was the same as purity. Since I didn't know what purity was either, I asked my mother

—What's purity?

one of my brothers got in before her

—You mean who's Purity?

referring to a family friend who smeared our faces with scarlet whenever she kissed us and after a certain point stopped visiting the house altogether because of some complicated business with the husband of a cousin. I heard someone say

—One day Purity will end up in the gutter

and I finally understood why the priests were so anxious to prevent me in turn from falling into such an unclean place. Saintly men. It was just a shame they didn't come to the riding school on Saturday mornings to keep me from tumbling into the rose manure of the horses and ending up in the gutter like Aunt Purity, thus saddening Salazar, that poor, kind, generous man who did so much for us.

MUSEUMS

They say that the painter Bonnard, briefcase under arm, used to visit the museums exhibiting his works. When the attendant wasn't looking, he would take a palette out of his briefcase and retouch the canvases. I like to think of the aging artist, dressed like a bank clerk from the 1920s, wearing a bookkeeperly tie and hat, and a beard that, in photographs, looks fake

(and who can say it wasn't?)

secretly amending his own work like a nervous child. On the very few occasions when I've visited a museum I've always harbored the absurd hope that I would find him there, glasses perched on his nose, correcting his paintings. Since I never did see him, I was almost always bored. In those places of contemplation and ecstasy, I'm more fascinated I think by the burglar alarms than I am by the pictures.

In this I resemble the Chinese man who used to go to concerts and, as soon as the musicians had finished tuning their instruments, he would stand up, applaud, and leave. As a child, when they decided it was time to teach me to like the important and beautiful things of life, I was trailed profusely around Spain, France and Italy. I retain the melancholy memory of endless corridors punctuated at intervals by tall spittoons

(I would love to have spat in them, but they wouldn't let me because this was, it seems, an activity incompatible with a love of what is important and beautiful)

endless corridors, as I was saying, aged attendants yawning in corners and, inside the picture frames, ladies and gentlemen from another age looking at me from the walls, grave-faced and accusing. There were chairs as well with a cord tying the arms together

(—Why can't I sit down?

—Because it's a Louis XVI chair

—That's all right, as soon as he comes back, I'll get up)

statues with bits missing, dusty fragments protected by glass from overdiligent cleaning women, detritus that as far as I was concerned wasn't worth two bits and yet aroused respectful admiration, naked Greeks, with very tiny weenies or else with their weenies covered by a vine leaf

(I never understood the connection between weenies and vine leaves and when I asked, people would just shrug. I still don't know)

Greeks with tiny weenies and with an enormous everything else— which makes me wonder when I see those bulging sinewy creatures from the world of bodybuilding—more spittoons, toilets with no graffiti in them where I was told to pee even if I didn't want to

(the only toilets without graffiti I have ever seen)

a wakelike silence, the echo of our footsteps like footsteps in an underground garage at night and then, thank God, the exit, thank God, the street

(before the exit there was a counter where bespectacled ladies were selling colored catalogues full of the very things that had just been tormenting me)

and out in the street were the real sun, real buildings, real trees and proper toilets full of obscenities and fascinating drawings. Years ago on a pedagogical impulse I took my daughter Isabel to the Gulbenkian Museum. I promenaded her past canvas after canvas, I explained, pointed things out, insisted, informed. Outside in the garden again, back in the natural light of day, back in life, I asked fearfully

—Did you enjoy it?

After a silence in which there trembled the fear of displeasing me, I heard

—I'm sorry, Dad, but I found it really boring

and I jumped for joy and carried her off to a really seedy café and ordered two vanilla ice creams. We spent hours licking them and mine was so good that I can still remember the taste.

IT PROBABLY WASN'T QUITE LIKE THIS, BUT LET'S PRETEND THAT IT WAS

W hat I most liked about Beira Alta was my grandfather's deafness. He used a kind of hearing aid from which emerged a coiled wire that ended in the huge battery that sat in his top pocket, and I always had the idea, given his intent expression, that he was communicating with the angels or with those disembodied voices I thought I could hear in the pine trees and which he was doubtless listening to as well. He never heard us mere earthlings: my grandmother would shout and gesticulate to tell him we were there, and my grandfather would look down and smile, make a movement as if to glance in our direction and then forget, distracted by the pine trees or by some celestial emergency. There was very little of the person about him: I can't remember seeing him laugh or eat; he would either sit silently on the verandah looking out at the mountains or he would read the newspaper, which arrived on the midday train and had to be fetched from the station. In his white linen jacket, he would lean against a pillar, making the noise of fluttering pigeons as he turned the pages, but his expression never changed. Perhaps he wasn't even reading it: he would linger over the news long enough for us to think he was reading, then abandon the paper on a canvas chair and walk down to the vineyard, avoiding stepping on the ridges between the terraces, with the absentminded lightness of the seraphim. His presence was a silent absence that smelled of brilliantine: in the evening, after my shower

(the water was pumped up from the well and the shower was a bucket with holes in it)

they would let me put a drop of that white cream on my hair which left it feeling crisp and stiff and bathed me in a perfume from Paradise. Contrary to my expectations, the sounds of the house did not diminish in intensity

(the chestnut trees continued to knock at the windows)

and the angels took no interest in me. I would have supper in my pajamas, feeling very annoyed with God.

I can't recall my grandfather doing anything apart from levitating. From time to time, he would put a cigarette in his cigarette holder and create clouds with his mouth. Perhaps the construction of clouds was his main job: the maids addressed him as Senhor Engenheiro and, in my view, engineers were people who built bridges and houses. My grandfather, who favored things weightless and insubstantial, preferred more gaseous substances that obeyed the caprices of the wind. His smoke-caravels, perfect and rigorous, sailed west throughout September, taking the wild ducks and the summer with them. When he wearied of weaving the autumn, my grandfather would fall asleep in his armchair in the living room.

Just as I cannot recall him actually doing anything, I cannot ever recall him saying hello to anyone. Visitors came and went, we came and went, the newspapers were screwed up and thrown in the rubbish bin announcing the following day

(the consignment of the newspapers to the rubbish bins signaled the coming of tomorrow)

and my grandfather would sit, silent and absent, sometimes asleep in his armchair and sometimes out on the verandah, constructing clouds, the one immutable thing in a world in which even the trees died. The same white linen jacket, the same white cream, the same white hair, the same white smile, distracted and, or so it seems to me now, all these years later, slightly sad, which is understandable because in the Heaven of the catechism, joy was a cavernous and gloomy thing, and Latin

(the official language of sacristies)

a difficult Esperanto. Spending one's day listening to a hearing aid, receiving declensions, must get boring. When I turned twelve, my grandfather died and Beira Alta came to an end. I don't know what happened to the jacket and to the cigarette holder that created those clouds, but much later on I found the hearing aid in one of those cupboards full of useless objects where the past is stored: albums, letters, broken cups, odd keys, exotic stamps, phosphorescent virgins who had lost their halo, everything that will allow future archaeologists to reconstruct us from this pile of detritus, thinking how backward we were compared to the days of three-masted galleys. At most, the hearing aid will intrigue them as it intrigues me. They will put the earpieces in their ears

(as I put the earpieces in my ears)

the enormous battery in their top pocket

(as I put the enormous battery in my top pocket)

they will connect the two things with the coiled wire

(as I connect the two things with the coiled wire)

and they will listen, astonished

(as I listen, astonished)

to the ancient murmuring of the pine trees and the conversations of the seraphim. The rest will be the echo of the water pump allowing me to have a shower, perhaps the fleeting vision of a child plastered in brilliantine negotiating with his mother over the soup he is served for supper, agreeing to eat it in exchange for a double helping of crème caramel. And with a little bit of luck, a deaf gentleman will create clouds for them on a verandah that looks out over the mountains before heading off with the clouds and the ducks in the direction of autumn. Now I'm the one who's deaf. And on sleepless nights the little bean that modern medicine has placed in my ear only brings me the amplified noises of an underground garage and the distorted squeaks of the universe. I must get back to Beira Alta as soon as I can and find those angels. In my white linen jacket and with my cigarette holder they will take me for my grandfather and ask, in Latin, how I am. I don't quite know how to answer

—Not too bad

but I substitute the words with a shrug of the shoulders and one finger indicating the tricks played on me by my bladder. Then I read the newspaper, light a cigarette and make a disastrous attempt at constructing a cloud: at fifty-seven it's time for me to leave too, en route to autumn, leaving in the cupboard for useless objects a dozen or so books, which are my equivalent of odd keys. The only thing you can open with them are doors that no longer exist.

WHO HAD TO MURDER ME TO
MAKE ME SO SWEET?

The huge, stupid finger of my primary-school teacher searching me out among the desks to question me about the tributaries on the left bank of the Tejo; my aunt's patience in trying to teach piano

using the Schmoll method

to my graceless hands; the gardener who used to kill sparrows, holding them behind his back and breaking their necks, all the while laughing at me; the girl I fell in love with when I was ten, who was going to be a dentist but who died before that in between the iron sheets of a car, horribly rumpled, on a bed of seats, wheels and chassis: which of those things murdered me first? Is it difficult to suffer or do other people think of it merely as an unpleasant commonplace, like old age and ill health? The girl, who was twenty then, was dragged from that mattress wrapped about a plane tree and I could have sworn that her mouth said

—António

but her mouth said nothing, the indifference of the dead that we call a smile but that isn't any kind of smile at all, it's a vitreous lack of interest, an irritating stillness. I want only what is impossible: a girl waving to me, a boat arriving, being able to use a hammer with my left hand, knowing how to dance the tango, seeing you far off, at the airport, waiting for me. My aunt taught me sol-fa, set the metronome whose finger, equally huge and stupid, moved to right and left with a cardiac obstinacy. In the restaurant the usual friends talk and talk. About what? I stopped listening to them when a retired couple came in: they took ages to sit down, their knees like the springs on a penknife whose blades, poor things, only bend with difficulty. When one of them started shouting, the other cupped a hand to one ear. The wife asked the waiter to put the leftovers in a plastic bag for the little dog stuck at home, desperately scratching at the door with its nails, piddling on the rug in its anxiety. Their apartment doubtless is full of ancient furniture, shadows and very old magazines. Perhaps the only time they don't need to cup a hand to their ear is to listen to the metronome. How do you starch rumpled iron sheets? Very old magazines to be read on rainy Sundays: *A Illustração Portugueza*, *Très Sport* and in *Très Sport* the world champion, Georges Carpentier, in very long shorts, his fists up, his hair parted down the middle. His opponent wore a mustache with curled ends, like the second lieutenants at the turn of the century who wooed young ladies standing on balconies draped with bedspreads on afternoons when there were processions. The very old magazines smelled of bandstands and revelry, of the stuffed bird owned by the Republican pharmacist who heaped insults on God as he filled prescriptions. My grandmother explained to me in a low voice that when the pharmacist was a young man

(and I'm sure the pharmacist was never young, my grandmother was lying to me)

he had been an ace at stick fencing, which, to judge by what she told me about the sport sounded like some kind of balletic brawl. If the pharmacist ever caught God napping he would give him the most almighty beating. On Christmas Day, he would go into the church, stand arms akimbo, hat on his head, and challenge God

—Come on, then, show us what you're made of

God, the soul of patience, put up with him for a few years and said nothing, but then he decided

(God takes a long time to come to a decision)

to make him fall down the stairs. It was, in my opinion, a treach-

erous death. On the day of his funeral my aunt stopped the metronome: she must have loved the pharmacist when he was young.
The proof is that when she bought cough syrup from him her lips
trembled, and the pharmacist's arms made meaningless gestures.
He addressed her as

—Senhora

and as long as we were there he left God in peace. Once, when my
aunt left her umbrella behind and I went back to the shop to fetch it,
I found the pharmacist blowing his nose. He thrust his sleeve into
the jar full of throat lozenges and, without removing the handkerchief from his nose, held out a fistful of cubes that smelled of euca-
lyptus and sugar, with a bearded gentleman

Professor Malinovski

printed on the wrapper, inside a medallion surrounded by little
flowers. My aunt blushed when I handed her the cough lozenges
and she lovingly put them away in her box of jewels, which consisted of a cameo that had become detached from its frame and her
parents' wedding rings. Then she asked me

—What was he doing?

I answered

—Blowing his nose

and she stood for ages in the living room staring at the piano. A
long time ago, I read in a book that a woman's homeland is wherever she fell in love. That night, over supper, I noticed that my aunt
was wearing perfume. And the wisteria beat against the windows,
saying good-bye. It seemed to me that the wisteria was making
meaningless gestures, it seemed to me that one cluster of flowers
was saying

—Senhora

it seemed to me that my aunt was listening, but I must have been
mistaken. Yes, I was obviously mistaken: since when have wisteria
blown their noses?

SEE YOU ON THE WAY HOME

In Rua Cláudio Nunes, along which all funerals passed en route to
the cemetery, there was a bar called See You on the Way Home.
And indeed, once the prayers, the flowers and the tears were over
and the coffin duly interred, the bar would fill up with relatives
of the male sex and within an hour it would be a pandemonium
of drunkenness, raucous laughter and community singing inter-
spersed with a few bouts of fisticuffs. As a child, I was astonished
at how easily dignified mourners became revelers with shirt collar
unbuttoned and tie stuffed in their pocket, cheering on Benfica with
glass in hand. Their wives, in rigorous black, came to fish them out
of there in the early evening, indignant at such carousing and at
such a show of disrespect for the dead, shepherding their husbands'
stumbling steps and joie-de-vivre back to the quiet of their homes,
where jubilant cries continued to be heard, albeit muffled by sleep,
until subsumed into the final snore of contented organs. The wives
complained to the prior, the prior had words with the Parish Council, the chairman of the Parish Council, who himself most evenings
knocked back a few glasses of wine at See You on the Way Home,
pointed out to the owner that the souls in Purgatory, depicted in the
catechism as being licked by flames, deserved the pity owed to bar-
becued souls. The owner, who, beneath his grimy shirt, concealed
a heart sensitive to second-degree burns, understood the prior's
scruples and took down the sacrilegious sign, spent a week ponder-

ing the matter with the help of a fruity young red wine that loos-
ened his synapses, then turned the sign around, inscribed upon it
a more decent name and hung it above the door. The prior was
reassured, the chairman of the Parish Council praised his perspi-
cacity and the delicacy of his feelings, the wives felt they had won
the battle, and the whole of Rua Cláudio Nunes applauded. See
You on the Way Home became Ye Olde Stopping-off Place. As I
said at the start, I was a mere child and consequently little affected
by the subtleties of the intellect. In my ignorance, it seemed to me
that there was no difference between See You on the Way Home
and Ye Olde Stopping-off Place. But I must have been the only
one to think so because Ye Olde Stopping-off Place continues, I
believe, to enjoy general approval, producing dozens of cases of
delirium tremens a day every time the waterwheel of fate, in the
form of the endless line of hearses, ceases its job of transporting
griefs. I was only a child and did not yet know W. C. Fields's retort
when someone asked him why he didn't drink water

—I never drink water because of the disgusting things that fish
do in it

and besides, in the domain of my parents and environs, Travessa
dos Arneiros, Travessa do Vintém das Escolas, Rua Ernesto da
Silva, Calçada do Tojal, I had become accustomed to living with
an extraordinary legion of Homeric alcoholics: Senhor Florindo,
the cobbler, Senhor Florentino, the porter, old João Paço de Arcos,
the retired tram driver, Senhor Carlos, the seller of caged birds, all
of whom I would sometimes find sitting in a row on the sidewalk,
interrupting their interminable debates to greet me

—Good afternoon, Master Antoninho

a sentence that took a good fifteen minutes to pronounce, requir-
ing great salivary control

(after the fifth glass the saliva gets stuck to the gums and the
upper gums to the lower gums)

as well as mental concentration if they were not to confuse me
with Master Joãozinho, Master Pedrinho and Master Miguelzinho

(Master Nuninho and Master Manuelzinho were, at the time, doubtless only future projects)

an easy mistake to make given the constant stream of babies being produced on the assembly line of that large red-brick house, only complicating Senhor Florentino and company's calculations still further. There are times when I wonder why it is I have never drunk alcohol, especially given the many numerous and illustrious examples at my disposal. And there are occasions when I regret not drinking. I'd like to sit on the edge of the sidewalk, after a fine funeral, cheering Benfica and, above all, saying

—Good afternoon, Master Antoninho

and find the doctor's eldest son, coming home from school, staring at me with a rapt admiration he has never shown me before. Master Antoninho for whom literature, with the exception of Sandokan, is a real bore, and whose sole object in life is to grow up quickly, so that he can wear the ring with the black stone on his little finger without anyone telling him off, so that he will never have to eat soup again and can dazzle the watchmaker's unattainable daughter with a pair of long pants. If I had started wearing long pants earlier, I would now be living, radiantly happy, in a constellation of cuckoo clocks and brass alarm clocks instead of all this dust from books which is bad for the lungs and doesn't tell me the time. And if I were ever to need a pacemaker, the doctor could fit me up with the saucepan that hangs on the kitchen wall and whose minute hand is a knife and whose second hand is a fork. If we were to add to this one of Snow White's dwarves from on top of the refrigerator, what more could a man need to feel happy?

O, ROSE, UNFURL YOUR SKIRT

When I was little, I often used to dream that I was flying. It was like this: I would be chatting away in the garden or the living room, and suddenly I would lose interest in the conversation

(people were always talking in my dreams)

I would turn my back on everyone, give a little jump, open my arms and take off. The dream seemed so real that even today I can still remember the clarity of things seen from above: our house, the trees, the other houses, the street, the family playing canasta beneath an umbrella, the pavilion by the lake, and me flying hither and thither like a birch leaf in autumn. The only thing I can't remember is how those dreams used to end. I must have grown up very fast after that because I didn't fly again for years, and my dreams grew dark and sad and despairing, leaving me, once awake, in a state of restless introspection. I was just starting to shave then and I was amazed that the hair on my head should be fair and the bristles on my chin so dark. I read once that Dom João de Castro,* on seeing a man with dark hair and a white beard, commented that the gentleman obviously thought more with his chin than with his head. This remark stayed with me for quite a while and yet, until today, I thought I had forgotten it. There is so much I thought I had forgot-

---

*Dom João de Castro (1500–48). Fourth viceroy of the Portuguese Indies.

ten that suddenly resurfaces in my mind. My mother's father, for example, reading the newspaper on the verandah at Nelas. Going with João to the pine woods in Beira Alta to eat wild blackberries and hoping to see the green flash at sunset in Caramulo. Senhor Casimiro at the grocery store who used to give us candy. Life then seemed so slow and vast. I flew again in Africa, during the war, but it made for bitter flying: hither and thither like a birch leaf in autumn and down below corpses and the chickens that the red kite would swoop down on, rising at once into the air again, its victim grasped in its talons. The house had disappeared and the family no longer played canasta beneath the umbrella. The gardener used to put the poles of the umbrellas in concrete blocks and each block had two holes in it, one vertical and the other slanted, which we chose depending on the direction of the sun. That's another thing I thought I'd forgotten, those concrete blocks, with iron rings, which I wasn't strong enough to move. And the stone table. And the processions on Sunday, with bawling children dressed as angels. My mother said that when I was a baby, she used to kiss me so much her lips would hurt. I didn't forget that, it simply never existed for me. My mother's grandparents were merely stern-faced generals in a photo, and my mother's father silently read the newspaper. The silence around him

(in my memory that silence was vast)

wrapped him in a second solitude. All silence, I think, is a second solitude increasing the first, and my mother's father seemed to me the most isolated person in the world. Now and then he would smile. My mother's mother told me that when he died he lay in his coffin smiling sweetly. That happened in 1955, when I wasn't yet thirteen and I don't know what will have happened to that smile now. Is it in the cemetery in Benfica? In Nelas? On the stone step facing the vineyard, with a lit cigarette in a cigarette holder? In the months following the funeral I found traces of lipstick on the glass of his photograph: the sideboard in my parents' room is a discreet graveyard of smiles. To the right of the silver-backed brushes, at the other end, there is a sort of metal tree with six round fruits on it, six little frames, and a son in each fruit, which hang in pairs. The brightness from the street, Travessa dos Arneiros, lights them from the side as it shines through the curtain. Six fruits. The fruit that is me also smiles: a slightly vain smile, slightly foolish, like the smile of all perennially shy people. I peer at him and I don't understand. It must have been taken around the time when those little dark bristles started sprouting on my face. If I say to him

—António

(a very ordinary name, my grandfather's name)

he doesn't answer. He remains there, vain and foolish, to the right of the silver-backed brushes, and so I prefer to say good-bye

—Bye, António

and move from my parents' bedroom to what we, as children, used to call the middle room, and from the middle room to the living room, where we are all sitting on sofas, talking. My mother says softly

—The soup's on the table

and when I take my place, I can't even remember that when I was a child I used to fly. All I'm thinking about is where those concrete blocks for the umbrellas are now.

THE GREAT BARRIGANA

For the last forty years, I have, with enthusiasm, fervor and admiration, seen nearly all the great Portuguese goalkeepers in action, from the unforgettable Azevedo, the Hercules of Barreiro, to José Pereira, the Blue Bird

(for months and months I kept with me a biography of his life, a lovely book full of huge portrait photographs, one of which showed a tiny, shrunken man standing beside a train and bearing the impressive caption: His father, Amadeu Pereira, working as a guard at the Rossio tunnel)

I saw the giant Ernesto, from Atlético, the bane of all wingers, I saw Abraão, from Olhanense, whose magical name had apocalyptic echoes of the catechism, I saw Cesário, from Sporting de Braga, one glorious afternoon on Benfica's dirt pitch, when he saved every attempt on his goal made by Palmeiro, Arsénio, Águas, Rogério and Rosário, I saw Capela, from Académica, and Sebastião, the blond Nero of Estoril Praia, famous for his acrobatic leaps, I saw the entire Francisco Lázaro Stadium bow down before the amazing Aníbal, with his sculpted, brilliantined hair, and about whom my Uncle João Maria exclaimed: He's the greatest Hannibal since Hannibal Barca of the Phoenician Wars, I saw mean and moody Carlos Gomes kicking out at photographers before his trade to Spain and, when he wasn't paid, threatening the club's president with the wise words: No money, no goalkeeper, I fondly followed Vital, of

Lusitano de Évora, who always used to gouge out a line on the pitch with the pensive heel of his boot to mark the center of the goal, and yet, to my great displeasure and frustration, I never saw a single match played by my idol Frederico Barrigana, The Man with the Iron Hands, the goalkeeper for Oporto Soccer Club. In an attempt to make up for such misfortune I would devotedly cut out any newspaper photos that showed him jumping up, usually at the same time as a forward from the opposing team was thrusting a dissuasive knee into his private parts

(why do we call them parts when they're perfectly whole?)

intending to cool his opponent's murderous intentions; I admired his bald head and the hat that covered it as precisely as a capsule; I collected all the interviews he gave

(one example of his prophetic statements: The Elvas lads are going to give their all)

and openmouthed, one hand cupped to my ear, I would sit glued to my father's radio every Sunday afternoon at three, as Artur Agostinho described in epic tones the exploits of the great Frederico Barrigana in a stadium packed to the gills with spectators. When I was twelve, if I hadn't wanted so passionately to become a writer, I would have wanted to be The Man with the Iron Hands: he is, by divine gift, perfect in himself, from the very beginning.

The pain of never having seen Frederico Barrigana in action accompanied me throughout my life in the form of bouts of periodic melancholy that made me dismiss with an impatient shrug all the other goalkeepers, Portuguese and foreign, that Benfica's Stadium of Light presented to me: it was the Barrigana Syndrome

(a nosological entity that I still hope to get accepted into the medical books)

working away at my brain: The Man with the Iron Hands became the unattainable ideal measure, like the platinum-iridium bar stored in the vaults of the Institute of Weights and Measures

(for further clarification, see the illustration in the physics manual used in the third year of high school) against which everyone was measured, be they politicians, poets, viceroys or sculptors.

In 1973, in Baixa do Cassanje* in Angola, the Almighty so willed it that my dreams and prayers should finally be answered. In an interval in the martial dramas taking place on the frontier with Congo, which are of no importance now, I happened to be passing the Ferroviário de Malanje soccer field when I noticed a man of a certain age, bald and paunchy and wearing a track suit, shooting at the goal defended by a mulatto boy with a part shaved down the middle of his tangle of tight curls, and behind the net, a group of small black boys enthusiastically applauding and shouting

—Come on, Barrigana

—Clobber him, Barrigana

—Finish him off, Barrigana

I approached, feeling first incredulous and then ecstatic: it was He. On a soccer field somewhere in Africa, in the midst of baobabs and mango trees thick with bats, The Man with the Iron Hands, with a whistle hanging round his neck, was teaching soccer to the children of the Luanda slums, gripped by a missionary zeal and a pedagogical devotion that transported and touched me. At each shot from the genius, the children yelled

—Sock it to him, Barrigana

with a familiarity that irritated my idol. No one, in his view and in mine, be they head of state, field marshal, pope or dentist, had the right to address the divine Frederico Barrigana in such familiar terms. Justifiably indignant at such an outrage, The Man with the Iron Hands made a patrician gesture that immobilized the mulatto with the shaved part, who immediately stood submissively to attention, then he advanced with forefinger raised toward the children, who respectfully froze, and, in a terrifying Last Judgment tone of voice, intended to make them bend the linguistic knee by teaching

---

*Baixa do Cassanje. A region in the north of Angola.

them the respectful courtesy due to the gods whom merciful Jupi-
ter very occasionally sends down to us in order to justify our existence: conquistadors, saints, surveyors and tax inspectors

—Don't call me Barrigana. I'm Senhor Barrigana to you.

And I never admired him more than I did on that day.

BEFORE DARKNESS FALLS

For reasons I won't go into right now, the last few difficult weeks have forced me to think about the past and the present and to forget about the future. Especially the past: I have rediscovered the smell and the echo of hospitals, the atmosphere like soft white felt through which the nurses glide like swans and that so thrilled me when I was an intern, the silence of rubber, the gleam of metal, people speaking in hushed tones as if in church, the sad solidarity of waiting rooms, the interminable corridors, the terrifyingly solemn ritual that I watch wearing a tremulous smile that serves as my walking stick, a fake courage barely disguising my fear. Especially the past because the future is getting narrower and narrower and I say especially the past because the present has become the past too, memories that I thought were lost and that return without my realizing they were lost, the Sunday markets at Nelas, the squeals of the suckling pigs

(I remember the squeals of the suckling pigs so vividly now)

a ring bearing the emblem of Benfica that when I was five I thought was beautiful and that my parents thought hideous, and that at fifty I still think is beautiful even though I also think it's hideous and feel that now is the right moment to start wearing it again given that I don't have that much time left for large pleasures. I want the ring with the Benfica emblem, I want my grandmother alive, I want the house in Beira, I want everything that I allowed to slip away and that I need, I want Gija to scratch my back before I go to bed, I want Zé Rebelo's pine woods, I want to play Ping-Pong with my brother João, I want to read Jules Verne, I want to go to the fair and ride on the figure-eight roller coaster, I want to see Costa Pereira save a penalty from Didi, I want to eat sweet eggy desserts. I want codfish cakes with tomato rice, I want to go to the school library and get a thrill from reading Fialho de Almeida's racy *The Redhead* in secret, I want to fall in love all over again with the wife of the Pharaoh in *The Ten Commandments* as I did when I was twelve and to whom I remained staunchly faithful for one whole summer, I want my mother, I want my little brother Pedro, I want to buy ruled paper with thirty-five lines a page from the grocery store so that I can write poetry counting out the stresses on my fingers, I want to play ice hockey again, I want to be the tallest in the class, I want to blow on my marbles for luck

ox-blood cat's eye rainbow and coral

I want Frias at Senhor André's school to tell us about the films he's seen, to talk about the Boy, the Girl and the Boy's Friend, in films I only ever saw through Frias's descriptions of them

(Manuel Maria Camarate Frias, where are you now?)

and his descriptions were much better than the films, Frias imitated the sound track, the noise of the horses, the gunfire, the brawl in the saloon, he imitated this so well it was as if we could see it all, and Norberto Noroeste Cavaleiro, the man who thought I was trying to break into his car and who boomed at me

—Dr. Cavaleiro to you, you young devil

the first time a grown-up had called me names and I felt like telling him that my father was a doctor too, and that when I first went into the locker room at Futebol Benfica, Ferra-O-Bico explained to the others

—Blondie's dad is a doctor

and a circle of respectful silence formed around me, Blondie's dad is a doctor, I want to get a cab at the door of my house and hear the driver ask

—Is this where a guy called João lives, the hockey player?

and I want to feel the same amazement that he should talk about my dad like that, I want to break one of my arms and have a plaster cast on it, or, better still, my leg, and have to use crutches and amaze the girls the same age as me, a small boy on crutches

I thought then and I think now

there isn't a girl who doesn't want to fall in love with him, what's more the cars stop to let you cross the road, I want my grandfather to draw me a horse, then get on that horse and ride away, I want to bounce up and down on the bed, I want to eat goose barnacles, I want to smoke a furtive cigarette, I want to read the *World of Adventures,* I want to be the Cisco Kid and Mozart at the same time, I want to eat Santini's ice cream, I want a flashlight with batteries for Christmas, I want chocolate umbrellas, I want my Aunt Gogó to give me my lunch

—Open your mouth now, Toino

I want a plate of lupine seeds, I want to be Sandokan, the Tiger of Malaysia, I want to wear long pants, I want to jump off trams while they're still moving, I want to be a ticket collector, I want to play all the plastic trumpets in the world, I want a shoebox full of silkworms, I want my soccer cigarette cards, I want there to be no hospitals, no patients, no operations, I want to have time to get up the courage to tell my parents that I love them very much

(I don't know if I can)

to tell my parents that I love them very much before darkness falls, ladies and gentlemen, before the final darkness falls.

PART II

PORTRAIT OF THE ARTIST

THE CONSEQUENCES
OF TRAFFIC LIGHTS

I hate traffic lights. First, because they're always red when I'm in a hurry and green when I'm not, and then there's amber, which provokes in me the most terrible indecision: should I brake or accelerate? brake or accelerate? brake or accelerate? I accelerate, then brake, accelerate once more and, when I brake again, a van has smashed in my door, hordes of people have gathered, hoping for blood, a man carrying a monkey-wrench has climbed out of his pick-up calling me You moron, the insurance company is urging me warmly to move to one of their rival companies, I have no car for a week, I stand on the sidewalk waving, like a man shipwrecked, to flag down a taxi, I pay a fortune for each trip and have, moreover, to put up with the magic firefly, the aluminum Our Lady on the dashboard, the plastic skeleton dangling from the rearview mirror, the sticker of the girl with long hair and her hat at a jaunty angle next to the warning sign: "Don't smoke, I'm asthmatic," a juxtaposition that leads me to suppose that her respiratory problems must have grown worse because of some perfidious secret on her part, although quite what I can't imagine.

The second and principal reason why I hate traffic lights is that every time I stop, the most extraordinary creatures appear at my window: sellers of newspapers, sellers of Band-Aids, virtuous ladies with a box slung around their neck who authoritatively stick the crab of Cancer on my breast, hefty supporters of the League for the

Blind selling raffle tickets alongside a truck bearing loudspeakers and the first prize of a flashy new car, the respectable gentleman whose wallet has been stolen and who needs money for the train to Oporto, the TB sufferer with a certificate to prove it, every conceivable kind of cripple

(the microcephalic, the macrocephalic, the lame, the hunch-backed, those with squints, divergent and convergent, the goitered, those with withered arms, hands with six fingers, hands with no fingers, the mentally retarded, leaders of political parties, etc.)

not to mention the volunteer firemen collecting money to buy an ambulance, graduates from Coimbra in cap and gown who have decided to make a graduation trip to Burma, and the heroin brigade that has failed to steal a single cassette player all day.

The result: by the first traffic light, I have no change. By the second, I have no jacket. By the third, I have no shoes. By the fifth, I'm naked. By the sixth, I've given away my Volkswagen. By the seventh, I'm waiting for the lights to turn red as I, along with a multitude of firemen, students, drug addicts and microcephalics, wait for the next car to appear. On average, I change clothes and cars five times before I reach my destination, and when I arrive, at the wheel of a cargo truck, wearing a pair of voluminous pants, several sizes too large, my friends complain that I'm late.

YESTERDAY, AT THREE
IN THE AFTERNOON

I've known Pedro as long as I've known myself. We both used to live in Travessa dos Arneiros, in Benfica, I down here, between Senhor Florindo the cobbler and the coal merchant's store that sold briquettes and red wine and was inhabited by a crow with clipped wings that hurled insults at the world from the sawdust floor, and he with his grandmother, close to the cemetery, in a little house with china Bambis on the shelves and a wild medlar tree in the yard trained against the wall.

We both went to the junior school run by Senhor André, together we collected cigarette cards with soccer players on them and the photographs of movie stars that you got in packs of chewing gum, we collected money for Santo António in Largo Ernesto da Silva and read the copies of the local paper, *Ecos de Pombal*, that Pedro's grandmother subscribed to, especially the deaths page, so full of surprising turns of phrase. I remember one obituary announcing the opportune death in Brazil of Commander Ernesto da Conceição Borges, "the uncle of our dear colleague Carlos Alberto Borges." Personally, I hope never to die an opportune death for any of my nephews.

Later, my father being a doctor, I went to high school at the Liceu Camões. Pedro, his grandmother being a subscriber to *Ecos de Pombal*, went to the Escola Veiga Beirão. Despite these different fates— due simply to my living in a house with twelve rooms and he in a

house with only two—we remained friends. We were both initiated on the same Saturday afternoon into the mysteries of the flesh, in a first-floor apartment in Rua do Mundo, in a room full of mirrors and torn velvet where estimable women in dressing gowns sat perched on rickety chairs and crocheted away like spinster aunts. A lady in slippers, shuffling along on varicose-veined legs like a disabled plantigrade, offered us a beer on the way in and emptied our pockets on the way out, and while we staggered down the stairs in a state of mind bordering on levitation, I thought about the young woman who had, for the first time in my life, given me the gift of flying: her name was Arlete, and she had been educated in a convent school in Penafiel and worked in Bairro Alto to support her blind mother.

(Even today, when I think of her, I hope that she subscribes to *Ecos de Pombal* so that she can one day read the news that a commander uncle of hers has died in Brazil, thus enabling her to complete her religious education and give her mother the comfort the worthy lady deserves.)

After the [Angolan] war, Pedro and I continued to see each other. He had left Benfica, rented a house in Amora and worked as an accountant for a tire factory, and I wrote novels that we discussed sentence by sentence, sitting on canvas chairs under an apple tree in the garden. I made him a character in one of my books, and made his grandmother a character in another. I used to visit him on Saturdays and we would talk for hours about the Benfica we had lost and about what we had failed to win in the meantime. I was recently divorced, Pedro never married.

Yesterday, as usual, I went to visit him in Amora. It was three o'clock in the afternoon. When I stopped the car, I saw him walking toward the apple tree, unaware that I was there, with a silk scarf around his neck. He climbed the tree and tied the scarf to a very high branch, full of tiny apples. Then he jumped and found himself hanging in space.

OLD AGE

I must be getting old: the Paula Cristinas are over twenty, the Bruno Migueis are fifteen, the Katias and the Sonias have given way to Martas, Catarinas and Marianas. Most policemen are now younger than I. I've started to like turnip soup. To fancy going home early. To observe in the morning mirror sagging flesh, unforeseen lines, my mouth between ever-deeper parentheses. To look at childhood photographs of myself as if I were staring at a stranger. To stop caring about soccer, I, who knew by heart the names of all the Benfica players, from the inimitable Fernando da Conceição Cruz, the Little Sparrow from Bairro da Liberdade, to the glorious Domiciano Barrocal Gomes Cavém, not forgetting José Pinto de Carvalho Águas, the Great Captain, and Mário Esteves Coluna, the Monster, who claimed in an interview that he was the Victor Mature of the soccer stadium. To lose interest in Santini's ice cream, which Dinis Machado,[*] a cigarette permanently clamped between his gums, believed was good for the chest. Quite soon, I'll probably be wearing a shoe on one foot and a plaid slipper on the other and go hobbling with my walking stick down to Praça Príncipe Real to count the pigeons pacing around the cedar tree with their hands behind their backs

---

[*]Dinis Machado (1930–). Portuguese writer whose best-known work is the comic novel *O que diz Molero*.

like department heads. Or playing whist with friends in berets in the Alameda Afonso Henriques, holding up my winning hand in a pose reminiscent of the Statue of Liberty. Or I'll be dispatched to Home Sweet Home, We welcome the Aged, the Disabled and Convalescents, and spend the afternoons at the window sitting in a wing chair, still in my pajama jacket, with my pockets full of toothpicks, domino tiles and biscuit crumbs, visited at Easter by nephews in a hurry bearing small bags of almonds. When I wake up, I'll find my smile on the bedside table mocking me in a glass of water containing thirty-two plastic teeth. I'll recognize my place at mealtimes by the little bottles of pills on the table-cloth, which will remind me of the flags stuck in the polar ice by pioneer explorers bundled up like race-car drivers from the heroic early days of motoring. I will be like that ancient, stone-deaf, once-pretty cousin of mine who kept an enormous radio by her bed, and to whom the male nurse, while giving her injections for her rheumatism, said

—That's a fine bit of apparatus you have there

and she, with a sigh, buttocks exposed, waiting for the syringe, proud and coquettish, replied

—You should have seen it forty years ago.

I must be getting old. And yet, without realizing, I still find myself feeling in my pocket for my catapult. I would still like to own a mother-of-pearl penknife with seven blades, corkscrew, scissors, can opener and screwdriver. I would still like my father to take me to the fair at Nelas and buy me a small round mirror with, on the back, a photograph of Yvonne de Carlo in a swimsuit. I still feel like writing my name on the window after I've misted it up with my own breath. I still walk along the edge of the sidewalk without stepping on the cracks in the pavement. I still wish my grandfather would come and kiss me goodnight. I still like solving the word puzzles in the magazines in the attic edited by Senhora Dona Maria Fernandes Costa and, when the clue is Great Portuguese Writer Now Sadly Dead, writing in the space left blank for answers the name of the emeritus poet General Fernandes Costa. When I think about it

(and I say this to the mirror)

I'm not an elderly man with the heart of a child. I'm a child whose envelope has grown slightly worn.

THE BOOK FAIR

The Book Fair involves sitting beneath a striped umbrella sign-
ing autographs and eating the ice cream my daughter Isabel
keeps bringing me from a booth three publishers away, concerned
about the tribulations of her perspiring father, who has suddenly
become the same age as she, writing dedications, tongue stuck out,
like an earnest schoolboy. Not that I'm complaining: I like people,
I like the fact that they read my books, above all, I like to meet the
people who read my books and help me feel that I'm not just casting bottles containing piratical messages out to sea, never knowing
where they might end up, and I like the novels I've written. I feel
proud of them and I'm proud of myself for having written them. So
here I am, pleased and shy, accompanied by Nelson de Matos,[*] my
patient shepherd, next to a sign with my name on it and the book
covers spread out in a fan before me, feeling rather as if I were selling Moroccan jewelry in the tunnels of the Marquês de Pombal
subway station or phosphorescent tracksuits at the Sunday market
of Feira do Relógio, which readers leaf through, buy, and hold out
for me to apply the official seal, and instead of explaining obsequi-
ously and confidently that the books won't fade or shrink in the
wash, I, lacking the gypsy spirit, merely put my label inside

[*]Nelson de Matos (1945–). Influential publisher (1981–2004) at the Lisbon publishing
house Dom Quixote.

(I'm sorely tempted sometimes to sign myself Hermès or Valentino)

and return them with the mercantile smile of one guaranteeing quality and good workmanship. As at the sales in Avenida de Roma, all kinds of things happen: there's the middle-aged gentleman with the sly eyes of a pimp who opens a copy of my novel *South of Nowhere*, leafs through it, first with curiosity, then with disappointment and moves off complaining to the man beside him, who has the long thumbnail of a guitarist

—What a gyp, it didn't even have any photographs

there's the young man with gelled hair and a crocodile at his breast, as Alexandre used to say, who asks with a knowing wink

—So which one has got the juiciest bits, I mean, sex scenes and all that

there's the virtuous aunt, with shoes like violin cases, preoccupied with the education of her nieces and nephews, the kind of aunt who is always asking if they need to go to the toilet and who regards me with apostolic severity

—What should I buy for my goddaughter, she made her first communion the day before yesterday, poor thing

there's the authoritarian who points at the title page and says in the commanding tones of a quartermaster

—OK, write there: For Fernanda on her thirty-eighth birthday with best wishes and then your name

there's the man after him, who doesn't trust me an inch and watches me as if I were filling out a prescription, leaning forward, his hands in the back pockets of his pants, and who says, outraged

—Elizabeth is written th, or have you got something against Elizabeths? Are you sure you're a writer?

At seven in the evening I strike camp. The sign with my name on it disappears, the books disappear, and since I'm fortunate enough not to live in Loures or in Damaia de Cima, I have time to celebrate the end of the sales with Isabel, by eating one last ice cream. We

sit down on the grass like a pair of lovers and observe from a distance the sellers of Moroccan jewelry and phosphorescent tracksuits authenticating their products as enthusiastically as any sales
clerk while we share the Donald Duck annuals we found on a shelf
devoted to difficult books and whose titles are a joy: *Psychoanalyze
Yourself, How to Get Rich Without Leaving the House, Adolf Hitler's Sex
Life, Five Famous Blind People, How to Cure Cancer of the Uterus Using
the Spiritualist Method*. A drunk nearby is snoring like a two-stroke
motorbike engine. The sky fills up with Magritte clouds. I propose
racing my daughter to the car and the last one to get there is a wimp.
In the car next to ours, the authoritarian gentleman who wanted
the book dedicated to Fernanda spoils our happiness: he has a mas-
cot hanging from the rearview mirror and two in the rear window,
and on the bumper a sticker of a girl wearing a hat, and he stops
talking to say

—That's the guy who wrote the book.

Fernanda, all frills and furbelows, casts me a distracted, mas-
caraed glance from the lofty heights of her glandular opulence, and
Isabel, who caught the indifference and the arrogance in full flight,
says to me pityingly as we drive to our hamburger supper

—You know, I think it might be better if you weren't a writer.

LIKE US

And so I wait for you down here, next to the post office in Estoril, or else stroll along the arcades without looking at the sea, ignoring the Casino gardens, indifferent to the lobster-red German tourists and to the straw hats decorated with plastic cherries worn by aging Americans. I lean against a low stone wall, the sun runs over me like a trickle of glycerine, and I think about your fair hair, your gestures, your mouth, your way of talking, while a dog comes to sniff my legs because, with age, I'm becoming more and more like an old tree, an elm, a medlar, a trunk of sad bones with its roots exposed to the air, and from the branches of my hands plunged in my pockets sprout the little leaves of an ancient spring, so ancient that it becomes confused with the portraits in the living room in the days when hope was a country the size of my family with its frontiers of young aunts and interrupted kisses.

I'm waiting for you down here while the blue patience of the waves writes your name with seaweed gestures on the beach and a watercolor face stares down at me, motionless, from a third-floor window, so real that there has probably never been a more surprised face, like my own surprise if no one answers when I knock on the door of the house where I live, a surprise that grips my shoulders like a borrowed jacket, I wait for you with the little light of a cigarette on my tongue so that you'll be able to recognize me in the darkness of this far-too-bright two o'clock in the afternoon,

I wait for you trembling with a fever I do not have and with my hair ruffled by the nonexistent breeze. The dog moves off, disappointed, the way everything moves away from my body, even the shadow kneeling ashamed at my feet, and when even shadows are ashamed of us, it's best to give up, lock ourselves in the bathroom and stand looking at the face we no longer are and never will be again. I wait for you, trembling, the way a very ugly boyfriend waits in the rain, clutching some autumnal chrysanthemums, intended for his equally ugly girlfriend who has forgotten all about him, nose pressed to the curtains, watching Sunday pass by. I wait for you, my dear daughter, and at this point, a car drops anchor by the curb, and on the back seat, alone, your smile discovers me, and I walk toward you, fearfully, knees shaking, in order to explain to you the giraffes in the zoo that stand indifferent to the blaring loudspeakers, as clamorous as the silence of my love for you.

THE GREAT MAN

I realized I was a genius when my novel began to appear on the shelves in bookshops; when my photo began appearing in newspapers; when I gave my first television interview. Conscious of my celebrity and my talent, I felt it would be wrong of me not to walk down the street or drive along in an open-top car, surrounded by bodyguards wearing Ray-bans, in order to show myself to the public and bestow blessings upon them.

It's true that as I passed, in a slow cortège headed by a phalanx of motorcyclists, men would doff their hats and cross themselves, bowing respectfully, it's true that some old ladies knelt down to pray. Convinced of my fame and of the admiration of my contemporaries, I resolved, since it was August, to go to the beach and offer Praia das Maçãs the gift of my presence, certain that there would be applause, autographs, ecstatic cries and the screams of fans on the verge of swooning.

I arrived at about lunchtime, after hours and hours in a long line of Sunday traffic clearly packed with enthusiastic readers, and I stopped at Augusto's restaurant where a multitude of my subjects were bent over their fish, poised to acclaim me with all the fervor of limitless love. No one seemed to notice my entrance: not a single jaw stopped chewing its steak, not a nose looked up from the cruet stand to observe me and wonder, and when I, annoyed by their incomprehensible indifference, coughed to attract their attention,

Augusto's voice boomed out at me from the bar at the back of the restaurant, so loud that it made the glasses of Colares wine tinkle and disturbed the hibernating lobsters limping over the pebbles in the bottom of the aquarium.

—Well if it isn't Antoninho! The times I had to give you a kick in the ass!

Half a dozen bored eyelids rose from their greens, and Augusto kept slapping me on the back hard enough to dislocate my ribs

—There you'd be trying to crawl under the wire fence to get into the swimming pool for free and there I'd be on guard, running after you, isn't that right, you young rascal? Oh, yes, those were the days.

Despite the precedent of illustrious colleagues
(Villon, Genet)
I found nothing to say. And Augusto, shoving me with his giant hands toward a table, next to the crabs and the lobsters, occupied by a weedy-looking bald man

—And what about that time you landed a punch on Zé Tó here at the ice rink? You were a real handful then. Oh, yes, the number of times I had to give you a kick in the ass. Those were the days, all right.

I could recall neither the punch nor Zé Tó, but the weed appeared to harbor resentful memories and muttered as he pressed himself against the aquarium as if to protect himself from some new blow

—He thought he was really hot stuff on the soccer field, but at the beach tournament he did nothing but let in easy goals.

To the left of the weed a toothless man, whom I also failed to recognize, wheezed lubriciously from the depths of his glass of *bagaço*

—His mother's maids, though, were really something. What legs!

the other customers' eyelids returned to their greens and Augusto, in a whisper, so that his wife, who was frying fish in the kitchen, wouldn't hear him

—Fan-tastic

and the weed, vengefully

—Not that he did anything about it, though, he was a little angel, a complete goof. Casimiro from the butcher's snaffled 'em all.

And from the distant past, as if in a dream, I see a motorcycle and a crash helmet that smells of steak patrolling our house, meanwhile Augusto, touched, and in a fury of nostalgia, continued to pound my poor bones

—So what are you up to these days, you rascal?

and I, shrunken and humiliated, in a little thread of a voice, amazed at the extent of his ignorance

—I've written a book

the weed, triumphant

—A rehash of someone else's work, I bet

I seized him by the collar with the idea of dumping him in the aquarium to keep the lobsters company, when Augusto proudly pinned me against the beer barrels

—Still fighting, eh, still causing a rumpus? Oh, the times I've had to kick your ass

one of the customers angrily removed a bone from his mouth and looked at me in disgust

—Send your little friend away so that we can eat our lunch in peace.

On my way to the door I realized with rage that the Portuguese did not deserve me. I considered emigrating, asking for asylum at the Colombian Embassy, committing suicide with cockroach poison. Once in my car, I could still see Augusto gesticulating, I could still hear the weed sneering

—Don't forget to send me a copy of that "book" of yours

and I was just about to start the engine when a little old man dropped his kebab and ran toward me waving his napkin

—Just a moment just a moment

finally, someone who had read me, someone who respected me, someone who knew who I was. I turned off the engine, put on my autograph smile, and the little old man leaning in through the window

—You're not by any chance
and me thinking, At last
—I'm I'm
and he, his face radiant
—the barber's nephew?
It must have been the climate
(I really cannot think of any other reason)
but I've never been back to Praia das Maçãs again.

PORTRAIT OF THE ARTIST
AS A YOUNG MAN—I

W hen, at around eight years old, I decided to devote myself
to literature, I imagined that all writers without exception
resembled Sandokan, Tiger of Malaysia

(my hero then and now)

by which I mean incredibly handsome, dark-skinned, bearded,
green-eyed and with a ruby fixed in the middle of his turban on his
forehead. The fact that I was fair-haired, blue-eyed and rubyless worried me and I even considered rubbing shoe polish on my hair to
make it darker: I experimented on one section of hair and resembled
nothing so much as a dwarf chimney sweep, my family said

—Are you stupid or something?

and ordered me to wash my face and hands and come to the
table and I spent the whole of supper with my nose in my soup
hating my parents for not having made me mulatto. In my view
I didn't really have the physique for drama, poetry, stories, and I
prepared myself to change careers and to be either retired, a martyr or a hostage

(the three alternative careers I had chosen to follow as an adult if
the arts failed me)

when, one providential Sunday, I saw in Benfica a plump gentleman, wearing glasses and a linen suit, standing outside Marijú's
store window eating a strawberry ice cream.

I was told that he was the poet José Blanc de Portugal,* whom I had never read because Sandokan and the *World of Adventures* provided me with more than enough spiritual nourishment, and I felt better. The poet was, at the very least, the antithesis of the Tiger of Malaysia: instead of a scimitar he wielded a considerable belly, he didn't wear a ring with a black stone on his index finger, he didn't give me the impression that he would board any passing ship, he planted an entirely unmartial kiss on my cheek, slightly sticky because of the ice cream, and continued to study the store window in which three mannequins in bridal gowns leaned toward him from the other side of the glass with all the solicitude of frozen muses offering him bouquets of orange blossom wrapped in gauze.

In my room, while my brother João was studying

(João and I shared the room for more than twenty years and during those more than twenty years he studied and I stared at the ceiling)

I reached the conclusion that writers were in fact all plump gentlemen nibbling ice-cream cones, wearing linen suits, and gawking at the clothes in Marijú's shopwindow. I gave up my plan to become Sandokan and started eating five bread rolls with cherry jam for breakfast every morning in the hope of growing a belly. I didn't get the belly, but to make up for it, I got an irritable bowel that, with touching loyalty, has stayed with me ever since. I struggled without success to acquire a few artistic spare tires but remained as thin as a rail and then I discovered in my first year at secondary school

(I think it was my first year, but I can't quite remember)

a teacher with a brow so furrowed and tormented he looked as if he had a pain in the lumbar region of his soul as he crossed the playground tortured by metaphysical doubt. A more educated colleague told me that the teacher's name was Vergílio Ferreira,† and

---

*José Blanc de Portugal (1914–2001). Portuguese poet and translator.

†Vergílio Ferreira (1916–96). Portuguese teacher, novelist, poet, and diarist whose autobiographical novel *Manhã submersa* [*Drowned Morning*] describes his years in a seminary.

that he published books: I took a closer look at his existential ulcers

(the man seemed to be riven by suffering)

and I spent months in front of the mirror nurturing stones in the urethra of my sensibility and trying to speak French like a concierge. As soon as I felt sufficiently Vergílio and sufficiently Ferreira, I appeared at supper looking deeply concerned about the meaning of life, ready to write another *Drowned Morning*, which had almost rotted away after all that time spent underwater. I refused the croquettes with stubborn melancholy, my family asked

—Are you stupid or something?

and I answered firmly

—That's how writers are

they told me not to be so foolish and to stop frowning because I did not, thank God, suffer from hemorrhoids, then my father showed me a picture of Byron and I decided to set off the next day for Greece and to die in battle reciting alexandrines. Since I didn't have enough money for the airplane, I took the bus to Vila Franca de Xira where there wasn't even a battle going on

(I vaguely remember a bandstand, a few spindly trees and some old men in hats on park benches in the middle of a pigeon-filled peace)

I got home very late, bursting with health, and received two slaps for having worried my mother and, instead of studying geography for the next morning's test, I immediately began

(at the same time as João was studying geography for the next morning's test)

a formidable novel entitled *Under the Sign of Capricorn*. I didn't get a single range of mountains or a single river right and scored only Average in the test

(João got a Very Good+)

but I finished the first chapter. There never was a second: the manuscript was confiscated, Flaubert was mentioned as a possible role model, but since I couldn't manage an epileptic fit

(frenzied kicking has never been my forte)

and there was no way I could grow a mustache, I decided in despair to do what I really wanted to do: be an ice-hockey player and produce masterpieces in my spare time.

I joined the ice-hockey club at Futebol Benfica and during that time and in between training sessions, I started to accumulate poems and bits of prose that have ended up who-knows-where. In the River Tejo I hope. And purely because I have no vocation to be retired, a martyr, or a hostage, I became a novelist. Which is odd, because I'm not fat or particularly ugly, I don't have a furrowed brow, I've never fought in Greece, I don't wear glasses or a beard, I don't dine at the restaurants for geniuses in Bairro Alto, I haven't got bad breath, I don't drink, and I'm completely oblivious to the successes or failures of others, which neither gladden nor sadden me in the least unless they involve the two or three friends I admire. This is fortunate because that way I don't run the risk of an inner voice asking me indignantly and sardonically

—Are you stupid or something?

were I ever to play at being the Portuguese intellectual as once I played at being Sandokan by daubing my bangs with shoe polish.

PORTRAIT OF THE ARTIST
AS A YOUNG MAN—II

Iwill never forget the beginning of my literary career. It was sudden, instantaneous, fulminating. I was traveling on the streetcar to Benfica, after another highly educational afternoon spent at the Liceu Camões, a kind of terrifying, futile concentration camp near Calhariz, when a surprising certainty blinded me: I'm going to be a writer. I was twelve years old, preparing for a brilliant career as an ice-hockey player, and unsure whether to be Spider-Man or Flash Gordon, but inclining slightly more toward Spider-Man because he could climb buildings, and in the midst of this came the call, the vocation, the certainty of a fate entirely unconnected with my plans, my dreams, my fantasies about muscles and fights. But the road to Damascus is the road to Damascus and people become St. Paul not out of pleasure but out of obedience. And obediently, before going home, I visited Careca's grocery store to buy a book of ruled writing paper, thirty-five lines, went up to my room, sat down at my desk, and plunged into immortality with a dozen quatrains. The following day I unleashed a few sonnets. They must have been pretty awful because, when I showed them to my mother, she gave me the pained look one bestows on cripples and hopeless idiots. Encouraged by this sympathetic stimulus from the author of my existence, I attempted a short story: another pained look. A poem in imitation of Camilo Pessanha,* which is, as every-

*Camilo Pessanha (1867–1926). Portuguese poet who published only one collection of poems, *Clepsidra*, but who was greatly admired by such poets as Fernando Pessoa and Mário de Sá-Carneiro.

one knows, dead simple: the pained look seemed to me tinged with alarm that she might have given birth to a moron. I sought comfort in my brother Pedro, who, having just turned nine, I judged, quite rightly, to be capable of evaluating my attempts. I was not deceived: from the height of his vast experience, Pedro, who never spoke, remained silent. But in that silence I could clearly see his admiration for my genius. I told him I was writing a book, and Pedro's silence deepened, a sign of agreement and admiration—even now, Pedro never argues with imbeciles. Occasionally, at most, he smiles. And in his smile I immediately saw respect and enthusiasm. I finished the book. I took it out to the garden and burned it. When the flames had died down, Pedro's smile widened. He only became serious again when I, scornfully stirring the ashes with my foot, threatened him with a new work. Naturally, I interpreted his seriousness as the eager expectation of a staunch fan. I immediately went upstairs to fill a new notebook. Through the window, I could see Pedro down below, studying the ashes and sucking a toffee. Toffees are only a problem for those with false teeth. Between the ages of twelve and thirteen I cooked up a dozen or so works of various types, all of them remarkable: novels, odes, plays. By fourteen, I was an experienced author. Convinced of the excellence of my secretions, I sent them to the *Diário Popular*. A gentleman whom I never met but who was clearly a benevolent creature

perhaps charitable would be a better word

published some of this rubbish in a section called something like "New Young Writers." A tiny sliver of good sense counseled me to use a pseudonym, which was in almost the same refined taste as the nonsense I sent him. Seeing my work in print filled me with doubts: I began nebulously to understand that there was a difference between writing well and writing badly. Later on, the realization that there existed an even greater difference between writing well and creating a work of art brought on a feeling of full-blown angst. I felt a complete fool

I was nothing but a silly little boy

I began again from the beginning and never showed anyone what

I was doing. For twenty years, perplexed and anxious, I labored every day over my ejecta, with the same sense of dissatisfaction I feel even now and the same occasional rare moment of joy that, when I reread objectively what I've written, I realize was unwarranted and cretinous. I started to shave. I finished a degree that had never interested me. I went off to the war in Angola. I came back from the war. I spent nine years on a completely worthless novel. And suddenly, although why or how I have no idea, some kind of fetus turned a somersault inside my belly and I began *Elephant Memory, South of Nowhere, Knowledge of Hell* and everything else, up until the book I started in July of this year. But the latter part of my apprenticeship is of no great interest. It's the other me I like, the one who wrote quatrains and patriotic odes, the customer at Careca's grocery store who, simply because he bought all those notebooks, deserved to have the red carpet rolled out for him each time he made his way past the beans and the potatoes clutching two coins in his hand. I hope that he still exists inside me with his innocence, his certainties and his unshakable imbecility, sacrificing the joys of Spider-Man for what

he considered

to be his destiny as a writer, that is, a bore holding a pen, incapable of climbing a building however small, convinced, with shoulders bent, that he has unveiled the mystery of people and of life and has no talent at all for being a limber, square-jawed Flash Gordon traveling from planet to planet, armored against the labyrinthine complexities of the soul.

BEYOND GRIEF
AN OPEN WINDOW

When I was thirteen, fourteen, fifteen years old I used to read any book I could lay my hands on, my parents' books, the books I stole and the books I could buy, for some reason I always came back, just as the tongue tirelessly searches for a missing tooth, to these lines from a French poem I had copied into a notebook

beyond grief an open window a lighted window

and I would close the notebook and smoke a forbidden cigarette beneath the lemon tree in the garden. When I was thirteen, fourteen, fifteen years old I used to read any book I could lay my hands on and because in my parents' house there was a simple and essential thing called good taste, I cannot reciprocate the stupid comments certain silly people make about me, comparing me to authors I simply don't know, because envy isn't my forte. I used to read the books I stole from my grandparents and from my aunts and uncles and the books I could buy, and I would go back to that notebook

beyond grief an open window a lighted window

I would sit down on the stone steps and look at the fig tree, at the well my mother had had covered over so that we children wouldn't fall in and at the window of Senhor Florindo the cobbler, repeating these lines that I couldn't understand because I didn't yet know what the word grief meant, just as later on, in the hospital, I would see the dying staring in horror at their own hands, and then, eventually, I lost the notebook and forgot about the poem. Or, rather, I thought I had forgotten it, because it reappeared in Angola, in the Land at the End of the World, six thousand miles from Lisbon and eight thousand from Moscow

(according to a notice hanging on the barbed wire)

in the midst of death, desolation, misery and that huge mistake of which Ernesto Melo Antunes* spoke in a letter the military censors neglected to open. It reappeared in Angola, in the Land at the End of the World, as it grew dark, as I was lying in my room

(let's call it a room)

when, suddenly, the voice of a Lisbon street vendor started shouting out the names of the evening newspapers, and the swamp of rifles and coffins in which I lived became a street in Lisbon's downtown, the Baixa. The voice was selling evening newspapers, the *Eva*

—Get your special Christmas edition of *Eva* here

it cried, like the sellers at a Corpus Christi procession

—Get your glass and candle here for ten *tostões*, a glass and a candle for ten *tostões*

the Corpus Christi procession in which I was a choirboy surrounded by little angels with musty wings and old ladies in tears. Suddenly in the middle of the night there were the Lisbon newspapers, the *Eva*

suddenly, blotting out the noise of the diesel generator, there were the sellers in the Corpus Christi procession

—Get your glass and candle here for ten *tostões*, a glass and a candle for ten *tostões*

suddenly there was my home city in the sand at the end of the world, in Angola, I went to the door of my room

(let's call that tent a room, I called it a room so as to pretend I had one)

---

*Ernesto Melo Antunes (1933–99). Portuguese army officer who played a major role in the 1974 Carnation Revolution in Portugal and had a key part in negotiating the independence of Guinea Bissau. He met Lobo Antunes when the latter was doing his national service in Angola, and they remained close friends.

and there, leaning against the flagless flagpole, a little soldier all
alone, his hands cupping his mouth
(beyond grief an open window a lighted window)
shouting out to the astonished guards the name of the city we
both came from. During that most difficult of times in Africa, when
everything got muddled up inside me, when I had no more tears
with which to grieve, after the mines, the ambushes, the boys without legs, the food thrown in a crate from a plane that couldn't land,
food that people had to fight over with the dogs, I beckoned the soldier to join me behind the ammunition store, behind what was left
of the columns of the post-commander's house
(Lisbon six thousand miles, Moscow eight thousand)
I said
—Call out the names of the newspapers
he cupped his hands around his mouth and started to call, and for
the next half hour we were both at peace, because
beyond grief an open window a lighted window
there was my parents' house, the lemon tree, the well, the stone
steps, the shade of the acacia tree, the photo of my mother as a
young woman wearing a necklace made from pearls, those seeds
that contain the seabed in their pale smile, then the generator was
turned off, and I said to the soldier
—OK, that's enough
I walked across a patch of night and went into the living room
(let's call that pile of bricks and dried grass a living room)
where the second lieutenants were playing cards on a table made
from barrel staves, where I stretched out in a chair also made from
barrel staves, and there was no war, there were no wounded, there
was no shooting, there was a choirboy, holding a small bowl of
holy water as he walked down to the cathedral, surrounded by little angels with musty wings and old ladies in tears.

GAS CYLINDERS AND ME

I have a kind of adolescent love affair with gas cylinders. At first, when I peer through the little window of the water heater, I see an exultant blue flame, firm, erect, resolute, joyful, determined to last whole eternities. The water from the shower is hot and I stand for ages immersed in the steam, which warms me to the point where my whole body smokes. With eyes closed, I let the jet play on head, neck, shoulders, chest, arms, legs, happy to stay there for the rest of my life, covering myself with soap and then rinsing it off, whistling as I pass slow hands over contented skin. I leave the shower reluctantly

(life is dreadful away from the bath, full of drafts, discomfort and superfluous people)

and I return to it the following morning in a state of voluptuous expectation. This state of grace lasts four or five days, days of exquisite pleasure. By the sixth day, more or less, the flame begins to waver, to lose firmness and impetus, the blue becomes tinged with an autumnal yellow, I have to press the reset button two or three times before the little window lights up again, I have to fiddle with the cold-water faucet to achieve what was, initially, instantaneous and easy, to find a progressively more delicate compromise on the mixer because at this point the gas cylinder begins to have incomprehensible caprices, hesitations, odd changes of mood that scald me one moment and freeze me the next (perhaps there is a third person using it without my realizing it, a thought that provokes in me deep feelings of resentment and jealousy, a third person, in the kitchen or in the other bathroom —But who, dear God?

more skillful than I at manipulating the faucets and to whom the gas cylinder now gives generously what, only a short time ago, it gave to me)

I step out of the bath wrapped in the towel of frustration, I run dripping to the water heater, skidding on the mat like some ridiculous duck

(suspicion makes such sad figures of us)

I find no one, the flame looks at me from behind the little window with a lukewarm, distracted, almost indifferent, almost extinguished eye, the next shower will be completely cold if I don't lay the cylinder on its side despite the warnings on its metal body

(to avoid explosions store cylinders in an upright position)

and even then the temperature vacillates, my body does not smoke, I do not feel hot, I do not, eyes closed, play the jet over head, neck, shoulders, chest, arms, legs, I doubt that I can spend my whole life there, passing slow hands over contented skin, I angrily finish my shower, pull on my clothes, and storm out of the house. Later, in one last effort, I turn the cylinder the other way, but with little hope that I will recover what I have lost, the reset button only responds after the tenth or eleventh attempt and then provides only a tiny tremulous flame that stutters, stops, revives very slightly, only to fade once more, my shower is unremittingly unpleasant

(I am convinced that the aforementioned third party has stolen it from me by manipulating the faucets more successfully than me)

Afterward, with an almost wounded brutality, I right the cylinder, which seems sadly inert, sadly empty, I make an angry muttered phone call, eager to have my revenge, I unscrew the rubber tube like someone removing from his finger a ring he had thought would prove eternal, the two giants whom I phoned and paid appear at my door, they carry away on their shoulder that great encumbrance whose departure I watch with loathing. I sit down alone in the living room pondering the prospect of years and years of melancholy ice-cold showers, I swear that so as to save myself future painful disappointments I will never wash again, I will, I decide, embrace squalor, I turn the television on, I turn the television off, I try reading a book or a magazine but they bore me, finally I pick up the telephone directory, wet one fingertip on my tongue, leaf through the pages and dial a number, I whisper, I murmur, I make requests, I'm given promises, offered guarantees, I hang up, and shortly afterward, in the little window of the water heater, a new gas cylinder ignites an exultant blue flame, firm, erect, resolute, joyful, determined to last whole eternities, and I, having forgotten all about the other cylinder, linger for ages immersed in the steam that warms me to the point where my whole body smokes.

LIFE, MORE OR LESS

I t seems you've been in the newspapers lately: they say you were
the greatest expert on Vieira* of the second half of the twentieth
century, that you were an exceptional teacher, a brilliant intellectual, that no one knew more about the Baroque period than you
and so on and so forth, and, as well as being able to read about you
in the papers, there was your photo

(I always felt there was something of the bird about you, your
eyes, eyebrows, nose, mouth)

lighting up the page. Yes, something of the bird: you didn't talk
very much, you didn't smile very much, and only when you said
certain words did you betray your Northern origins, my father's
voice on the phone

—Margarida just died

my mother's voice

—There was always a special empathy between you two

I had never heard my mother use the word empathy before and I
realized then that she was upset because my mother never normally
speaks like that. When we reached the hospital, Miguel was just

---

*António Vieira (1608–97). A Jesuit priest and brilliant orator who defended Portu-
guese Jews and protested the treatment of blacks and Indians in the New World.
He was himself imprisoned by the Inquisition but was subsequently pardoned.
His published sermons fill sixteen volumes.

coming out, I don't think we have ever hugged each other so hard, then I shut myself up with João in his office

(I hadn't seen João in his white coat for ages)

and

(you know what we Lobo Antunes men are like, you know what João is like)

we said almost nothing to each other and yet we were both so sad, but when we went out into the corridor I think we disguised it well. That night I sat down at the kitchen table with my parents

(the days of servants are over)

my mother was serving supper, we talked about Herculano[*] the whole time

(you know the family strategy: as soon as anyone gets upset we start to discuss some famous Portuguese writer, Herculano or Antero[†] or Eça de Queiroz[‡])

and then my father got up with his usual brusqueness, we heard his footsteps on the stairs and when he came down, without saying a word, he showed me a book in which you had written a dedication saying how much you cared about him: I was amazed that you should transgress one of our rules, which is to love without actually mentioning the word, out of modesty, out of discretion, because it isn't necessary. When I left the house in Benfica I thought

—I'll go to the church

but I couldn't

(you know I couldn't)

first, because it made me feel odd

(and so on and so forth)

---

[*]Alexandre Herculano (1810–77). Portuguese historian, journalist and poet credited with bringing Romanticism to Portugal.

[†]Antero de Quental (1842–91). Portuguese poet and political agitator who was the guiding light of the reformist, modernizing group of writers and thinkers known as the Generation of 1870.

[‡]Eça de Queiroz (1845–1900). Portugal's greatest nineteenth-century novelist and a member, with Antero de Quental, of the Generation of 1870.

second, because I didn't want to acknowledge the fact that you had died. I have a photograph of you on the beach with Zé Maria when he was little and you look very pretty, standing up and look-ing affectionately down at your son, in a pose, slightly leaning to the right, that you preserved all your life.

The funeral was on the Saturday. I drove my father, and the blue of his eyes

(like the blue of all our eyes)

shocked me. I don't remember which writer we discussed

(I can imagine you smiling when you read this)

and I can still remember wanting to hang back, and Miguel beck-oning me to join them. And so at the head of the cortège went your mother, your brother and Miguel, and me behind them, clinging on to Zé Maria and to João Maria, terribly upset, not seeing anyone, my brothers immediately behind me, I'm Zé Maria's godfather, I'm your eldest son's godfather, we were rather tense

(when I say rather you know what I mean)

and because you were at the front you didn't see me cry. You can't imagine the number of funerals there are on Saturdays. Anyone would think that people

(you weren't very original, at least in that respect)

wait until Friday to die so that they're less of a nuisance to their family because people don't usually work on a Saturday. If you go to the supermarket it's a real madhouse. The rest passed quickly: they lowered the coffin into the grave, covered it with earth, put the flowers on the earth, I can still see Miguel at the edge of the grave

(I will always remember Miguel, very erect, at the edge of the grave, I wanted to touch him or give him a kiss

and so on and so forth

but I didn't, of course)

and then, that was it, we left. I have a vague memory that there were quite a lot of people, I have a vague memory that I shook hands with some of them, I have a vague memory of damp cheeks, I have a vague memory that the gearshift in my car didn't work. On that day of all days, the wretched gearshift, which always works. Now I'm sitting here waiting for Christmas. Because it's traditional

at Christmas

for you to come and see me so that I can autograph a book for you to take to Oporto for your father. It may not seem like it, but February to December is a long time. Perhaps you'll phone before

(you do sometimes phone)

on the pretext of telling me that in your opinion I'm a great writer. You phoned quite often lately. Obviously I'm not going to repeat what we talked about, but I can just say that at the end of our last conversation

—I'll phone you later

you let it be understood that I would hear from you soon. And now, forgive me, but the doorbell is ringing and it might be you

—António, it's Margarida

it had better be you because

and so on and so forth

even though I may not show it, and I make every effort not to, I miss hearing your voice. How stupid that I miss hearing your voice so much.

HOMAGE TO JOSÉ RIBEIRO

There are people who love books. There are people who sell books. There are people who publish books. I know only one person who, out of love, sells them, publishes them, collects them, reads them, and, even more unusually, despite not being particularly wealthy, gives them to those he feels share his passion: his name is José Ribeiro, José Antunes Ribeiro, and beneath his gray curls, his broad smile, his glasses almost as transparent as his eyes, his small precise finger perusing the spines of books, he has the generous innocence of a child. He founded the publishing houses Assírio & Alvim and Ulmeiro and, apart from the rare moments when he chances to surface, so jolly in his shy, tender way, he can be found in a tiny basement apartment in Benfica, three or four small rooms that resemble corridors, pantries, cocoons, cells in a honeycomb where his large body moves with unexpected agility past pages and pages and pages of print, showing, searching out, giving

—Do you have this?

—Do you know this?

—Have you read this?

in the humble, fraternal pride of which his friendship is so purely made. If it weren't for José Ribeiro I would hate Avenida do Uruguai. They've erected buildings and more buildings where I, as a child, would go with the maid to buy milk from a farm that used to be there, they've erected buildings and more buildings on top of my past, they've drowned with boutiques and patisseries the places where once I was happy, they've destroyed a whole row of houses inhabited by people who, although they weren't actual members of my family, became part of it, the aged general wrapped in a blanket, the fierce lady, tiny and electric, who taught me English in between yaps from her tiny electric dogs, Grandma Galhó and her vast, tremulous collection of glass cats, her poems by Gomes Leal, her one-eyed cook

Rosa

garden gates, pillars, plots of land, bougainvilleas and dark hallways stagnating in perpetual winter, impermeable to the sun, a gentleman with white hair lying ill in bed

(but there was no death, for a long time there was no death, death was the little oval images of saints in my mother's prayerbook, I was eternal, at what precise point, I wonder, did I cease to be eternal, I who was eternal for so many years)

the cart belonging to the man who sold olive oil, the flocks of sheep, afternoons longer than a history lesson. They've erected buildings and more buildings and where once there were churns and foaming milk now there are people who never address me as sweetheart, who never address me as António, I traipse from shop to shop like a dog searching for a bone it buried in some now-forgotten place, and I end up, lost, ringing the doorbell of José Ribeiro's basement apartment. I go down the steps in the dark

(I don't know why there's no light on the stairs, but when I think about it, I prefer it like that, a mysterious darkness, a sense of imminent surprise)

a faint light appears somewhere inside and suddenly, framed in the doorway, are the gray curls, the glasses, the smile, the study like my grandfathers' studies, piles of books, bundles of books, boxes of books, shelves of books, the smell of books

(Paradise)

and that kindly, unassuming St. Peter

—Do you have this?

—Do you know this?

—Have you read this?

with the delicate attentiveness that only country people have, with the calm solicitude of friendship, the two of us ferreting about among all those books nine or twelve feet below floor level, bent like miners, rejecting, gathering, discovering

—No, I don't have that

—No, I don't know that

—No, I haven't read that

we come to the surface laden with sacks like happy Father Christmases, the buildings in the Avenida do Uruguai have disappeared and flocks of sheep can be heard again until the moment when we part, and José Ribeiro's absence restores me to adulthood, with no exuberance and no wit, a poor grown-up in a battered car, waiting for the lesson of childhood that his eyes teach me.

TALKING TO THE ROSES

B ecause I know it would please her, I kiss her photograph: the
elderly ladies straighten up and look at me as gratefully as if
it were their smile I had kissed. When they're not in the cemetery
or the church, they sit crocheting outside their front door and life
passes by without even touching them: not a single hair moves.
One day they'll turn up here in a hearse, accompanied by half a
dozen dry-eyed relatives.

In March and October I usually go to the cemetery to visit
my aunt's grave. Cancer carried her off on her birthday. Outside
the wrought-iron gates there are always flower-sellers sitting on
benches beside great wicker baskets, women who argue, laugh and
talk with each other then look suitably sad when they hand us the
flowers. As soon as we move off, they put the money in their apron
pocket and resume their chatter. The cemetery is in a square on
top of one of the city's hills from where you can see country vil-
las, the castle, the river in the distance and fields of sheep and olive
trees and, if the weather's fine, a distant tractor that, for some reason, makes the enormous noise of something very close. I've never
understood how that distant tractor can roar and labor as loudly as
if the piston rods were grinding away only a few yards from us.

I like the cemetery. I like the trees and the sparrows on the paths
between the graves, the strips of sunlight on the ground between
the bushes. There are always a few stray dogs around, sometimes

gathered together in a puddle of murmurings behind some bitch in heat, its snout down, looking terminally depressed. The gravediggers eat their lunch in the shade of an oak tree, its trunk stripped of bark, and throw stones at the dogs, chewing all the while, offending the elderly ladies maternally cleaning angels with a dustpan and brush. My aunt was maternal too. On Sundays she would dust the crucifix and the enameled photograph of my grandfather on his grave, she would go to the faucet on the wall to change the water in the glass vase and when she dusted the crucifix, she seemed to be stroking my grandfather. She explained to me that, on summer nights, the spirits of the dead release blue flames. Because I know it would please her, I kiss her photograph: the elderly ladies straighten up and look at me as gratefully as if it were their smile I had kissed. When they're not in the cemetery or the church, they sit crocheting outside their front door and life passes by without even touching them: not a single hair moves. One day they'll turn up here in a hearse, accompanied by half a dozen dry-eyed relatives.

My aunt's grave is in the most recent section of the cemetery, which was added only two years ago, almost next to the soccer field in the new subdivision. The poplars haven't had time to grow yet, there are no paved avenues, and they haven't covered over the well that has been here for centuries, since long before I was born. A fig tree persists, leaning over the well, and a few yards from my aunt's grave is a bathtub with lion's feet, half buried, slowly rusting away. Cats with eyes the color of gasoline make their nests nearby and the gravestones overgrown by weeds are starting to list in the soft, crumbling earth. There was no bath in our house: we had to stand in a tub in the kitchen and wash ourselves there. I hated standing naked in front of my family because I was ashamed of how small my genitals were. I was convinced that they would never grow and there I stood, dripping soap, exposed to everyone's disapproval, while my mother, with her back to me, removed saucepans from the stove and a smell of stew mingled with that of the water and the brilliantine they applied to my hair to keep it from sticking up.

In the mirror I looked, I thought, like a miniature singer of tango songs and this helped me overcome my embarrassment. Not much, but a little, enough to be able to sit down at the table without blushing. But that must have been a long time ago because people's faces were bigger than they are now. Gigantic faces, enormous noses, vast handkerchiefs, Jesus in a frame displaying his heart surrounded by thorns. Wherever I was, he was looking at me. I sometimes think that he's watching me here in the cemetery or when, back home, I point the hose at the roses. On such occasions I remain absolutely still, motionless, like those objects that stay just where they fall. Like the bathtub, for example, listening to the cats or the drunk wandering about humming the old song my aunt used to sing as she dusted the crucifix and my grandfather's round photo.

THE ROAD TO BENFICA

If you were to ask me what I feel, I would find it hard to say. Physically it's a kind of lassitude, the apathy and tiredness that precedes flu or some other illness, or death. My legs ache and feel heavy, my skin has become more sensitive to cold and to heat, to the hardness or rigidity of things. Nothing interests me, I feel uncomfortable being still but would feel even more uncomfortable if I moved. I don't know whether speaking is painful or just boring. I sit here, staring straight ahead, with no desires, no needs, hollow. I'm not even sad. I feel only passivity and indifference. My intestines stir gently. I listen without pleasure to my breathing, to the pulsing of blood in my ears. Yes, I think that's it: hollow. Made of plaster like those replica deer that people buy as garden ornaments. Out of the open window I can see other windows, a woman in a sleeveless blouse hanging out washing, taking wooden clothespins from a small wicker basket. Shirts and socks hanging up inside an enclosed verandah. An open umbrella waiting. For what? Alone, turned toward the light on an empty terrace. To the right of the umbrella a rusty TV aerial. Suddenly, I don't know why, I remember being small and being held in the arms of one of my aunts to watch soldiers marching past in the street, following behind some drummers. We lived in the north of the city where the city ended, and almost immediately beyond my grandparents' house there were fields, olive groves, flocks of sheep. Whenever I could, I would lie down on the grass to listen to the birds and the leaves that shone in the light, even when there wasn't any wind. I remember the tiled benches, the ceramic statues. My grandfather would arrive back from his club, swap his jacket for a white linen one and sit smoking and saying nothing. When he noticed me, he would smile. It's strange, but that smile is still important to me today.

But if you were to ask me what I feel, I would find it hard to say. I would probably shrug or say

—Nothing

and that wouldn't be true because vague images and memories appear and disappear, tiny meaningless scraps, rather like what happens before I start writing a novel, when filaments of characters start to crystallize into filaments of words and the plan of the book slowly comes into being, things start to connect. The woman in the sleeveless blouse, the open umbrella, the rusty TV aerial: perhaps there's some connection; perhaps there's a connection between this and my memory of the soldiers. Long after they had disappeared from view, the drums continued beating in our heads. Even during the night. Or the following day when I went to see the toads in the garden, and the Alsatian would gallop the whole length of the wire fence to which it was chained, beside the door of the tenant farmer who still looks after my parents' trees and flowers. He's lost nearly all his teeth and he's very old now. He greets me and takes off his hat.

—Good morning, sir

tries to focus on me from behind the awful clouds of his cataracts. Because I am the eldest son of the eldest son of the person she still calls

—Our master

the farmer's wife tries to kiss my hand and takes the opportunity to grieve

—Ah, sir

over times past, wiping her cheeks with her apron

—Ah, sir

as if she had been happier then. There she is, a young woman, running after her children and throwing her clogs at them, but always missing. Always jealous of the cooks, of the maids making scenes in the courtyard, threats, shouts. At the time, I used to spend every moment I could in the hayloft. I loved the smell of the hayloft and the locked chests that were stored up there. Through the holes in the roof I could see the sky. And the skeins of ducks in September on their way to Morocco. If you were to ask me what I feel, I think that's what I would say: I feel like the skeins of ducks in September on their way to Morocco. Or the bats hanging from the rafters in the hayloft, waiting.

ANTÓNIO 56½

The thing that we call circumstances, and that is, quite simply, what we allow life and people to do to us, obliged him to reflect ever more deeply upon himself. At twenty he thought time would resolve all his problems: at fifty he realized that time itself had become the problem. He had gambled everything on the act of writing, using each novel to improve on the previous one, in his search for the book that he could not improve on, working with such intensity that he had no recollection of the events that had taken place while he was producing these books. This intensity and this work meant that he remained untouched by any influence but his own and created no model outside of himself, even though this left him more alone than a jacket forgotten in an empty hotel room, while the wind and disillusionment made the shutter that no one had bothered to close creak in the night. Although unfamiliar with sadness, he knew about despair: his own face in the mirror when he shaved in the morning or, rather, not a face but parts of a face reflected in a troubled surface, incapable of constructing the present, returning to him loose fragments of a past that did not fit together

(afternoons in the garden, children's smocks, tricycles)

and conveying more a feeling of strangeness than any particularly touching memory, something that he judged could be an aid to those who did not have the courage to dream unaided. He countered the ethics of consumption with an ethics of production, not out of any kind of virtue

(he had no virtues)

but because he was incapable of using the practical mechanisms of happiness. His scorn for money derived from a distortion that bore no relation to a love of poverty. He regarded his bank account much as he did the dull books that stood in piles in a back room: one day, in a sudden desire to clear the decks, he would simply sell off the notes by weight.

He was bewildered by the admiration of the young writers and aspiring writers who sent him manuscripts and letters: it was incomprehensible to him that there should be men and women prepared to live from day to day in a permanent state of affliction and anxiety. He had never made a conscious decision to be a writer: something or someone had made him write, and he thanked God that those he loved were free beings who treated him with the kind of indulgence one feels for someone who has lost an arm or a leg in the service of some madcap cause. His friends tended to lead him with the friendly hand with which one guides a blind man, warning him about any bumps or potholes in the road, convinced that he was possessed of a kind of helpless innocence that left him defenseless, at the mercy of almost everything, principally himself. If they could, they would have confiscated his shoelaces and his belt as guards do with prisoners to prevent them from escaping who-knows-where or else dying from sheer incompetence, given that he could not tell sugar from sand or diamonds from glass, busy as he was with engraving words so deeply that they could be read, like Braille, without the help of one's eyes. So that one could run one's finger over the lines and feel the fire and the blood. If others were to feel the fire and the blood, it was necessary for him to burn and bleed. Did aspiring writers realize the price one paid for each page? The difference between the pure and the impure? When one should work and when one should stop working? That success is worthless, first, because we have already moved beyond it and, second, because qualities are, almost always, defects in disguise, and because it's dishonest to take satisfaction in receiving praise for those skillfully concealed defects? Did aspiring writers know that our most bitter triumph is, at best, not to achieve what we want? That finishing a novel leaves us too exhausted to feel happy and that we are immediately troubled by the fear that we won't be able to write the next book?

Afternoons in the garden, children's smocks, tricycles. Once time had resolved all problems and

time itself

had become the problem, he noticed that his daughters had grown into women and that night had fallen. But, with a little luck, he will leave behind him not a trace, not a shadow, not a memory, only what he had hidden deep inside him, what he had and others did not. And then, when the time comes, he will be able to lie down in peace, close his eyes and sleep: and finally he will have become just like you.

CHRONICLE TO BE READ
ACCOMPANIED BY A KISSANJE*

The loveliest thing I've ever seen wasn't a painting, or a monument, or a city, or a woman, or my grandmother Eva's bisque shepherdess when I was a child, or the sea, or the third minute of the dawn of which the poets speak: the loveliest thing I've ever seen were fifty thousand acres of sunflowers in Baixa do Cassanje, in Angola. We set off before dawn and, with the coming of light, the sunflowers, as one, raised their heads in the direction of the rising sun, the whole earth full of huge yellow eyelashes on either side of the path, and on one occasion

I recall

a band of mandrills on a slope, sitting perfectly still, observing us. Then they grew bored and vanished into the shade of the stems. The loveliest thing I've ever seen was Angola, and despite the poverty and the horror of the war I still love her with a love that does not die. I love the smell and I love the people. The moments when I have perhaps been closest to what is commonly called happiness occurred when I was delivering a baby

I solved any problems that the women or my witch-doctor colleague

*Kissanje is a kind of lamellophone or thumb piano common in many parts of Africa. It is made up of a series of thin plates or "tongues," each of which has one fixed end and one free end. The musician presses the free end with one finger, then allows the finger to slip off, so that the "tongue" vibrates.

euá kimbanda

could not, and when I emerged from the infirmary hut as if I were still holding in my hands a small tremulous life, I felt happy. The vast mango trees rustled above my head, Senhor António was watching from the mess. It's odd, but during difficult times the memory of Baixa do Cassanje helps me. I remember chief Macau

euá Muata

I say to myself

—Tumama tchituamo

and I feel calmer. If I went over to the window, I swear that, even here in Lisbon, there would be fifty thousand acres of sunflowers as far as the eye can see, golden eyelashes, mandrills. The incredibly beautiful girls, their soft, soft skin, Tia Teresa, enormously fat, who was in charge of a hutful of whores in Marimba, and who knew more about the human condition than anyone I've ever known.

—Euá Tia Teresa

euá the drums at night in the village of Dala, the marijuana smoked at funerals:

euá liamba.

I used to talk to Tia Teresa as darkness fell and be filled with a nostalgia for everything. Sometimes she would press one of her girls on me, but I could never bring myself to accept. She would send for a basin of water, soap, a towel, and we would both solemnly wash our faces. One day she gave me a tin of talcum powder, to protect me from the evil eye. Perhaps it worked. And from palm leaves the color of chalk we ate moamba together. She and the kimbanda Kindele, the white doctor. And in Africa I was often so ashamed of being just that. My clumsy body. If I put my ear to the trunk of a tree I wouldn't know, as Tia Teresa did, who was about to arrive. But the chief Kaputo invited me to be his son's godfather, the greatest honor I have so far received, and, out of politeness, no one made fun of the way I danced. An old lady holding the lighted end of a cigarette in her mouth squeezed my fingers with her fingers

euá Velha

she squeezes my fingers again: I'm writing this with great joy, the same joy I felt on Sunday mornings when I smoked a mutopa

a pipe made out of a gourd

along with the other men, listening to them talking, playing a kind of backgammon with pebbles as I watched the raft crossing the River Cambo, beneath the bats at twilight, with the lights of Chiquita off in the distance. The sunflowers bowed their heads to go to sleep, owls flew into the headlights of the Jeep on the road. Senhor Gaspar's tobacco plantation, Senhor Gaspar with his long, gaunt hippopotamus face. Senhor Gaspar smiled into his mustache

euá Senhor Gaspar

we sat on the verandah

—Tumama tchituamo

with his pet monkey shrieking and rattling its chain because it was afraid of the dark. Out came the basin of water, the soap, the towel. In the midst of the poverty and the horror there were moments of deep contentment. A feeling of eternal peace I have never recaptured. What I want most in the world are the sunflowers of Baixa do Cassanje and me walking

flying

through them.

—Euá Velha

squeezes my fingers again.

CONTRIBUTIONS TO A BIOGRAPHY
OF ANTÓNIO LOBO ANTUNES

I think I inherited from my grandfather a taste for sitting quietly and looking. He used to do this in the garden. Since I don't have a garden, I do it at home, on benches in the street, in parks, in shopping malls. When I was at the university, as soon as the lesson at the morgue was over, I would walk down to Avenida da Liberdade and, with a little shuffle of the hips to the right and to the left, conquer a small space on the wooden bench between two retired gentlemen. Retired gentlemen don't talk much and neither do I. All I lacked was a slipper on my right foot, a hand-rolled cigarette, and a walking stick. I was usually the last to leave. With my white coat folded on my knees I would watch the city lighting up. The pigeons would migrate to the rooftop that bore the Sandeman advertisement, a man in a broad-brimmed hat and cape and a glass of port wine in his hand. In my opinion, one I have held since I was five or six, there has never been anything lovelier. The main reason I was drawn to Mandrake the Magician was because he looked like him: "Mandrake made a magic pass. . . ." When it raised the glass of port, the Sandeman advertisement made a magic pass too, and the night appeared. This daily miracle still enchants me. Then there were the façades of the cinemas and the little lights racing round and round the names of the actors: Esther Williams, Joan Fontaine, Lana Turner. I developed an undying, exclusive passion for Lana Turner. In moments of doubt, I almost think that she did not reciprocate this passion. But such moments, of course, do not last, and the platinum blonde hair, the elusive penciled-in eyebrows, perfect semicircles, the vertiginously plunging necklines in satin, the scarlet lipstick, all speak to me of eternal love, eternally requited.

I didn't like her kissing other men in films. But perhaps it was better that way because if I had arrived home with lipstick on me and said to my mother

—It was Lana Turner, she's crazy about me

I don't think she would have liked the idea

no, not the idea, the fact

that her eleven-year-old son was going to marry a divorced woman, because that would have meant we couldn't get married in church and my family were Catholics.

This argument

—She's a divorced woman, dear

unnerved me. When I tried to talk about it to Lana Turner, with her on the screen and me in the balcony

—My mother's going to make things difficult for us because you're divorced

a spectator, three rows in front, told me to shut up, but I could see that while she was locked in an embrace with Jeff Chandler, Lana Turner shook her head before closing her extremely long eyelashes

(not out of pleasure, but merely because it was her job, after all what was Jeff Chandler, with his white hair, compared with me in my short pants?)

assuring me that she herself would speak to my mother about the inevitability of our marriage while Nat King Cole, singing "Imitation of Life" in the background, would melt away that overanxious parent's final doubts. I even tried an exploratory conversation: I walked nonchalantly over to the sweater she was knitting and touched its sleeve, she stopped counting stitches

—What's wrong?

and I announced in a casual tone of voice

—I think Lana Turner and I are engaged

my mother went back to counting her stitches, seventy-six, seventy-seven, seventy-eight

—Oh yes?

proof that she accepted the fact without argument, I went back to my room, told my fiancée, who was on a poster on the wall, wearing a fur coat

—It's all settled

and I made the engagement official with the aluminum ring I had found in my slice of Christmas pudding. I should add that it was a happy marriage, unspotted, until I met Anne Baxter when I was twelve, in *The Ten Commandments*, the wife of Yul Brynner, the Pharaoh, and in love with Moses, Charlton Heston. I flicked aside Yul Brynner and Charlton Heston and forgot all about Lana Turner. Not exactly nice, I know, but the human soul can be ruthless. I feared my mother's reaction, because she had been with my father for centuries and I assumed she would be somewhat conservative. I fearfully explained the matter to her, again touching the sleeve of the sweater she was knitting. Fortunately she, a freethinker, merely asked

—Oh yes?

and added

—If you don't give up this playboy lifestyle of yours, I'm going to ruin this sweater

and then forgot all about me. I went back to my room and told Anne Baxter, pinned to the wall with four thumbtacks, in the place formerly occupied by Lana Turner

—It's all settled

Yul Brynner and Charlton Heston proved to be good losers and resigned themselves to the situation. I even noticed that in the film, Yul Brynner took to kissing her less passionately

well, that's life, and there's no arguing with feelings

and I didn't worry much about Charlton Heston, given that he died before he reached the Promised Land, and Anne Baxter and

I only parted after *All About Eve*, when I realized how wicked her character was, hurting poor Bette Davis who looked like my grandmother. In despair I tried to go back to Lana Turner, but she, in her grief at my rejection, had vanished from the screens. If you see her, tell her I'm terribly sorry and ask her please to forgive me. And tell her to phone my parents' house: there's probably a little boy there wearing an aluminum ring found in the Christmas pudding who is waiting to take her call.

IN CASE OF ACCIDENT

Today I feel like I could simply leave: pick up the car keys for
no reason at all
(the keys are always in the dish by the front door)
go downstairs
(I wouldn't take the elevator, but the stairs)
to the basement garage, make the locking device on the car
open with two beeps and two flashes, see the automatic door of
the garage slowly rise up and then, once I was out in the street,
put my foot down, drive through the lights on red, heading for the
freeway, not even looking at the signs showing the cities and the
distances in miles, without an idea in my head, with no destination,
with nothing but this desire to leave, to put the greatest possible
distance between myself and myself, to forget my name, the names
of my friends, of my family, of the book I can't finish and that torments me, to stop in one of those restaurants next to the toll booths
and eat alone, not looking at anyone, not seeing anyone, not even
the children running up and down between the tables screaming,
and then get in the car again and drive off, feeling empty, holding
the wheel just as I used to hold the handlebars of my bike when I
was a boy, while my father, running along beside me, taught me to
pedal.

Today I feel like I could simply leave: the walls of the apartment
are closing in on me, everything seems so small, so pointless, so

strange. Writing novels. Publishing them. Waiting months for the next novel. Writing it. Publishing it. Receiving phone calls from my agent about contracts, translations, prizes. Receiving reviews from the publisher, screeds of incoherent compliments and praise written by someone who hasn't understood and yet praises what he or she hasn't understood. Or am I the one who doesn't understand? At any rate, I never read my work: I simply produce it and, once it's finished, my head turns to see the next book as it arrives. Only to abandon those pages too. Now I really could just leave, before I go as crazy as the dogs running around in circles all night. If I walk over to the window I'll find that the cold has left the lids of the trash cans wet with dew and that there's only one window lit in a building down below. It's as if I were the only person alive. I and the telephone, which, although it's silent now, looks as if it might start shouting at any moment. My ribs breathe against the window. In the empty parking lot opposite is a dead pigeon. Or a seagull. Some bird or other. The lids of the trash cans reflect the streetlights in fixed, coagulated stains. I make a face at myself in the window.

Today I feel like I could simply leave. I would put all the money from the drawer in my pocket, I wouldn't take along my wallet, my documents, anything that might identify who I am. If anyone asks me what I do, I'll say I have no profession. I am merely a man in a restaurant next to a freeway toll booth, silently chewing. I might come back one day, I might not. What will my French publisher, my German publisher, my Swedish publisher say? Desperate letters from my agent that I will never receive, unopened telegrams in the mailbox demanding a book for which I have been paid and that I abandoned, half finished, at the penultimate chapter, uncorrected, unedited. What is it that torments me? All those useless spines of books on the shelves, by authors I used to enjoy but who now leave me cold: Felisberto Hernández,[*]

---

[*]Felisberto Hernández (1902–64). Uruguayan writer whose short fiction influenced Gabriel García Márquez and Julio Cortázar.

William Gaddis,* Eliseo Diego.† Felisberto Hernández and Eliseo Diego are dead. Felisberto Hernández is playing the piano in the photograph I have of him. Eliseo Diego stares at me, pipe in hand. Perhaps along with the money from the drawer, I'll take with me Felisberto Hernández, one author and no more. Or Juan Benet.‡ I could read them while I'm chewing. Eliseo Diego, who was a poet, isn't right for restaurants, he demands the kind of privacy you get only when you're alone in your living room. He wrote a very short poem about his grandmother, in which his grandmother asks him to cover all the mirrors. My departure is a way of covering all my mirrors. Today I feel like I could simply leave. With no fuss, no talk, no explanations, without that last quick glance at myself that we all give to check that our hair is OK. When I was a very young doctor, I treated an elderly lady who was dying. Halfway through the afternoon she asked me:

—Don't you think I look a little tired?

and the following morning the men from the funeral home came and put her in her coffin. Her daughter told me that after she had asked that question

—Don't you think I look a little tired?

the elderly lady, unbeknownst to me, had asked for a glass of port. She spilled half down her front, but the half she swallowed cheered her up. She had been a widow for years and didn't expect much from anyone. If I ever visit Tomar again, I'll take a bottle of port wine to her grave and leave it on the marble slab, among the little vases of flowers. I go over to the window and see the lids of the trash cans still damp with dew. The trees in the park have grown calmer at last. I turn on the TV. I don't understand what's happening on the screen, but I keep

*William Gaddis (1922–98). American novelist.

†Eliseo Diego (1920–94). Cuban poet, writer, and translator.

‡Juan Benet (1927–93). Spanish novelist and essayist.

watching. A child smiles out at me. Unfortunately, the smile doesn't last very long. Perhaps it wasn't a smile. Perhaps it was just me feeling in need of a smile. There are times in life when we desperately need a smile. For lack of anything better, I touch my reflection in the window with my finger.

STILL LIFE WITH WOMAN

E very September, after the death of her husband and after
her children had left home, she used to rent a tiny first-floor
apartment on the same beach where once she'd owned a huge
house. The first-floor apartment was squeezed between two buildings, opposite the butcher's, in a street with no sea view. And she
spent her afternoons in a canvas chair, surrounded by furniture
not her own, holding a cigarette and facing the wall on which a
blue china plate hung on a nail. She left the door open because of
the smoke, but what with the comings and goings outside, everything shook all the time, the canvas chair, the plate, herself, a glass
cabinet containing cups and colored glasses, the newspaper on her
lap that she didn't appear to read. At supper time she would heat
up on a little stove two meatballs and a spoonful of rice, which
she ate alone, at a table covered with oilcloth, watching the television news with the sound off. Then came the evening dampness,
as always in September, and she would go back to her canvas chair.
She didn't turn on the pink ceiling light that tinged the room with
a pale, flickering exhalation: she sat there listening to the waves or
not even listening to the waves, listening to nothing. The photo of
her late husband, placed on a kind of sideboard, took no interest
in anyone. In the next room was what looked almost like a child's
bed where I suppose she slept. Did she sleep? In the next room was
what looked almost like a child's bed where I presume she contin-

ued to smoke as she waited for the morning to come. At eighty years old, what morning was she waiting for, I wondered? She was thin, her short hair brushed back, her old-fashioned clothes too big for her. She used to play the cello and gave classes during the winter in an apartment in Estrela that reminded me of flotsam from a shipwreck. She didn't speak much and she never complained. Why should she? After all, her life hadn't been so very bad, had it?

In September, the gulls left the beach and perched, screaming, on the rooftops, frightened by the rough equinoctial seas. The summer visitors gradually left, the butcher, with no customers, stood at the door scratching himself, and almost nothing shook the street now. Occasionally rain fell on the remains of summer, and the dogs emerged in groups from the empty lots and the dunes, heads bowed in hunger, sheepdogs with nowhere to go, sniffing the gutters. The butcher used to shoo them away with a broom and they would trot off down to the beach in search of any forgotten scraps. You could see them from the seawall investigating fishing rods, baskets, boots, and whatever had been washed up by the waves. As evening fell or during the night, the dogs howled at the mountains, which were crowned by the first clouds of autumn. The streetcleaners hosed September away. No buses arrived now, no cars. The cold of October was one of the few things that did arrive. In the first-floor apartment squeezed between two buildings, in a street with no sea view, the cigarette held between her fingers never burned down. Her husband an ever more distant presence in his photo. There he was, wearing a tie, in what looked like a garden. Still young, with dark hair and glasses. She had thought him handsome. She didn't think anything now, but she still brought the photo with her in her suitcase and took it back again, placing it on the bedside table, next to the clock, which told the time but never made sense. Thirteen twenty, seven twelve, one ten: what difference did it make? Sitting in her canvas chair, she continued to smoke. Until when?

I used to visit her as a break from the book I was writing. I would walk down the hill, almost all the way from Tomadia, knock on her open door, and go in. There was another chair next to the canvas chair, and I was feeling bitter and disillusioned with my work. I would rest my arm on the table's oilcloth and smile at her. The smile she gave me in return resembled a crack in an old wall. A boy was doing tricks on his bike on the sidewalk, a man shouldering a gas cylinder was crossing the road. The cups and colored glasses in the cabinet intrigued me. Who would use them in January, in March, in May? Then I would remember some line that wasn't working and go back and rewrite it. It was a particularly difficult novel whose words were taking a long time to arrive. I was writing, at most, three pages a week, getting up early and spending my whole life on it. A blackbird in the pine woods, doubtless the same one as when I was young, distracted me. Blackbird, blackbird. The man carrying the gas cylinder stopped to rest, the boy on the bike had disappeared. I was sorry to leave her there in the canvas chair, in front of the blue china plate hung on a nail. What could I do? Stop October and the gulls shouting on the rooftops? Shoo away the stray dogs with the butcher's broom? Wind everything back and say

—There you are

the vast house with the garden and the swimming pool, with the marble statue at the entrance? I felt like forgetting her and her door left open because of the smoke, and the newspaper on her lap that she didn't appear to read. To forget about the meatballs and the spoonful of rice. The television news with the sound turned down, where a fish wearing a jacket and opening and closing its mouth alternated with shots of forest fires and government ministers. And so I said

—See you tomorrow, then

and, once outside, I stuck my hands in my pockets. I stuck my hands as deep as I could in my pockets, clenched so tight that when I picked up my pen I realized that my joints were hurting. Not that it mattered: I rubbed them as I read through what I'd written and very soon I was ready to start again. All I had to do was forget that smile like a crack in an old wall. But that, thank God, is easy enough to forget. Isn't it?

NOT SO CLOSE TO THE SURFACE

Guez de Balzac* tells a story about a Norwegian who had never seen a rose bush and who, when shown one, was astonished to see a plant sprouting flames. Over the years, years that sometimes seem too many and sometimes far too few for me to feel as I do, either so weary or so unprepared that when I think about them, suddenly I'm not entirely sure how many years they are

(I catch myself counting on my fingers like a bad pupil who has forgotten his times tables)

on most such occasions, I've felt like a Norwegian who has never seen anything. If events repeat themselves, I respond with equal amazement, which, out of innocence or stupidity, makes me the ideal audience, enthusiastic and ingenuous, of the kind who doesn't even complain that his seat is uncomfortable, whose degree of discomfort serves as a barometer to measure the quality of the show: a good play is one that doesn't make one's bottom ache. An uncle of ours read the same novel for months on end, arguing that one of the advantages of old age consisted in reaching the end of the book having forgotten how it began, then starting all over again with no idea how it ended, which meant that those three hundred pages contained an entire library eternally renewed. I presume I have inher-

*Jean-Louis Guez de Balzac (1597–1654). French writer known as "the restorer of the French language."

ited his capacity for surprise: when I change my shirt I put on an
entirely new one, when I shake the proffered hand of an acquaint-
ance, I introduce myself, I enter my house each evening with all the
ceremony of an occasional visitor, perching on the edges of chairs
out of shyness with myself and I never fumble in my pockets for
anything because I was taught, as a child, that one shouldn't touch
other people's possessions. Prevented, therefore, from paying for
anything

    (the money I have on me belongs to someone else)

people interpret as meanness what is merely a horror of theft
and an acknowledgment of the precept that it's very hard to earn
one's living. It must be difficult for them and for the person they call
António Lobo Antunes and who lends me his name, face and clothes
with a generosity I find hard to comprehend. I get mistaken for him
every day as if we were very alike, his old school friends greet me,
his family invite me to supper, people ask me to autograph books
he has written: out of force of habit I can now imitate his handwriting fairly well and, from time to time, I even help out on a chapter,
written very slowly, wondering what António Lobo Antunes would
think and trying to reproduce what I'm told he feels. This is the first
time I've written for a magazine because they asked me to write
this chronicle thinking that they were asking him. In order not to
embarrass anyone

    neither the people at the magazine nor the aforementioned
António Lobo Antunes, whom I see only fleetingly in the shaving mirror each morning and who is under the impression that he
doesn't have to write this article,

    I decided to write it myself. I began with the Norwegian and
the rose bush and simply carried on, slightly randomly, hoping that
they will accept it without realizing the deception. With a bit of luck
no one will notice: the people at the magazine might, at most, comment that António Lobo Antunes seems to have lost his talent and
his qualities as a writer, his readers will hope he recovers them in
time for his next article, his friends will wonder if it mightn't do him

good to take a week or two's break from writing and thereby rest his pen. They're too polite to say anything to him and since António

(I occasionally allow myself the familiarity of using his first name)

is too fastidious ever to read what he writes, there's no risk of his getting annoyed with me. He won't read it, but I will. And I confess that I've decided to filch a few coins from his pocket

(despite my guilt, despite my fear that he might have counted them)

so that I can buy the magazine and find in black and white these scribblings that cost me an hour of grammatical anguish. I hope I haven't split any infinitives, that my subjects and my predicates go together relatively correctly, that I've got my tenses right, and finally, that the people at the magazine fire him and commission me to write any future articles, given that I'm more docile in temperament and have a readier smile. When I think about it, if his jackets fit me, maybe my prose pieces will fit his readers. And it will be António

(there I am slipping into familiar mode again)

who, when he glimpses me in the morning shaving mirror, embarrassed to find me there still in my pajamas, apologizes as he disappears out the door for being in my house.

HERRN ANTUNES

Today is Wednesday, April 25, 2001, and I'm on the top floor of a hotel in Munich. I don't have a room: I have a room, a bathroom, a corridor and a kitchen-dinette, and whenever I'm in a hotel with a room, bathroom, corridor and kitchen-dinette, I always remember the worst year of my life, 1976, when I lived in a place like this in Lisbon, with my suitcase in the kitchen area and guys from the Soviet Embassy as neighbors, with eyes as pale as wolves' eyes, and who seemed full of fear and mysteries. They didn't talk to anyone: they each occupied their own little cubbyhole, and a one-legged man who appeared to be the boss walked along the corridors with the air of a prison guard, checking that all the doors were locked. Sometimes I would come across him sitting on a chair at the far end of the corridor: I never quite understood why he didn't shoot me. I felt the man's eyes on my back while I put my key in the lock.

This hotel is different: during breakfast the guests eat boiled eggs and look as if they were painted by Lucas Cranach the Elder. The same hands, the same noses, the same thin lips, facial expressions that cross the centuries to wrestle with the blocked holes in the tops of saltcellars. The air fills with the cracks of old paintings and all the waitress needs to do is put a carved wooden frame around them. In 1976 I went over to the window and saw Rua Luís Bivar, trees, parked cars, trash cans, streetlights. A cockroach watched me from the baseboard, waving its antennae. The guys from the Soviet Embassy must have been tormented by nightmares about surplus value. Once, I ventured onto the landing at dawn. The one-legged man leapt out of his chair and I thought he was about to start barking. He walked by propelling himself forward with his left leg, piloting an invisible skateboard, and looking at people suspiciously as if they were about to steal his toy.

1976, a hard spring, a hard summer. I wasn't writing, I wasn't reading. People must have been able to smell my loneliness a mile off. The male receptionist, in whom dwelled a uniformed St. Francis of Assisi, handed me the viaticum of the sports newspaper, retrieved from the depths of the counter with a conspiratorial smile. According to the thinking of that particular lay friar, kicking a ball around must have seemed an aid to dissolving anxiety. He shifted a match from one side of his mouth to the other with one rapid movement of his tongue. Senhor Fernandes, with two wedding rings on his finger and a rather grubby shirt. Virtue is not incompatible with a scorn for laundries: even Cardinal Richelieu's eminence was grise. Proposal for an advertisement for detergent: the cardinal pointing to his spotless white eminence

—I thought my eminence was grise until I used (add name of product)

1976, a hard autumn. I was constantly assailed by memories of events in the war, perhaps because, at the time, I was living through an even worse war. The prisoner who had been strapped to the fender of a land-mine destroyer and was screaming in terror. Ernesto Melo Antunes who arrived back in despair from committing acts of piracy with the South Africans:

—We destroyed everything.

In 1976 I had destroyed everything in my own life, with mortars, bazookas, offensive and defensive grenades, G3s, napalm, exfoliants. I don't think I had a single friend left: an act of complete piracy. Somewhere in the darkness, the little light of a woman's love and me fleeing that little light. Why? While Ernesto despaired, the South African got drunk. I heard them singing until dawn, in Afrikaans.

Today, April 25, 2001, the wounds have still not healed completely, but I'm in Munich, which is tantamount to saying that I don't exist. I spot my photo in the newspaper that the guest at the next table is leafing through: it doesn't look anything like me, just as I don't look anything like myself. Nerval* used to write on the back of photos of himself: I'm the other one. Anyway, at least there's no danger of me being recognized.

Tomorrow I'm going to Vienna to collect a prize: with all the fuss, all the ceremony, the lunch with the chancellor. The other one is going to Vienna. I'm staying here: characters out of Lucas Cranach don't go strolling along by the Danube. They hang around museums, studying people. This boiled egg should last me years; don't even consider eating it. I should have worn a tie to please my mother:

—They'll think I didn't bring you up properly.

You did, Mama. The problem is that when I wear a tie I look like a provincial bridegroom at a fairground booth. And don't worry, I'll make sure everyone knows how hard you tried:

—I'm wearing a tie because my mother wanted me to.

I promise I'll even tell the chancellor, so don't worry:

—I'm wearing a tie because my mother wanted me to, you know.

And I'll be polite, pleasant and attentive instead of merely smiling absentmindedly. And explaining:

—Nerval was the other one, Mama.

—Nerval wasn't my son.

What can you say to that? It's true, Nerval wasn't her son. And having reached the final argument the only thing I can do is to say

---

*Gérard de Nerval (1808–55). French Romantic poet who greatly influenced Symbolists and Surrealists.

nothing. The guest at the next table has passed the page with my
photo on it. I pick up my spoon and strike a first blow at the eggshell:
nothing happens. A second blow: nothing happens. An unbreak-
able egg. My eternal struggle with inanimate objects. A third blow,
really hard this time: the egg leaps onto the floor and the Lucas
Cranach characters start to take an interest. A wary woman recoils
a few inches, just in case. I look at the egg, the egg looks at me,
demanding

—Pick me up.

I pick up the egg, but my napkin slides off my knees. I pick that up
too, I have an egg in one hand and a napkin in the other, like a bull-
fighter ready to display his trophies to the public. I hear my mother's
voice declaring to those present

—Honestly, I did my best.

And you did, Mama. You did do your best. When I get back
from this trip, I'll come and have supper at your house and show
you my best table manners. I'll wear a tie and everything. You'll
see, you've never had such a well-dressed son. A model son to
show off to visitors:

—His brothers are all the same.

The problem is that it's too late for that. And the model son is just
a fifty-year-old boy fumbling in his pockets for some marbles that
aren't there. Or perhaps they are. If they are, I'll make three little
hollows with my heel and then you'll see, I'll show these Germans.
Once, I was given a cloth bag for the marbles, do you remember?
It had a drawstring and everything. If I had the bag here, I would
take out of it not just the marbles but my laugh as well. If I stay
very quiet and very still, I can hear it. You can hear it too: just press
your ear to this page. My laugh hasn't changed a bit since primary
school, has it?

THE SCENT OF
MIMOSAS FROM THE HILLS

When she was a little girl, she used to play in the cemetery in Abrigada, pretending that the tombs were dolls' houses. Perhaps they were: they had shelves with doilies on them, paper flowers in blue glass vases, and frilly curtains at the windows. You could mark up the gravestones with chalk squares, number each square, throw a stone and play hopscotch. The wind brought with it the scent of the mimosas from the hills while she hopped her way to the end of the game. At night, her grandmother used to tell her stories about her father, who had worked as a navigator in the Azores, and meanwhile her grandfather did crossword puzzles as he sat amid the dark furniture. Once she woke up to find a tawny owl beating its wings against her bedroom window. Or perhaps it was a barn owl.

—I don't know what time it would have been then

she said to me the night before she died, looking at her own hands with slow surprise. She could barely manage to breathe, propped up against a pile of pillows, and sometimes she moved so far away from us we could hardly see her. She had stopped eating: she would simply drink a little liquid from a cup, take a cigarette from the pack and then forget about it. The two cats would curl up together at the foot of the bed.

—I don't know what time it would have been then and I don't know what time it is now because she couldn't turn her head to see the clock on the bed-side table. Her hair, once thick and dark, reminded me of the straw-like hair on a doll. She again left for a moment and returned with difficulty.

—What time is it now?

We attached the oxygen tube to her nose with a kind of elastic band while her sense of astonishment walked about the room. Sometimes she would pick up a little mirror and paint her eyelids and her lips. She didn't seem sad. Merely distant, sunk in a sleepy indifference. Now and then she would smile.

—What are you thinking about?

—I don't know. What time is it now?

The plastic clock said it was twenty to five.

—Twenty to five.

Her hands touched the newspapers the people at work had sent her, then gave up.

—What an unlikely time

she said. I'll never forget those words:

—What an unlikely time.

A dozen or so bottles of pills amid the general confusion of the sideboard, morphine, tranquilizers, cough syrups, anticoagulants, a kind of pump that helped her to breathe, a couple of blind wooden Christs, without arms or legs, necklaces dangling from a wooden knob, an empty hanger on one corner of the screen, clothes draped willy-nilly over the rocking chair. That smile.

—What are you thinking about?

—I don't know

and her fingers feeling for nothing on the sheet. All the lights on, even though it was day. Suddenly she sat up in the bed. When I went over to her, she said

—Don't be frightened

and disappeared again. She took a long time to come back, fiddling with the buttons at her throat. The border of tiny flowers on her blouse, a bony knee sticking out from beneath the blanket. She didn't seem sad.

—Who's going to love me now?

She looked at the statue of the pipe-smoking black woman who could be taken apart to reveal the wooden children she carried in her belly. The pipe fell from the woman's mouth, rolled among the papers on the floor, and came to a stop on its side.

—I should go back to São Tomé,* don't you think?

I agreed. She should go back to São Tomé, to find the sharks on the beach again, Governor Gorgulho's massacre.† A pair of blue-rimmed spectacles and a pair of green-rimmed spectacles lay on the newspapers she didn't read. No tawny owl, no barn owl. A plump pigeon on the verandah of Olaias, pacing the rail with pontifical slowness. That odd bunioned way birds have of walking. She tried to go to the bathroom on her own and we found her sprawled on the tiles, exhausted, unable to move:

—Don't be frightened.

That Sunday the hearse drove at about eighty miles an hour from Lisbon to Alenquer, passing nearly all the cars it met on the road. After Alenquer, a secondary road, factories, the homes of immigrants, what people in the city call the peace of the provinces. Once we reached the village, everything slowed down because the people of Abrigada accompanied the coffin on foot. I leaned against a large tree growing behind the church. The priest advised the congrega-

---

*São Tomé. A former Portuguese colony off the coast of West Africa. São Tomé e Príncipe consists of two islands and a number of smaller islets. It was granted independence in 1975.

†Governor Gorgulho's massacre. This took place in February 1953 in the then-Portuguese colony of São Tomé, on the orders of Governor Carlos Gorgulho. The colonial police, with the support of white colonialists and African contract workers, unleashed a series of violent attacks on the native Creoles, who had always refused to work in the fields but who feared being forced to do so because of labor shortages.

tion to be good and told them that in Our Father's house there are many mansions. I don't remember the rest of the sermon. Then we walked behind the hearse. I felt like an automaton. It was very hot. I understood nothing and I remembered Jesus's words in the Gospel according to St. John: "Why do you not understand my speech? Because you cannot hear my Word." The priest said good-bye and left, taking with him the cross and his assistant with the little bowl containing holy water. In my Father's house are many mansions. It was nearly twenty to five, that unlikely time. Speaking of houses, there were no children playing in the cemetery, pretending that the tombs were dolls' houses. There they were with their shelves, their paper flowers, their frilly curtains. It didn't seem to me either that anyone played hopscotch on the gravestones now. But the wind brought with it the scent of mimosas from the hills, so much so that long afterward when I was back in Lisbon, I could still smell it.

GOD AS JAZZ FAN

I grew up with an enormous photo of Charlie Parker in my room. I think that for a child whose one ambition was to become a writer, Charlie Parker was in fact the ideal companion. That poor, sublime, wretched, brilliant drug addict, who spent his life killing himself and who died of youth the way others die of old age, continues to embody for me those words from Horace's *Art of Poetry*, which sum up what any book or painting or symphony should be: a fine disorder preceded by a poetic fury is

he says

the basis of the ode. Whenever anyone mentions words and literary influences, I laugh quietly to myself: the people who really helped me mature as a writer were all musicians. My road to Damascus happened about ten years ago, watching a TV program in which an English ornithologist was explaining birdsong. He slowed everything right down, took the songs apart and, by comparing them to works by Handel and Mozart, proved that birdsong was structured like a symphony. By the end of the program I had understood what I had to do: use characters like the instruments in an orchestra and transform the novel into a score. Beethoven, Brahms, and Mahler were my models for *The Natural Order of Things*, *The Death of Carlos Gardel*, and *The Inquisitors' Manual*, until I felt capable of composing something for myself, putting together what I had learned from jazz saxophonists, principally Charlie Parker, Lester Young, and

Ben Webster, the later Ben Webster, in "Atmosphere for Lovers and Thieves," where you can learn more about direct metaphors and about holding back information than in any handbook on literary technique. Lester Young taught me phrasing. He was a man who began as a drummer. When a critic asked him why he swapped the drums for a wind instrument, he explained that by the time he had finished packing up his drums after a gig, his fellow band members had already made off with the prettiest girls.

The fact that he also wanted to get the pretty girls led him, among other masterpieces, to "These Foolish Things," in which each note sounds like the last sigh of an illuminated angel. The photograph I have of him shows a man sitting on the edge of the bed in a hotel room with a tenor sax beside him. Thin and old, he stares at us across the years with the saddest, sweetest eyes I have ever seen. His tie is crooked and his jacket rumpled, and probably few people were closer to God than that celestial hobo. Ben Webster, on the other hand, looked like a plump storekeeper transfigured by an invisible but obvious halo. These three men sat at the right hand of the Father and it astonishes me that they don't appear on the altars of churches. Perhaps there's no room in those marble and plaster heavens for promiscuous alcoholics and hopeless sinners. Perhaps some people feel more comfortable in the company of edifying creatures who edified nothing apart from joyless lives that ended in virtuous deaths perfumed by lilies. Since I believe that God is no fool, I'm sure He would be driven crazy by all that melancholy goodness and pointless prudery. I would even bet that He plays drums so as to let the other guys go off with the prettiest girls while He stays behind and quietly packs away snares and cymbals, leaving Charlie Parker, Lester Young, and Ben Webster to head blithely off with the gin, the marijuana, and the best-looking chicks to a recording studio where Billie Holiday has just begun singing about His power and His glory world without end.

CHANCE IS THE PSEUDONYM
GOD USES WHEN HE PREFERS NOT
TO SIGN HIS OWN NAME

Almost every day after lunch, I park the car next to an olive tree in the hospital grounds and sit there thinking about nothing, feeling nothing, looking at the tree trunk and listening to myself breathing. It's an old tree, hunchbacked, moss-covered. Even on sunny days, night seems to linger there. A little bit of night hidden in the branches. Beyond the wall, poor people's verandahs closed in with sheets of cardboard instead of glass. A shirt drying, cheap clothes, brightly colored. I've never seen anyone out on those verandahs. It makes me think of the places where I grew up, the palm tree next to the post office with a blind man crouched in the shade. I am the olive tree's blind man, waiting. What's missing is the man who used to sell wild birds, his hands full of cages, arguing with himself even in the deserted street. At fourteen or fifteen I wrote a poem about him. He used to catch the birds with nets laid near the elementary school, chaffinches, hoopoes, sparrows. They were nearly all snapped up by the owner of the bar, to be fried and served, still dripping oil, to customers who made a sandwich of them with bread, washed down with a glass of wine. A stray feather floated above their heads.

When it rains, the olive tree grows still more wrinkled. Once when I was on duty, I went to visit it after dark: the day seemed to linger there, a little bit of day hidden in its branches. It must have been June or July. A patient had hanged himself. He used to bum cigarettes off me, money to buy a cup of coffee, things like that. His wife used to visit him with a basket of peaches and those peaches were the color of the cheap clothes hung out to dry on the verandahs. The nurse had cut the rope and laid the man on the ground. I went to the first-aid room to complete the paperwork. My pen refused to work. The nurse offered me one from the pocket of his white coat. Blue. I took longer than usual to fill in the form. From somewhere, perhaps from beside the scales, the blind man from the post office was watching me. For some reason he was always surrounded by cats. One line in my poem was about those cats. Obviously no newspaper ever published it. I used to buy them all, ever hopeful, but no luck. There I was, the best writer in the world, and no one even noticed me. I'd had the devil of a job writing that poem about the palm tree, the blind man and the cat: I counted out the syllables on my fingers and there was always one or two too many. I had to do quite a few versions. I ended it with an exclamation mark. Then I changed it to three dots. Then, in order to solve the problem, I removed the punctuation altogether and felt very modern. The wound inflicted by the unfairness of those literary pages lasted a very long time, well, a day or two. When you're fourteen the days are endless.

I wonder how old the olive tree is. I like to run my hand over its bark, to touch the little razors of the leaves. On one of the verandahs there's a cactus in a pot. The pot sits on an aluminum saucer. I feel a childish desire to throw a stone at the pot. If I threw a stone at the pot, would they complain to my mother? Would she appear on the verandah to tell me off? I could always tell when she was angry with me by the way she said António. My name, in her mouth, bristled with knitted brows. We know we've grown up when no one tells us off anymore. They simply shake their heads in silence. They wrapped the man who had killed himself in a sheet from which one bare foot protruded. Stupidly I started counting his toes. They brought a stretcher and carried him off. When his wife was told the news, the little basket of peaches started to tremble. I watched her leave, taking the fruit with her. Seen from behind she seemed thinner. The darkness of the corridor swallowed her up. Little thin legs, tennis shoes. I wonder where she lives? I repented of my desire to throw a stone at the pot: cactuses really keep a person company.

Today is Saturday, January twenty-something. A grubby sky, a grubby day, clouds that make you want to take a brush or a damp cloth to them and scrub out the stains. The night before last I had supper at my parents' house. The little waterfall is broken, the garden neglected. The times I played ball there! The windows with wooden shutters, the little limestone bench, the table whose top had been a grindstone, me hunting for lizards in the nooks and crannies. One afternoon, I found a toad next to the fig tree, puffing out its throat. It looked like the tailor in Calçada do Tojal, plump with emphysema, drawing chalk lines on his customers' lapels. When I went out into the street I had the feeling that I was doing more than just going out into the street. Someone called my name. I could swear someone called my name. António. No knitted brows. Just António. Who could it have been? The creeper? The balcony? The plants in the flower bed? I turned round and saw myself watching me. Good-bye, António, he whispered. I hadn't seen myself for ages. I answered

Good-bye, António

and hoped never to meet him again. Whatever for?

TEXT FOR A BOOK BY
PHOTOGRAPHER
EDUARDO GAGEIRO*

I've always been terrified of photographers: they order us to sit still and then start to examine us, to stalk us, to approach, to move away, half hidden behind that horrible mechanical, myopic eye socket that blinks its circular eyelid from time to time, they ask us to be natural while they study us, all camera and hands

(a second camera, slung around their neck, stares at us, swaying, from belly-button level)

and then there's a click and they devour us, that mechanical eye socket suddenly swallows us, we are transferred, like the dead, onto a square of paper where we are not us continuing to be us, where we become a face outside time or a smile that belongs to no one

(I don't smile like that)

and that conceals and adorns me like a false mustache, it's impossible to be natural if I have ceased to exist, frozen in that wave of the hand, that expression, that attitude, none of which was ever mine, no one is like that, no living being is like that, those serious features overlying my features pretending to be happy, this man so much older than me

(always so much older)

---

*Eduardo Gageiro (1935–). Celebrated Portuguese photographer.

in whom I discover a future I never thought would arrive, when the session is over it isn't me they talk to, it's the shadow I've become, and who, for obscure reasons, the mechanical eye socket has decided to spare, a small useless remnant, a shadow, the kind of thing washed up at night on the beach and scorned by the retreating tide, then I ask myself

—And now what?

or rather

—How am I going to carry on now?

how am I going to carry on now that they've stolen everything from me, now that I inhabit an album, a drawer, a frame in the living room, I don't get up, I don't sit down, I don't respond, I don't exist, I have become a creature I don't recognize

(but who?)

suspended against an uncertain backdrop, trees possibly made of cardboard, since no wind stirs them, the walls of houses that no one lives in, more ghosts

distant

and indifferent, I return to my childhood when someone would point out to me on the sideboard a swarthy gentleman in uniform, wearing a medal and a mustache

—Your great-grandfather

staring at me across decades and decades like one vast question mark, the same great-grandfather in Mozambique or in India, impossible countries that only existed on maps

(Mozambique pink, India green)

or rather that never existed at all, my mother had a baby book for each of us and on a page in my book, tied with ribbons, was a lock of my hair from when I was one year old, the past reduced to a lock of hair in a book; after a session at the photographer's, or rather after the photographer has put away the mechanical eye socket in cases and bags and has finished pursuing, devouring, and swallowing me, that is what remains, that useless remnant, that shadow, that thing

scorned by the retreating tide. Nerval wrote on the back of a litho-
graph of himself

—I am the other one

Je suis l'Autre

—I am the other one

the other one, but where, when, how, and, more important, what
other one, which other one, the others that you assure me are me,
but that aren't, I'm not me, I'm not even what you see because I am
only me if I'm seen by someone; the photographer or, rather, the
camera is saying

—Don't move now, that's great

and although I don't move I'm gradually shrinking inside because
the photographer

—Forget about me, pretend I'm not here

meaning

—Let me kill you

let me blink my circular eyelid and kill you, let me approach,
move away, walk around you and kill you, devour you, swallow
you, turn you into a face outside time or a smile that belongs to
no one, any day now I'll be just another gentleman on the sideboard en route to the chest in the attic and final oblivion among
old clothes, hatboxes, chairs the upholsterer will never mend, and,
after the chest in the attic, the selling-off by weight to peculiar
individuals who buy detritus and dust and sell them to even more
peculiar individuals who are proof against allergies and adore
detritus and dust, and there I'll be: a great-grandfather to a lot of
fake great-grandchildren in some antiques store somewhere, no,
don't tell me to keep still, don't start studying me, please don't
encourage me

—Perfect, just perfect

don't turn my body to the left and my nose to the right, don't
suggest that I light a cigarette or rest my chin on the palm of my
hand, don't point that fairground magician's finger at me

—Concentrate on my finger

when I concentrate on that finger there's the click of the eyelid and after the click only the bench where I was sitting, only the window behind, only the buildings, but no me, perhaps the cigarette you suggested I light burning out on the floor while a little smile like a false mustache slowly evaporates with the last ray of sun.

LIFE SURPRISES US SOMETIMES

L ife surprises us sometimes. There I am struggling with a book,
burdened down with anxieties and doubts
(writing is not usually an activity I associate with pleasure)
the same doubts I had when I began in October 1998, the same
doubts that will accompany me when, in a few months' time, I
hand the book to my agent and the agent hands it to the publishers, the fear that this time I'll be found wanting, that I'll have
failed and have reduced to ashes the incandescent material I had
in my hands
(and this time, dear God, I had so much incandescent material in
my hands)
there I am suffering through this novel for fifteen hours a day
every day, anxious, angry, wanting to give up, to throw it in the
trash, to do something else, and yet, finally, like an ox plowing
words, like a man engaged in stripping away all excess fat from
those hundreds of pages, falling asleep with them, waking up
with them, investing time and health, feeling furious, discour-
aged, hopeful, exhausted, and along comes the surprise, the miracle of a letter, a pause in my fate as self-appointed burning bush,
a pause for friendship, affection and peace. It comes from Oporto,
with a photo of my daughter Zezinha, when she was still tiny,
in Angola, and it speaks, in a language that goes straight to my
heart, of things I had forgotten, births, autopsies, the cholera epi-

demic, camaraderie in the face of suffering, sickness, the misery of war and death, it speaks, in a language that goes straight to my heart

(why don't I write like that, with that spare simplicity, that unforced tenderness, that energy?)

of the shared courage, or, rather, the not being afraid of being afraid, of the one hundred or so young men lost in the jungle while trying to survive in the midst of a paradoxical joy. He was a quartermaster, his name was Firmino Alves, and we spent a whole year together in Baixa do Cassanje, on the frontier with Congo. Marimba, Marimbanguengo, Mangando, and when I recall those names, a row of mango trees trembles in my veins. His name is Firmino Alves and by a miracle he survived a horror that, after twenty-four months in Africa, took from us several of our comrades. And yet what a lesson in hope he always gave me and gives me again with his words now. A book is, in fact, nothing compared with what he suddenly lit up inside me: the River Cambo full of crocodiles

(do you remember, my friend?)

and the people, who were also crocodiles, slow, opaque, cruel, many pairs of little eyes adrift on that stagnant water. And yet, how odd that we feel nostalgic about it. Perhaps because the cruelty was not malicious and the violence not perverse. After months and months of war, we took on the unaffected simplicity of animals. No thoughts, no dreams, no problems of conscience: just the desire to survive on the surface of the days. As far as I was concerned, the Fatherland could go screw itself, along with fascism, democracy and everything else. I was an animal who took more interest in a sunset than in an idea, and who carried another immediate instinct for survival inside me. I wasn't fighting for anything apart from making sure the rest of our company stayed as alive and as animal as I, so that the inhabitants of the villages between Marimba and the frontier remained as alive and as animal as I. Because the people who weren't there with us and who were not therefore dying were the bastards in Luanda and Lisbon, the politicians, the gener-

als, the big businessmen, the sons of bitches of Portugal from the
Minho to Timor.* Those sons of bitches didn't exist: we existed. And
it was just as well they didn't exist because they might have ceased
to exist if they'd ever turned up there in the jungle. Do you remember, my friend, how easy it was to fire off a shot? Do you remember
when they had to take away our guns so that we didn't start killing
each other? Do you remember the card games with a pistol on the
table and the feelings of deep hatred? The dealer transformed into
the enemy and we capable of blowing out his brains if he won a trick?
And yet

(do you remember, my friend, you speak of this in your letter)

I fought for hours to pull living babies out of half-dead mothers, I
disappeared for weeks on end into Baixa do Cassanje trying to save
complete strangers from the wretchedness of cholera. When faced
by the sickness of some poor unfortunate, I did what I knew I could
and what I didn't know I could. Who can explain that to me, who
can explain that to us? How is it possible to be, at one and the same
time, so brutal and so compassionate? It's funny how we imagine
we've forgotten. Convinced that I had forgotten, there I was grappling with a book

(I'm still grappling with the book)

as once I grappled with a child that wouldn't leave its mother's
womb, fumbling for it with anxious fingers. And once or twice,
Quartermaster Alves helped me. Now that he's not here, I have to
do it all alone. Now that he's not here is just a manner of speaking.

---

*Minho to Timor. Minho is the former designation for a province in the north of
Portugal, on the border with Spain, the principal towns being Viana do Castelo
and Braga. East Timor is in Southeast Asia, part of the island of Timor, situated
about 400 miles northwest of Darwin, Australia. After East Timor was granted
independence by Portugal in 1975, Indonesia promptly invaded and only very
reluctantly allowed a referendum on East Timorese independence in 1999. The
overwhelming vote in favor provoked more violence from Indonesian loyalists; it
was eventually brought under control by a UN peacekeeping force.

He arrived yesterday in a letter from Oporto, and the mango trees of Marimba began trembling in my veins. They're still here, they were always here. That and the two of us in the improvised infirmary, thrilled by the sound of that first victorious, urgent cry. What sinister, touching, pitiless, marvelous creatures we were.

THE TWO OF US

The trouble with getting older is that we grow younger. For example, barely have we woken up in the morning than we approach the shaving mirror and find in the glass a middle-aged gentleman saying to us, with the kind of startled, reproving look we haven't seen in ages

—My, how you've grown

then he disappears very slowly, razor in hand

—Tell your parents it was lovely to see you again

until we realize that it's us holding the razor, that grown-ups' toy

—Leave it alone, António

which we'd better put down quickly before someone tells us off, and then we realize that the middle-aged gentleman is us as well, that where once there was a smile there are now wrinkles, that in place of the fair hair are a few grizzled strands, that no one tells us off for smoking, that we can reach the highest shelves without the aid of a stool, that the house is a different house, without our mother's dressing gown hanging behind the door, that we're no longer thinking about writing books, we're actually writing them, and that we don't, after all, have a math test in the second period at school.

The trouble with getting older is that we grow younger, but young in a way that young people reject. The adolescent girls of today don't even notice us, fascinated by boys far less handsome than we were than we continue to be

out of nowhere emerge children much older than we thought and who insist on considering themselves to be our daughters, whatever happened to my cigarette cards of film stars and soccer players, who took my copy of *Sandokan, The Tiger of Malaysia* from my bedside table, where have my silkworms gone, my chocolate wrappers, the ring with the Benfica emblem that my grandmother bought me in the market at Nelas, much to my aunt and uncle's disgust

—It's hideous

after I promised, for hours, never to pee in the flowerpots again or to hide the walking stick belonging to the cook who has been living with us for fifty years

fifty years is an unimaginable number

and who doesn't do anything except sit on a bench sucking her gums and addressing my ancient cousin

who's so old she's pregnant

as Miss. When I think about it, I can't have gotten older: I merely dreamed I got older and as in all dreams everything appears to be true, but isn't. I didn't buy this apartment

I'm not old enough to buy apartments, what clerk would draw up the title deeds to an apartment for a boy in short pants?

I've no interest whatever in all these dull books on the shelf, paintings that are nothing but daubs, sofas my feet mustn't dirty, the decrepit old man who has just finished shaving and is examining a mole, his nose pressed to the mirror

he probably wears glasses,

he doesn't have false teeth, fortunately, so it's obviously not me although there is something about his eyes, something about his mouth

no, of course it's not me

the decrepit old man resigns himself to the mole, gives me a surprised, reproving look

—My, how you've grown

he seems to be looking for himself in my amazement

no, not in my amazement, in my annoyance

he seems to be looking for himself in my annoyance, he parts his hair where I part my hair except that he does it more slowly, as carefully as a geometer, and even though no one has told him to, he wastes a ridiculous amount of time putting everything back as it should be

lids screwed back on, the towel in its correct place, the washbasin clean

and finally leaves me in peace in the bathroom and slouches back down the corridor like some slow, vanquished elephant. Now I can lock the door, feel in my pajama pocket for the crumpled cigarette I stole from my father, sit down unseen on the bidet, open the box of matches I swiped from the pantry without anyone's noticing, apart from the cook with the cane whom no one notices anyway, and start coughing at the first puff, spluttering and happy. Then all I need to do is bat away the smoke with my hands, drop the cigarette butt into the toilet bowl, pull the chain several times because the cigarette butt spins round and round and refuses to disappear

it finally does, thank heavens

leave the bathroom wearing a look of complete innocence, still coughing and wiping my streaming eyes on my sleeve, creep up on the old man wrestling with his shirt collar, slip into his body as if into a baggy suit

grown-ups' clothes are way too big for me, when I wear their shoes I make a hell of a clatter on the floorboards

and sit there very quietly inside his gestures, rereading this with him, feeling very bored, unable to sing the praises of Sandokan, Tiger of Malaysia, who could at least sail a parau

whatever a parau is

wielding a scimitar

a scimitar is a sword or something I think

instead of this idiotic pen, which would never frighten off the corsairs.

THE HEART'S HEART

The novel I would like to write would be a book whose every page, as in the final stages of Chinese wisdom, was a mirror in which the reader would see not just himself and the present in which he lives but also the future and the past, dreams, catastrophes, desires, memories. A story in which, as I leafed through it with the intention of making numerous emendations, armed with a red pen primed to create a bloodbath of corrections, I would suddenly find, waving gaily to me, perched on a paragraph as if on the garden wall, my grandfather and the caretaker's son who taught me to trap birds and to steal figs from the neighbor's orchard and who is probably now a body-shop guy living in a third-floor apartment in Alverca, with no room for the storks of Benfica, for the trees in the woods, for that captivating, religious, auroral dimension between heaven and earth where the orange trees breathe slowly and the fish in the pond enter and leave our body through the pores of our skin. And not only the caretaker's son, but the piano music from Vila Ventura, home to a couple of ugly spinsters whom Chopin transfigured, softening their eyes until they took on the unbearable, exquisitely beautiful sweetness of sick animals who converse with us in a language that, over time, we grow too deaf to understand, opaque to the angelic condition of cripples, orphans, and married women, the only beings I know who are capable of flying over the mystery of things.

In the novel of mirrors that I would like to write, I would stumble, at the edge of a chapter, upon the years I spent at Nelas, tennis courts, the Serra da Estrela strewn with lights, the branch of the chestnut tree that frightened me by beating against the shutter of my insomnia, Dona Irene playing the harp with the tame doves of her fingers, the widow installed at the top of the stairs like an obese Buddha, and the bachelor cousin hunched over the phone and whispering into it with the gestures of a romantic lead

—Send me half a kilo of rump steak, Senhor Borges.

Given that the pages are mirrors, I would find in them my present face and all the faces I have had up until now and that I revisit in the baby book that still preserves, mummified like the braided tress of a saint, a little lock of hair from the child, now dead, that I once was, looking at me across the ages, accusing and suspicious, hair I dare not touch for fear it might crumble into dust like the orange-blossom bouquets of ancient brides, and that with it would vanish the child I was and the people I loved with unequaled passion, my paternal grandfather, my maternal grandmother, Flash Gordon, Sandokan, Captain Haddock, and the little girl with long eyelashes who played Our Lady in the Nativity tableau at the church.

Given that the pages are mirrors, it would be a rough and troubled book like the houses in the Beira region in September, the wind in Zé Rebelo's pine woods, the first rains beating against the granite walls, my mother frowning, her hand cupped to her ear, asking loudly

—What?

and, tucked away in one corner of the room, where no one will hear his seductive whisperings, the bachelor cousin, eyes shut, cooing into the phone, manly, persuasive, irresistible

—All right, Senhor Borges, if you haven't got rump steak, make it a kilo of loin chops.

Given that the pages are mirrors, there I will find my years as a choirboy, the hypnotic choreography of the mass, the lugubrious mise-en-scène of processions, the fear of a terrifying God who spied on me, hoping to catch me lying or swearing or with my thumbs in my pockets attempting sinful maneuvers, in order to propel me into a universe that resembled a rusty kitchen full of pans of boiling vegetable soup and maids with phosphorescent pupils and goats' feet, ready to plunge me for all eternity into the torment of those steaming broths. There I will find the priests with cheeks as wax-smooth as women's cheeks who came to lunch on Saturdays at my grandparents' house and transformed the meal into a solemn sacrament, where the duck served with rice took on a liturgical density that their Northern accents and wafer-laden breath only underscored. And indifferent to the priests, to the devil, to Hell, trilling away in velvet tones, his face half in shadow like Humphrey Bogart's, his hat tipped forward over his eyes, incantatory, magical, shadowy, the bachelor cousin, lips pressed to the mouthpiece, was saying in resigned, languid, swooning tones

—Fine, Senhor Borges, if you don't have loin chops, you don't have loin chops, bring me half a pound of ham instead.

Given that the pages are mirrors, if I move closer to the book I will find, behind my grandparents, Sandokan, Flash Gordon, the girl from the Nativity scene, my mother cupping her hand to her ear, and the adolescent I have ceased to be, aflame with embarrassment and pimples, a desperate man laboring over his novel word by word until he hands it to the publisher who, from the other side of his desk, receives it with pastoral benevolence, as an ecclesiastical dignitary might accept the offering of a believer. I reverently place the bundle of paper on his desk, he blesses me with the crosier of his silver pen, and once out in the street I realize that, having lost the novel, I have lost an essential part of my identity and so, once home, I immediately start preparing my notebooks for the next story, in my haste to see myself once more reflected in the paper from which a new hope slowly emerges, stubbornly insisting that there will always be more early mornings and that, for them alone, it is worth believing not in politicians, those pathetic administrators of the ephemeral, not in economists, those absurd managers of the contingent, but in all those beings whose prestige lies solely in a kind of hesitant vehemence and in staying alive. After all, I might always, when I least expect it, come across the bachelor cousin embracing the phone as if it were a woman's body and speaking conspiratorially into it so that no one else can hear

    —A quarter of a pound, Senhor Borges, at least a quarter of a pound of ham for my breakfast sandwich.

MEMORIES OF THE
YELLOW HOUSE

My parents who, as regards their sons' education, had clear and enlightened ideas, chose to send me for my primary education to Senhor André's school in Avenida Gomes Pereira, in the days when the Simões factory was still there, when the headquarters of Benfica stood where the municipal building now stands

(I was astonished that a sports club should consist of two dark rooms full of elderly gentlemen with chesty coughs smoking roll-up cigarettes and playing billiards and cards)

and when ladies in dressing gowns and curlers chatted to each other at their windows complaining about their husbands' rheumatism.

The four main components of Senhor André's school were, in descending order of importance, Senhor André, his Wife, his Wife's Mother, and their dog. The dog, named Pirate, thanks to one of those flashes of humor in which Senhor André was always so prolific, wore a red collar with a bell that made no noise

(the usefulness of a silent bell was a mystery to me)

never barked

(it was as silent as the bell)

wandered about the flower beds in a state of chronic melancholy and, as well as being ugly and obese, had the face of a worker-student or perhaps a labor-union official, which comes pretty much to the same thing. The Wife's Mother, from whom, likewise, I never heard a peep

(don't despair, there will be some sounds later on)

spent all term crocheting while seated on a small canvas stool beneath the apple tree, and her sole function was to allow me to dream that if she died, there would be no school for a whole week. While I was at the school, she did not, alas, die, despite a touch of bronchitis whose progress I followed anxiously and hopefully, and I bet she's still there crocheting away in some suburban school and still suffering from that same touch of bronchitis that, to the despair of the students, never quite develops into anything more serious. The Wife, the daughter of that perverse centenarian tortoise and married to Senhor André, had a pockmarked face

(misfortunes never come singly)

taught the first- and second-year students and took no notice of me at all: for that alone, in my opinion, she deserved both her husband and her spots. Senhor André taught the third and fourth years, was bald, beat us often and methodically by means of kicks and slaps and raps with a ruler and drummed into our heads, by dint of many whacks around the ear, the mountains in the Galaico-Duriense Massif, the railroad lines of the Beira Alta, and the rivers of Mozambique. An example: Peneda (slap), Suajo (slap), Larouco (slap), Gerês (slap), and so on and so forth

("and so on and so forth" was one of his favorite expressions)

like someone hammering nails into a wall.

The lessons of this pedagogue began according to an immutable ritual: Senhor André would arrive, we would stand up, Senhor André would sit down, we would sit down, Senhor André would tug at the hairs sprouting from his nose, we would not

(Senhor André had more hairs sprouting from his nose than you can possibly imagine, and it seemed to me that instead of brains inside his skull, he had an endlessly sprouting palm tree)

and after his harvest of bristles, which he discarded scornfully on the floor, rubbing together his index finger and thumb, he would issue an order to Nicolau

(Nicolau had ginger hair: there's always one in every class)

meanwhile feeling for change in his pocket, Nicolau go and buy me a pack of Três Vintes. Nicolau left at a trot, thus avoiding having to recite the names of the islands of the Azores, and a tremor of envy ran around the rest of the class, who, during the lunch hour, assuaged that envy by kicking Nicolau in the shins, and while Senhor André waited for the aforementioned Nicolau to bring him his cancer sticks, he would summon Vasconcelos to the blackboard and give him a slap even before the lesson began, because, as he explained to us in his subtle head-on way of tackling things, this simply saved time given that Vasconcelos never studied anyway. In fact, no one ever knew whether Vasconcelos studied or not because Vasconcelos never managed to open his mouth: as soon as he came within range of Senhor André, his head was already being hurled against the board. The board fell down, Vasconcelos was dealt an extra kick for having brought down the blackboard, and then, after Vasconcelos, it was Norberto's turn, and after Norberto, it was Nelito's turn, Nelito was the son of the woman who ran the vegetable stall and he became famous later on as Nelo do Twist, a rival of the great Victor Gomes and Zeca do Rock, the kinds of performers in which Portuguese music abounds. When blood was pouring in gallons down the walls and a dozen broken legs lay moaning among the desks, Senhor André would soften. With an ominous smile he would announce

—Now since today is Sunday . . .

the dying hastened to correct him with what remained of their mouths

—No, Senhor André, it's Monday

the smile gave way to a terrifying snarl, Senhor André grew angry

—Oh, so you know the days of the week, do you, you rascals

and he would resume the massacre, furious that this useless knowledge should, out of pure malevolent stubbornness, have taken up the space in our minds reserved for the names of the tributaries flowing into the left bank of the Douro River.

My parents, who were not easily impressed, considered Senhor André to be an excellent teacher: after all, with a broken arm I might quiet down a bit and minus one tooth I would eat less meat. They very nearly placed in the living room, in a ceramic frame, a photo of that local hero, whom I met many years later in Rua dos Arneiros. He recognized me at once and greeted me with surprising affability—Good morning, sir. Terrified, I responded by listing all the principal towns of Angola, and when I told my mother about this, the lucid author of my days replied:

—Apparently the poor man has some horrible disease. It always seems to happen to the best of men. At least you remembered the names of the towns in Angola. Your old teacher is a real saint.

INWARD SIGNS OF WEALTH

When, on December 25, 1863, Victor Hugo wrote in one of his notebooks: I am a man thinking about something else

he was, of course, referring to me. When I have lunch with someone, for example, I leave my smile sitting in my place and tiptoe away to another table in the restaurant, where I doodle trains and ships on the paper tablecloth while I wait to set off, in an ink locomotive or a steamboat, to somewhere far from that world of saltcellars, bottles of white wine, and fish heads. When I was small, in the days when they tried to teach me the catechism, I thought of God as a gaseous vertebrate: it took me ages to understand that the gaseous vertebrate was me.

The result is that I observe the objects of daily life with as much bewilderment as a caveman: I've never yet managed to play a video, I cut myself each morning when I shave, and writing a check is almost as hard as solving one of those problems involving faucets: If a tank is nine feet long, how much time will it take a faucet that lets out 25 fluid ounces of water per minute, etc. etc. I was the despair of my instructors during military service, turning toward them with a loaded rifle and asking

—What?

in genuine incomprehension and surprised to see them hurl themselves to the ground screaming

—Point that fucker somewhere else
gripped by an anxiety I still don't understand. Perhaps I inherited
this from an absentminded uncle who, at a wake, astonished to see
the widower so upset, patted him consolingly on the back and said
—Anyone would think someone had just died
I am a man thinking about something else, who tries to open the
door with a cigarette and smokes a pack of keys a day: if I get lung
cancer they'll have to call in a plumber to operate. Large, important
words like Work, Family, Money, pass me by without touching me.
This might sound as if I don't know how to live with those I love or
that I reject their affection: that's not true. It's just that sometimes
when they're fondly caressing me, I'm watching the storks in the
jungle of Aunt Madalena's attic, or I'm on the esplanade at Praia das
Maçãs, beside my grandfather, eating strawberry ice cream. And I
like modest people because what I find most touching are purely
inward signs of wealth.

Speaking of inward signs of wealth, I saw a young woman of
about forty during office hours at the Hospital Miguel Bombarda
last week: she had a lump in her breast and the doctor didn't want
to operate because the disease had spread to her bones. Chemother-
apy. A pretty, intelligent woman. She said to me
—I'd like to live a bit longer
and she's going to die any time now. Then she smiled and asked
—I'm going to get better, aren't I?
she knew she wasn't and she knew I knew she wasn't
—Of course you'll get better
I said
—You're looking very pretty, you know
—Everyone tells me that now. I'll be forty-one next month.
She was wearing her Sunday best, necklace, rings, blue eyeliner.
The nurse opened the door and peered in, saw that I wasn't alone
and vanished. And her smile
—Perhaps we'll see each other again

and me shaking her hand

—Perhaps we will.

As she left, even her way of walking was elegant. And then I thought: it's just as well I'm a man who thinks about other things. If I wasn't, I would feel like crying.

And so by the time the next patient came in, I had already forgotten about her. I had already forgotten about her. I had already forgotten about her.

I had, thank God, already forgotten about her.

CHRONICLE OF THE
POOR LOVER

The sacristan went over to the ragged vagrant kneeling in prayer and leaning against a pillar. He tapped him on the shoulder to tell him that it was time to close the church and the vagrant dismissed him with a howl whose indignation was somewhat colored by red wine

—*Je n'aime pas qu'on m'emmerde quand je prie.*

The vagrant's name was Verlaine,* and I often remember that indignant howl when I sense that someone is about to speak to me, because the people who speak to me either pull me or push me.

Those who pull me grab me by the arm and shake my sleeve as if to emphasize the importance of what they have to say, in such a way that after two minutes, nose to nose, I receive from them both their opinions and their breath and I can even calculate how many times they've been to the dentist while I struggle not to be swallowed by those gigantic mouths with little sponges of saliva at the corners.

This proximity also allows me an infinite series of not particularly agreeable discoveries, blackheads, pimples, nasal hair, sties, scars, strange wrinkles, balls of spit, as I try in vain to free myself

---

*Paul-Marie Verlaine (1844–96). One of France's greatest and most prolific poets, closely associated with the Symbolist movement. Although he continued to write, he spent the last ten years of his life ill and alcoholic and living in abject poverty.

from the fingers clutching me and as the person speaking looks more and more like a monstrous, carnivorous insect, ready to bite into me with his enormous mandibles.

Among those who pull, there is a subtle category of ones who, instead of seizing my arm, stroke my lapel, remove from my jacket, all the while talking nonstop, hairs and threads that they delicately detach with thumb and forefinger, or else they dust off my shoulder with the back of a hand. These sweet seducers, who improve my appearance by picking off impurities like those birds that keep rhinoceroses clean, hopping about between neck and rump

(they even scrape away, with an efficient fingernail, stains missed by the laundry)

as I was saying, these sweet seducers do not normally devour: when they have finished their confidences, whispered into an ear that they would love to clean out with a little finger, they step back, regard me with one critical raised eyebrow, and announce sternly

—You've gotten thinner

as if being thinner deserved to be punished by the Civil Code, and they suddenly cease their caresses and forget about me, ready, in their need to communicate, to commence cleaning work on another victim.

The people who push use either a forefinger or the palm of a hand

(there is an equal number of both species)

in order to add extra weight to the opinions with which they attack me. Determined and affirmative, they advance on me with little blows of friendly loathing

(in boxing terminology, they prefer to keep a safe distance rather than get into a clinch)

asking from time to time

—What do you think?

in the threatening tones of someone asking

—Do you want a smack in the mouth?

obliging me to walk backward for an entire block, nodding and hoping that the bell will save me from the inevitable knockout. If I try to look behind me for fear there might be a hole in the sidewalk, they immediately ask, redoubling their blows

—Am I boring you?

and I, incapable now of defending myself, completely beaten, dizzy with punches and arguments, reply breathlessly

—No, of course not

agreeing with everything, accepting everything, putting up with everything, longing for a corner of the ring with a bench and a trainer with Q-tips in his mouth who, with a sponge and in his Italian-accented English, would heal me of all explanations and bruises.

Apart from those who pull and those who push, there are those who put a passionate elbow around my neck to breathe whispered misfortunes at me, those who stroke my knee at the restaurant table spattering my beefsteak with spit and resentment, those who look nervously around like political dissidents under surveillance before making the dangerous confession that their wife has run off to Caldas da Rainha with the concierge's husband, those who phone me at four o'clock in the morning not in order to reveal to me, as Cocteau said, that God is the cool part of the pillow, but to announce that they have just been to the bathroom cabinet to look for the Valium and are about to kill themselves with a dinner of pills, which actually happened with my friend Reinaldo Arenas,* the Cuban novelist, who called me from New York in the small hours and stammered drowsily over and over

—I'm going to die, António

Reinaldo whom AIDS had reduced to a sulfurous wound, and hours later our agent rang to say

---

*Reinaldo Arenas (1943–90). Cuban poet, novelist, and playwright. His writings and openly gay lifestyle brought him into conflict with the Cuban government and, in 1980, he fled to the United States as part of the Mariel Boat Lift. Diagnosed with AIDS in 1987, Arenas committed suicide in New York in 1990. His autobiography, *Before Night Falls*, was later made into a film starring Javier Bardem.

—Reinaldo is dead

and me looking out at the river, looking out at the river, looking out at the river and remembering the advice given in Cocteau's*
Parade

given that events are bound to overtake us, let's pretend that we were the organizers

looking out at the river trying as always to transform melancholy into fantasy, as if life, ladies and gentlemen, were not cheerfully painful and we did not always plump all too often for the bad side of happiness. Looking out at the river when, this evening, I dropped Isabel off at her mother's and she gave me a kiss

—I love you, Dad

and I tried to keep her with me a while longer

—Are you sure you haven't forgotten anything?

and watched her as she walked away, watched her as she walked away from the car carrying a bag of clothes that was much too heavy, watching her fair hair, her T-shirt, her shorts, and, you know how it is, I felt such a pang. If, at that moment, the sacristan had come over to tell me that the church was about to close, I would have remained on my knees in front of that house in Setúbal and dismissed him with a howl whose indignation, since I'm a teetotaler, no red wine would color

—*Je n'aime pas qu'on m'emmerde quand je prie.*

And since there was no one else around, at least the sun, at least the trees would have understood.

---

*Jean Cocteau (1889–1963). French poet, novelist, dramatist, theatre designer, playwright, and filmmaker. He is best known for his plays *La Voix humaine*, *Les Enfants terribles*, and *Les Parents terribles* and for the films *Beauty and the Beast* and *Orpheus*.

THE CHRYSALIS AND I

Adaughter of eleven is a real pest: she no longer likes the zoo and she's not yet interested in the bars on Avenida 24 de Julho; she won't sit in the back seat, but she's not yet reached the stage of asking me to borrow the car; in between reading Scrooge McDuck, she's demanding precise explanations about the anatomy and profession of the transvestites in Rua Conde Redondo and the type of clientele that frequents them; she sits on my lap like a baby and then locks herself in the bathroom to get undressed for bed; she's neither a child nor a woman; she's an indecisive chrysalis, part larva and part butterfly, who wants to stay up until four in the morning and then falls asleep with her thumb in her mouth, finding Kevin Costner and Gladstone Gander equally attractive. How can a poor father spend holidays and weekends with such a creature, who still hates brushing her teeth but is always telling me off indignantly if, out of tiredness or distraction, I put on the same shirt I was wearing yesterday?

I have just spent two weeks at Praia das Maçãs with this strange, contradictory being, who asks me for money to buy ice cream and then, between licks, her mouth all smeared with ice cream, demands in the tones of a very stern publisher

—So when are you going to finish that novel?

making me feel horribly guilty because, instead of editing the final chapter, I've secretly been reading the sports pages with the same delight an adolescent might take in poring over a magazine of naked ladies.

Two weeks at Praia das Maçãs is hard work: and I don't mean the permanently red flag, the permanently rainy days, the permanently damp sheets, the permanently coughing vacationers: I am speaking of the difficulty of being both father and mother to a mutant with a face covered by a bubble of pink gum and with grubby fingernails who advises me to eat fish and vegetables to improve my digestion and in the restaurant demands, at the top of her voice, to know what charisma means, and epistemology and fag; I am speaking of a creature whose beauty products consist of two different types of sun cream, various bracelets and necklaces that she forces me to buy for her at the newsstand and a special shampoo

(—Don't tell anyone)

in case of head lice; I am speaking of a being whose smile is so like mine that I feel as if I've been sent back to a time when I used to examine myself in the mirror in my parents' bedroom, surprised to be inhabiting a face that I had the greatest difficulty in accepting as mine, since in my mind I was none other than Mandrake the Magician, not a little boy with bangs and a mole on his cheek condemned to the torments of grammar.

Two weeks at Praia das Maçãs, believe me, is hard work. Two weeks at Praia das Maçãs with an eleven-year-old girl borders on the epic: I've played table soccer, I've stuffed myself with hamburgers, I've watched her splashing around, as impassive as a lifeguard

(why not a beachguard, a seaguard, a waveguard, I wonder)

with a cigarette clamped between my lips as if it were a whistle, I've listened to interminable descriptions of her girlfriends' boyfriends

(hairy little squirts who show their affection by tripping up their beloveds and filling their mouths with sand, which, I suppose, is the height of sensuality and passion)

we've slept in the same room and I've found myself

(in moments of weakness)

feeling touched by how sweet she looks when she's asleep, by the shadow cast by her eyelashes on her cheeks, by the comic book fallen from her fingers like the breviary of a priest having forty winks.

Two weeks at Praia das Maçãs is hard work, a real epic, a bore, a torment. There were times when I felt like strangling her, there were times when I truly wished she had never been born. It was a relief to return her to her mother, a joy to be alone again. Quiet. At peace. Free. I don't miss her. Of course I don't miss her. I just can't understand why she isn't with me. It's not a question of love

(don't be ridiculous, please)

it's just that, what with my being so absentminded, if she's not here, I might well end up wearing the same clothes for a whole month.

COMPUTERS AND ME

O
ne afternoon in Marimba, in Baixa do Cassanje, in the year
of the Angolan war 1973, I showed the tribal chief Macau
(Sebastião José de Mendonça Macau)
a toy belonging to my daughter Zezinha, who was still a baby
at the time, a small plush toy deer that, if you pulled a little cord in
its belly, emitted a few hoarse squeaks. The chief raised his staff of
office, pointed it at the tops of the mango trees, and fled in terror,
and I started to laugh until suddenly I understood and the laughter
dried in my throat. I flung down the deer in panic and went chasing
through the grass after the chief.

That infinitely wise old man, capable of guiding his people
unscathed through the tyranny of the police and the demands of the
MPLA,* the Popular Movement for the Liberation of Angola, understood more quickly than I did the infinite perversity of machines,
even those hidden in the cotton entrails of a small toy animal. He
understood that machines, endowed with the ingenious and almost
elegant treachery that Pasolini attributed to Machiavelli, bite us or

---

*MPLA, Movimento Popular de Libertação de Angola. A socialist organization
founded in the early 1950s that sought to free Angola from Portuguese rule. After
independence was declared in 1975, civil war broke out between the MPLA and
its former allies, UNITA and FNLA. The fighting lasted for sixteen years. A peace
agreement with UNITA was signed in 1994. MPLA, under the leadership of José
Eduardo dos Santos, remains the ruling party of Angola.

cut us or give us electric shocks out of sheer stubborn, inhuman, impenetrable wickedness. He realized that machines and gadgets hate us and that our survival requires us to keep well away from them, not to plug them in or read instruction manuals with their explanatory diagrams in eight equally incomprehensible languages, and never to give in to the temptation to press a button.

As far as I'm concerned, I don't know how to use any of those symbols of progress, from the vacuum cleaner to the pencil sharpener, from the microwave to the Black & Decker drill, from the video player to the corkscrew that gradually raises its two perfidious metal wings. I avoid cell phones like the plague, I will go to any lengths to avoid getting too close to a pocket calculator. The ignition on the pilot light frightens me with its rapid, instantaneous little blue flame, the shaking of the dishwasher makes me break out in a cold sweat, as if I were standing blindfolded before a firing squad. And I've managed to survive all these years despite machines and thanks to an obsessive degree of prudence and a caution worthy of a blind man, until, that is, computers arrived.

I don't believe I'm afraid of death, or the dentist, or leprosy, or politicians, but I am afraid of computers. I'm afraid of their feigned innocence, of their apparent submissiveness, of their murky efficiency, of their silent, tortuous hostility. They've already swallowed a whole novel of mine, transformed entire chapters into experimental poetry, extracted the bones from my paragraphs and reduced them to a puree of adjectives.

That's why I write by hand. I write by hand so that any mistakes are mine alone and so that the characters are as they appear in my head and not the result of the wild, aseptic imaginings of a schizophrenic disk, inventing awkward, aberrant situations like the ones you get in flu-induced dreams. I imagine computers lying sleepily in a cage at a circus, with their claws unsheathed, creatures one can only confront wearing knee-high boots and braided jacket and carrying a whip, and who reluctantly obey the orders of whoever comes near and pokes them with a stick, forcing them to perform the difficult trick of producing a perfect sentence. When I unwittingly press a key or when I find myself with someone else who presses a key, my skin grows dark, my shoulders hunch, my shirt gives way to a Congolese loincloth, my feet slough off socks and shoes, the sounds of Africa fill the room, I point with my official staff at the tops of the mango trees in which the bats hang upside down all day, and I flee, terrified, through the grass, toward the river where the eyes of the crocodiles dance on the surface of the mud as they wait for some small unwary goat to approach.

BACK SOON

In shopping malls, the stores that make me dream are the ones
with the door closed and a sign announcing
BACK SOON
stuck to the glass. Rather than the bare belly button
(a belly button that stares implacably at me like a Masonic eye of
providence)
of the clerk who stands smoking scornful cigarettes, as motionless as if she were a sign lit up by the spotlight of her glorious future
career as a guest on TV talk shows or as a soap star, it is the closed
shop door, concealing its treasures—knickknacks or videos—in a
darkness worthy of the confessional, that helps me to imagine that
I was the one who hung that sign
BACK SOON
on the glass doorknob and then escaped past pizzerias and shoe
stores selling army boots where adolescents seethe with excitement
and acne like febrile parachutists, shouting out passwords in the
language of heavy metal, which makes me feel like some kind of
ancestor from the Tertiary period, a Jurassic creature incapable
of overcoming the obstacles of existence with two jumps on a pair
of in-line skates and the refrain from a rap song. I was the one who
hung that sign
BACK SOON
on my life so as to reassure my family, my friends and people who

face danger by turning their backs on it, and here I am again, brand
new, in Nelas, in Praia das Maçãs, in Benfica, armored against anxiety and death by the visits made to Fátima by my grandmother—a
close friend of Our Lady, who listened to her promises in the days
when the future was not yet behind me—and determined to begin
the world afresh the way someone begins a chapter again and to
organize my emotions in accordance with my moods, the one irritation being the light brown fringe of hair that gets in my eyes and
stops the bouncers outside the nightclub from letting me into cellars full of old men with bald heads and big tits, every one of them
the spitting image of General Franco

(my great-uncle to my uncle

—Aren't you a bit young to be here, nephew?

and my uncle to my great-uncle

—Aren't you a bit old, uncle?)

folding up banknotes and slipping them down the cleavages of
generous Andalusian women, who are very clever with their ruby-
encrusted fingers and happy to leave the generals and lead me to
the toilets out back as solicitously and benevolently as a godmother
whose perfume used to make my head spin in delightful intoxica-
tion. I was the one who hung the sign

BACK SOON

on the door of the room where I'm usually to be found staring
at the ceiling or writing, the two identical ways of being useless in
which I have spent my days, to the great displeasure of those who
worry about me, accumulating words instead of credit cards and
ridiculous literary prizes

(all literary prizes are ridiculous)

shares in respectable companies or posts as financial advisor. I
was the one who hung the sign

BACK SOON

on some handle or other, on a nail, on the key I left in the door,
and I arrived at my grandmother's house where her smile hears the
elevator coming up, mistaking for a visitor someone she knows to

be an exile. I must have gotten the time wrong because the building has ceased to exist and my grandmother's smile has disappeared, I have been abandoned to hopeless orphanhood in Avenida Grão Vasco, which has lost in blackberry bushes what it has gained in boutiques pandering to suburban vanity and in bars serving spider crabs, eaten to the accompaniment of hammer blows and manly eructations. And so I stand there, hands in my pockets, uncertain whether or not to leave, reluctant to stay, with the suspicion that it wouldn't be a bad idea to tie a knot in life just so that I don't forget it.

ON GOD

When Voltaire was asked about his relationship with God, he answered
—We're on nodding terms, but we don't speak
and I feel rather the same, because there are things that seem to me quite simply wrong. When I was a choirboy, I found the church frightening, so large and solemn, so full of mysteries and drafts, leading me to think that religion was simply a windy place from which one departed sneezing. The candle flames on the altars were always being bent this way and that by contradictory breezes, the slightly worn hangings were in constant movement, the uncomfortable choir stalls bruised my back. Many of the ladies brought cushions to kneel on, and the men, when they got up, would brush the dust from their pants, which led me to believe that God was either not very fastidious or else employed a highly incompetent cleaning person. My mother was much better at choosing staff, and this failing on God's part confused me. I found the idea of God as a negligent employer most off-putting. The sacristan, for example, wandered about languidly dusting the martyrs on the altars, infecting St. Roque's wounds, which cried out for hydrogen peroxide not the dusty hairs of a broom, and there wasn't a single saint who didn't wear sandals and didn't have at least one broken toe. Horrible sandals, too, worthy of a Dutch tourist, not to mention faded tunics, which made me imagine Heaven to be a cross between the

beach at Cruz Quebrada and a rundown campsite, where the fortunate ate canned food and left litter everywhere. This suburban side of God displeased me, and his portrait, in the little catechism book, only increased that displeasure: a hirsute gentleman perched on a cloud and grasping a lightning bolt in one hand as if he were an electrician, one to whom no one with a grain of sense would open the door if they found him standing on the doormat. It was hard to picture him in the living room with my family: the visitors entering in a flurry of effusive kisses, only to stop short at the sight of that disheveled vagrant, and my father's embarrassment

—Allow me to introduce God, Senhora Dona Ângela

the vagrant getting up from his cloud in an unexpected show of politeness, holding out one vast hand with fingernails of such dubious cleanliness that our visitors would be obliged furtively to wipe their hands on their handkerchiefs and then have to spend the rest of the afternoon in the company of a strange creature who did not so much speak as launch into labyrinthine prophecies, who boasted about having killed his own son and who said good-bye with

—See you tomorrow, myself willing

having first given us all stinking colds with the aforementioned treacherous drafts, and who, instead of making his exit via the porch, would sail across the ceiling on his plaster cloud, bending our chandelier in the process. My mother would make her apologies as she poured the tea, excusing God

—Poor thing, it's his age, he's so many thousands of years old now

the visitors would pass comment on his clothes and his unkempt appearance and suggest that someone have a word with the prior about getting up a collection for Christmas to buy him a decent suit, while the prior, for all his subservience to the pious rich, would argue

—What can you expect of someone who likes locusts and wild honey

and because anyone who eats locusts is clearly not quite right in the head, the visitors would suggest putting him in a home, staffed by vigorous caregivers immune to colds, who would serve God plenty of soup with lots of cabbage and not much meat

(cabbages are cheaper than meat and true charity should take such details into account because money isn't elastic, as my mother never tired of repeating, thus teaching us to distinguish between a 500-*escudo* note and a stick of bubble gum)

remove the dust left by the sacristan's broom with a good shower and put him to bed between clean sheets and out of reach of any bottles, so as to keep him from launching into another string of prophecies, for we know how easily wine can lead to *folie de grandeur* and elaborate speeches. An impeccable God dressed in tweeds, with no glimpse of skin between pants and sock when he crossed his legs, capable of playing a hand of bridge if anyone needed a partner, his kitsch cloud replaced by a wing chair, a God who dismissed locusts as bad for the digestion and who preferred a jar of reliable home-made jelly to wild honey. Someone to whom you could safely open the door if you found him standing on the doormat

—Do come in, God

and introduce to your visitors as an aged but dignified relative, instead of hustling him off to eat with the servants in the kitchen

—You'll just have to put up with it

where he would place the bundle of thunderbolts on his lap like a battered umbrella missing a few ribs.

THE FAT MAN AND INFINITY

For more than an hour now, I've been trying to think of an idea for this chronicle, and I haven't come up with one. I hear footsteps in the corridor, cars out on the street. From time to time, voices. I'm writing on a sheet of letterhead paper and since I don't know what to write, I'm filling in all the o's with my ballpoint pen. I take off my glasses. I clean my glasses. I put on my glasses. Underneath the letterhead are various telephone numbers, so I fill in the zeros too. Fortunately, there are six telephone numbers with loads of zeros. Given that no idea comes, I deal next with the smaller circles of the eights. I put down the pen. I brush my hair back with my fingers. I open the window and see trees. The sound of cars out on the street grows louder. An elderly man in a white hat stops and feels his pockets. Has he forgotten his key? For the nth time I use first my tongue and then my little finger to probe a broken tooth. Even while I'm writing this, I continue to probe. A lady who lives in a yellow building opposite is watering a window box. Tomorrow the dentist will say

—You can spit now.

The dentist's office is the only place in the world where people tell us to spit. With a bib around our neck we bend over the sink. I could spit beautifully when I was in elementary school, but I am reduced now to a clumsy dribble that runs down my chin and embarrasses me. Then, I could hit a grasshopper at six feet and was the envy of my class. Now I'm worse at spitting than the class fatso, who might have been the best student but wasn't worth a bean when it came to spitting. To avenge himself, he would state confidently that parallel lines never meet. I always thought that parallel lines never met because they had better things to do. The teacher did not agree and assured us that they met in infinity. Infinity, a recumbent eight

I fill in the circles on the recumbent eight

which hasn't even got the strength to stand up. On which point of that lethargic eight would the parallel lines meet? I saw Fatso a few weeks ago, in a restaurant. He was just the same, except now he was wearing a tie, not short pants. He owns two companies

—I'm an economist

a smug, authoritative voice, his bottom lip protruding over his top lip. When I asked if he had learned how to spit, he said

—Nice to see you again

and sat down with the other fatsos, who appeared to respect him, doubtless because of his knowledge of parallel lines. Each fatso placed his cell phone where his napkin had been, ready to solve any problem involving time zones that the teacher might present over lunch. The class fatso would occasionally proffer some definitive utterance to this deferential assembly. My tongue and my little finger poked around in the hole in my tooth. If I'd had a ballpoint pen, I would have filled in all the o's on the menu. The way in which he said

—Nice to see you again

the way in which he said, as he was sitting down

—Oh, not too bad

the fact that when the dentist tells me

—You can spit now

and I, with the bib around my neck, will obediently dribble into the sink with no panache at all. God, the abilities we lose with age. Fatso arranges his food on his fork, raises the fork with majestic slowness, makes an o with his mouth, one circle I cannot fill in. Since I cannot fill it in

(there is no broken tooth in that circle)

I smile. He smiles back at me, from above his tie, not realizing that I am calling him a son of a bitch. He picks up his cell phone. I cannot understand what he is saying, but he is doubtless talking about infinity. His fat colleagues gaze at him adoringly. They are eating poached cuttlefish. How I wish there were bones in their cuttlefish, the sort that you have to spend hours searching for, passing the food from the right side of your mouth to the left, your eyes staring and anguished. But no such luck: the fatsos triumphantly swallow them down, while my finger, poor thing, once more probes my ruined tooth before returning, humbly, to my salt cod. Now getting back to this chronicle, what shall I write about today?

PART III

MA PETITE EXISTENCE:
STORIES

MA PETITE EXISTENCE

In the old days, at Christmas, I used to be taken to the circus. Later, I took other people to the circus. Now that there's no one to take me or for me to take to the circus, Christmas has become no more than the happy-holiday signs from big companies in the store windows and municipal lights in the trees, reflected on the sidewalk in small colored smudges.

I live right here, on the third floor of this building, behind the church. Sixteen years ago, when I first started renting the room, the façade was green. It's faded a bit now, some of the decorative tiles have fallen off, the gutters are broken, and the manager of the building, who is the cousin of the owner of the grocery store downstairs, has already warned Dona Berta that she risks being fined: Dona Berta actually came outside in her dressing gown and looked up at the house

(I hadn't seen her out in the street in ages)

put on her glasses to examine the damage and promised him that by March, without fail, as soon as she'd received the interest on her savings, she would phone the plumber and the mason and get the damage repaired.

I get on well with Dona Berta: she does my laundry, I have a right to two baths a week, she doesn't mind if I fiddle with the electric meter so that I can read the newspaper until late, and on Sundays, she invites me to lunch with her daughter and her son-in-law. The daughter wears men's sandals and braces on her teeth like the kind schoolchildren wear, the son-in-law works behind the counter at a firm selling electrical goods in Bairro das Colónias, and although Dona Berta is older than my late mother would have been were she still alive, I could swear they're hoping I'll marry her.

In the living room, apart from Dona Berta, the doilies, and the plastic roses, there's a photo on the wall of her late husband in his fireman's uniform: it's clear that he was a fat man, but the peak on his cap means that you can't really make out his features. It seems that he left one Saturday in a hurry, still buckling his belt, to put out a fire in Martim Moniz and hasn't been seen since. The daughter swears that he's living in Argentina with a manicurist; Dona Berta fears he may have fallen down a hole that the workmen then sealed up without first checking, as was their duty, to see if they could spot the glint of a helmet or an axe inside. At this point in the conversation, the son-in-law, a pragmatic fellow, says that it makes no difference whether he's in Argentina or down a hole, Dona Berta is a free agent. The daughter agrees, Dona Berta wipes away a tear with the sleeve of her dressing gown, and since there's nothing more to be said, we eat our *bacalhau*, gazing at the photograph of that hero of the flames.

The daughter and the son-in-law disappear immediately after we've all had a liqueur, Dona Berta installs herself on the wicker sofa between the plants, unwraps her crochet work on her knees, the way builders unwrap their packed lunch while perched on the scaffolding, and I stand leaning at the window, not knowing what to do, then Dona Berta, who knows my tastes, poor thing, points at the radio with her crochet hook

—If you want to listen to the match, feel free, Senhor Adérito

while the pigeons return to the church opposite, multiplying the number of shadows on its façade.

Yesterday morning, when I left for the shop where I work, I noticed an advertisement for a circus on ice. All around are the happy-holiday signs from the big companies, all around are the municipal lights swaying in the trees, and the advertisement for the circus on ice is a really lovely poster with a clown and a girl in a swimsuit, both of them on skates, smiling, against a backdrop of trapeze artists and magicians. Perhaps Dona Berta, despite her age, is not so very different from me. Perhaps, as a child, she was taken to the circus, perhaps, later on, she took her daughter to the circus. Perhaps, from time to time, she feels as lonely as I do.

When I got back from work, at supper time, I knocked on her door: she was in her dressing gown, of course, with plastic rollers in her dyed hair and her crochet work in her hand, and I thought she looked pretty. There are times when I do think people look pretty. I didn't dare tell her. I didn't dare talk about the circus, and after waiting a while, she finally asked me, with eyebrows raised

—Did you want something, Senhor Adérito?

Feeling terribly embarrassed, I replied, stumbling over my words

—Do you happen to have a little bit of soap you could lend me, Dona Berta?

and then I sat on my bed for I don't know how long, without taking off my tie, sniffing the soap in my open hand and thinking about the clown in the shiny leather shoes and the checkered socks smiling at me from a backdrop of trapeze artists and magicians.

MY SUNDAYS

On Sundays after lunch, I put on my purple-and-green tracksuit and my blue sneakers, Fernanda puts on her purple-and-green tracksuit and the high-heeled shoes she wore at our wedding, I zip my tracksuit top right up, with my gold chain and medallion on the outside, Fernanda zips her jacket right up, with her two gold chains and medallions on the outside, plus the necklace her godmother gave her, and we get Roberto Carlos out of his crib, put a white satin bow in his hair, drive out of Alverca, pick up my in-laws in Santa Iria de Azóia, and spend Sunday at the mall.

Fernanda sits in the back of our Seat Ibiza with the baby and Dona Cinda, Senhor Borges sits next to me, sports paper under his arm, and wearing a suit, a tie with silvery flowers on it, and a Tyrolean hat; at the parking lot in Amoreiras, he helps me get the stroller out of the trunk, and all the other cars parked there are Seat Ibizas too, they all have an Alentejo car rug on the back seat, they all have a sticker in the window saying Don't Follow Me I'm Lost, they all have a sticker on the right fender saying Short Life and one on the left fender saying Long Life, the same teddy bear dangles from every rearview mirror, they all display on the license plate, next to the little circle of stars representing Europe, the same girl with long hair wearing a Stetson, they all have a sports newspaper, their in-laws and a child, they probably all live in Alverca and spend the whole afternoon trudging around the mall in exactly the same way as we do: ahead go Fernanda and Dona Cinda, who is wearing a fake fox fur and limping slightly because of an ingrown toenail, pushing Roberto Carlos who is kicking and screaming, his pacifier hanging around his neck on a chain. Senhor Borges and I are sixty yards behind, discussing Olivais Moscavide, who lost in Alhandra despite having bought a new forward from a Cape Verde club called AC Arrentela, and who, instead of playing soccer, spends his nights snacking in the bar, an earring in one ear, surrounded by his black friends, facing a table cluttered with empty beer glasses.

Because Fernanda and Dona Cinda stop to look in every window of every furniture store or boutique to study this brand or that, I make a mistake and swap them for another acrylic mother-in-law, another purple and green wife and another child with a satin ribbon, and end up spending hours on a bench, without noticing the difference, with a Fátima and a Dona Deta, discussing the payments on a microwave and a new fridge, then go back to Alverca, have a chicken supper at a local restaurant and my usual bottle of Sagres beer, and it's only on Tuesday, when I'm about to leave for work, that my wife informs me, with great embarrassment, that she lives in Loures or in Bobadela, that Roberto Carlos is called Bruno Miguel, and that she only realized her mistake five minutes ago because my *Last Supper* wall plaque is made of tin and hers is made of bronze. Obviously, we straightened out the matter the following Sunday, when I return home with a Celeste and a Marco Paulo in the Seat Ibiza to which I have added

(is it really my Seat Ibiza?)

a new sticker that says I Hope Not to Meet You by Accident.

This week, my wife is called Milá, my son Jorge Fernando, and I'm paying off an apartment in Rio de Mouro. Since this wife cooks better than the others, I do not intend to return to the mall again. Besides, she's so keen on TV soaps that we probably won't leave the apartment for years, by which time the boy will be wearing a purple and green tracksuit, I'll discover in my closet a fake fox fur coat and a Tyrolean hat, and hear downstairs, after lunch, the sound of my daughter-in-law honking the horn of her Seat Ibiza. By then, I'll be on a low-salt diet because of my blood pressure, so just a bit of grilled fish will do.

A LETTER FOR
CAMPO DE OURIQUE

Yesterday, Ana, I went to see the house. I mean, I knew there *was* no house now, but nevertheless, I insisted on going to Campo de Ourique. You know the house, the one where my parents used to live, behind the church, the little two-story place where we used to play in the garden, kneeling in the rabbits' clover, near the wire-mesh cage at the far end, where eyes, ears and nostrils trembled. In fact, when I think of the house, that's what I remember more than anything: a silent agitation of shadows in the cage against the wall, beneath the wild medlar tree, little red pupils, eyes watching me, watching us, secretly, from childhood.

Where once our house stood and the house next door

(the one owned by a colonel in the artillery, that very tall gentleman, leaning on a cane, looking like a sharp breeze that had run out of puff)

there is now a minimart where the widows of Campo Ourique buy soap, detergent, candy—dozens of widows pushing their shopping carts along aisles of diapers and jellies, but I continue to imagine that our house still exists, and so I go into the minimart, put a fifty-*escudo* coin in the slot, remove my cart from the other carts all nested into each other in a long expectant line, and as if I, too, were a widow

(men can be widows, can't they, Ana? especially men of my age, gray-haired and silent, as hopeless as rain in a courtyard)

I walk along aisles of oatmeal, candy, yoghurt, just as I used to walk weightlessly through the rooms in the house, across the islands of light that the afternoon sun scattered over the carpets.

It's so strange not to have a home, Ana. We haven't seen each other for such a long time, we stopped talking to each other such a long time ago that you don't know, can't know, where I live: suffice it to say that to reach Campo de Ourique I have to take three different buses, the last of which drops me quite a way from the house, next to the cemetery and its pure white gladioli. But I come here every Sunday. I need to come home even if no home exists, even if I have to push the cart across the tiled floor of the minimart and buy oregano, sage and mints I don't eat, just so that the employees don't realize who I am, so that they don't grasp why I come here, so that they don't hear the faint, soft, stubborn, persistent murmur of the past that pursues and accompanies me, so that they don't notice the rabbits in the wire-mesh cage devouring the clover beneath one branch of the medlar tree. I would hate them to notice the rabbits. Just as I would hate them to notice the portrait of my parents over there, in its usual place, above the chest of drawers, which has been transformed into a pile of bottles, beer labels and orange soda.

Sometimes, I have the feeling that it isn't ham or milk or chocolate that the widows of Campo de Ourique are pushing around in their metal carts, I have the feeling that what they have in their carts are photographs, knickknacks, little woolen jackets, my grandfather's gold clock in its glass dome. I have the feeling that they are buying my past at the checkout, that they're storing it on pantry shelves, that they're eating away at it through the winter, that, in some way, they're feeding off what I was, what we were: bike rides out to Ajuda, Friday nights at the movies, the taste of tangerine candies, a huge corpse wearing patent-leather shoes in the room upstairs. How odd these widows are, Ana: all in black, wearing a little hat with a veil, trotting along, one after the other, carrying in their plastic bags what belongs to me, what, for endless years, belonged to me. From here, where I'm writing to you (a modest snack bar near our house, with a blank TV set perched above the boxes of cookies) I look across at the minimart, which the last of the widows is leaving, and I know that if I go in there, if I put a fifty-*escudo* coin in the slot, take the cart and push it down the avenues of cans of tomatoes and sliced bread, I will find dozens and dozens of rabbits nibbling, for lack of clover, the patterns on the carpet, in a house in whose empty rooms absence is multiplying. The woman at the checkout is leaning on the counter, oblivious, reading a photo tabloid.

I will stroll among the shelves searching for an odor that isn't there, I will catch the bus at the stop next to the cemetery and return to the apartment where I live in order to finish this letter, put it in an envelope, and sit staring at the wall opposite for ages and ages, just as, on that evening we went to the theatre, I gazed at your profile beside me, without your realizing it, and wanted to tell you that I loved you and never could.

MY OLD MAN

By the time I was ten, my old man had already given up boxing: instead, he sucked on Dr. Bayard's throat and chest lozenges and coached amateurs at the Académico. The Académico was in a cellar, next to the basement apartment where we lived, and where, instead of my mother sitting doing her crocheting between the stove and the radio with a photograph of our cousin's wedding on top, there were two sandbags hanging from the ceiling, a roped-off square made to look like a boxing ring, and my old man with a plastic bucket full of water, a sponge, and a whistle, telling the boxers what to do. Otherwise it seemed no different: the same posters on the wall, the same smell of rotten rubber and sawdust, the same pigeon house out back, sheltering beneath a dead walnut tree. You couldn't see the river from the Académico or from our house, and I was happy.

My old man had to give up boxing because of a lung disease. When he was the local welterweight champion, he developed a cough and started to lose weight dramatically, and my mother said to him then

—You should go to the doctor, Arlindo

but he took no notice, he put his title up for grabs with a mulatto boy from Chelas, went into the fight on an empty stomach because he was getting chills that took away his appetite, and right from the first round, the mulatto started pummeling his liver, and my old man's second said

—Throw in the towel, Arlindo
and my old man, in pain now from his gallbladder, said
—No way
and in the third round, of course, he started coughing, his mouth-guard jumped out of his mouth, the mulatto threw him one hell of a hard hook, and the doctor at the sanatorium, during the months when my old man was there with his chest, did his darnedest to persuade him to get some dentures to replace the teeth that had been knocked out by the straight punch of that guy from Chelas. When he came back to Penha de França, he couldn't even attempt to regain his title because of the scars on his lungs, so he set up the Académico with my godfather and started training welterweights in the hope that one of them would give the mulatto the battering he deserved and send him off to Alto de São João cemetery with one avenging blow.

The stained posters on the wall all had pictures of my old man in shorts, staring out at us angrily and threatening us with his gloves, each poster bearing the caption: Arlindo da Conceição Martins, Penha de França's Man with the Iron Fists. But he wasn't in the least frightening because my old man was quite short and a bit scrawny, and a whole head shorter than my mother, who was a big, strong woman, and if she'd ever decided to swap her crochet work for the boxing ring, she would just have had to breathe on that mulatto to dispatch him to the undertaker. But my mother never got angry and, besides, the male nurse from Oporto had told her not to make any physical effort because of a nerve in her spine. My old man often tried to get the nurse to allow him to enter her in the women's free-style wrestling
—My wife's got a real gift for it, Senhor Borges
and the nurse would point to my mother's spine
—And what if she damages a nerve and is stuck in a wheelchair, a cripple, is that what you want, Martins?
And so my mother worked as a maid during the day and, when she wasn't crocheting, looked after the pigeon house. One of the

pigeons was a carrier pigeon, except that it never left the yard because it was too nervous and sometimes at night we'd hear it cooing outside the back door.

After school, I always used to go and see my old man at the Académico. There was a single, very dim lightbulb hanging from the ceiling

(to save on electricity)

a couple of determined guys punching the sandbags, a loser in whom my old man nevertheless had high hopes jumping rope next to the chamber pot, a couple of welterweights in the ring, hopping back and forth, and my old man shouting

—Go on, get in closer

and they, terrified of each other and hoping to go back to the café with all their teeth intact. At supper time, my godfather would turn up, having had a few beers too many, and complain that if we didn't find a champion soon, there wouldn't be enough money for the rent of the gym

(my godfather liked to call the basement a gym)

to reassure him, the loser started furiously jumping rope, the two men punching the sandbags punched even faster, and my old man urged on the fearful pair in the ring

—Go on, get in closer

my godfather, sitting down on a bench, shook his head in despair, wiping the beery sweat from his neck

—We won't get anywhere like this, Arlindo

and at the end of the month, the landlord, who owned the coal dealership, closed down the Académico because we were behind on the rent and kept the plastic bucket, the sponge, and the sandbags on account.

That was when my old man really changed. He hasn't left the house for five years now, he just sits on the bench in the kitchen next to the fridge, sucking on Dr. Bayard's chest and throat lozenges and showing no interest at all in the music on the radio. The loser comes to visit from time to time to cheer him up, and he shows him the posters on which Arlindo da Conceição Martins challenges the world with his iron fists, and my old man just shrugs and says nothing. He sits there for ages and ages, not saying a word, and my mother

—Come on, off to bed, Arlindo

and my old man doesn't even respond, unwrapping another lozenge and jumping every time the fridge has one of its asthmatic attacks and shudders and changes its tune. Yesterday, I woke in the middle of the night feeling thirsty and went to get some water and I came upon him in the dark, absolutely still, leaning against the sink. The male nurse who lives next door assured my mother that my old man died of a heart attack, painlessly, suddenly, but I know that's a lie because he had his eyes open and his ear cocked toward the back door, listening to the cooing of the carrier pigeon. In my opinion, the two of them were talking about the best way to beat the mulatto. And this morning, when they laid him out on the bedspread, in his suit and tie, there he was, not talking but discussing fights with my weeping godfather. My old man's like that: whatever happens, he never forgets an insult and, if necessary, despite his age, he'll go out in the yard and start training and recover in no time from that lung disease and from the men coming, any moment now, to close the coffin lid. I know what I'm talking about: my old man's never let me down yet.

EDGAR, MY LOVE

Please, Edgar, don't just leave me like this, what's happening to us, why haven't you phoned? Here I am waiting like an idiot, I didn't even go to the hairdresser's because I was afraid you might phone while I was out, I've smoked eight cigarettes one after the other, and my head's spinning, I've asked the phone company to check if there's a fault on the line and there isn't, I tried killing time by painting my toenails and I've made a real mess of it, I even got nail varnish on my heels and on the carpet, I even got some on the arm of the chair, you haven't been to the café, you haven't been to the club, what's wrong, Edgar? It's not right, it's not like you, don't leave me like this, I keep going over and over in my head trying to understand, and I don't, I mean, only yesterday you came to supper here, only yesterday you complimented me on my eel stew, only yesterday, on the sofa, do you remember?

—I love you, sweetheart

only yesterday, on the sofa, you remember, how one thing led to another, with me getting tipsy and you tugging at my pantyhose

—You naughty girl, you

and me showing you the wineglass I was holding

—I'll stain the new cushions, Edgar

you on your knees, your hair all over the place, your tie all awry, you remember, don't you

—Who cares about goddamn stains, I can't unhook your bra, it's stuck if you don't help me, I'll have to call the locksmith

and of course it wasn't stuck at all, Edgar, you just have to know how it works, you just have to keep calm, and you looking at me and unbuckling your belt, you getting in a tangle with your shoelaces

—Wait a minute, Deolinda, I won't be a second

and I did wait, but you were digging into my leg with your elbow and I said

—Move your arm, love, you're hurting me

from the window I could see almost the whole of Laranjeiro because my apartment's on the top floor, Laranjeiro, Cova da Piedade, Almada, another six months and I'll have this two-room apartment paid off, and there I am, thinking that, if you wanted, we could live here together, buy a dog and be happy, but then you went all quiet, all embarrassed looking down

—I must be tired, Deolinda, it must be because I worked late at the office last night

and you not a flicker, not a spark, and me helping you and you, ashamed, your pants around your ankles, in a tiny thread of a voice

—It must be that late night at the office, no leave me alone, let's stop for half an hour and I'll be fine

we stopped for half an hour, we watched that show where people beg their family's forgiveness and then everyone flings their arms around everyone else and they all cry and the audience applauds and cries too, and even the woman who presents the show, such a nice woman, she's moved too, the whole of Laranjeiro is moved, and then I kissed you

—Do you feel more rested now, Edgar?

and you angrily, and very far from fine

—Oh, shut up

in a voice that wasn't like your voice at all, my love, no sweetheart, no naughty girl, no pussycat

—Oh, shut up

and I lovingly stroking you, concerned because you were so tired

—Edgar

and you still with your pants around your ankles moved to the other end of the sofa

—Don't touch me

and I, because I adore you, put my hand on your thigh and you as if my hand had burned you

—Don't touch me, for Christ's sake, don't touch me

you got dressed in an instant, you put on your coat, and as you were leaving said

—If you tell anyone what happened, I'll kill you

and me still trying to get over the shock, me stumbling after you

—Don't leave me all alone, don't go, Edgar

you walking down the street to the bus, all stooped as if you were carrying the world on your shoulders, and me from the steps

—Edgar

and you didn't even turn around, didn't even say good-bye, didn't even smile, didn't even phone, I wanted to say Don't be angry, I wanted to say It doesn't matter, I love you anyway, let's try again, I won't tell anyone, Edgar, I swear I won't tell anyone, they won't make fun of you at work, they won't make fun of you at the café, we can live together here in Laranjeiro even if you're tired forevermore, I don't mind, we could buy a little dog, on Sundays we could go to Ginjal, it's quiet here in Laranjeiro, you can see Cova da Piedade, you can see Almada, my head's spinning from all those cigarettes, I already asked the phone company to check if there's a fault on my line and there isn't, I've made some eel stew, I bought some ice cream from the supermarket and I'm wearing a black lace bra today that opens at the front, Edgar, so you won't have any problem taking it off.

I REALLY NEED TO
TALK TO YOU

It might all be over, but I'm not such a fool that I'm going to break down in front of you. On the contrary: I turn up wearing a smile as if nothing was wrong, I sit down at the table, I tuck my napkin into my collar because I don't want to splash my shirt

(my mother, poor thing, whose eyes aren't what they were, has a terrible time getting stains out)

I say

—Good evening, Manuela

and I drink every drop of my soup, talking of this and that, not letting on that I'm sad, that I have a lump in my throat, that I feel my life is in pieces because I promise I'm not such a fool as to break down in front of you. You get up, take my spoon from me, put my plate on top of yours, bring the braised rabbit and rice from the kitchen and I open a bottle of beer, which can sometimes help a little to dissolve the sadness and the lump in the throat and while I help myself to rice I wait for you to talk about Carlos.

It may be my fault for always putting off getting married, coming here on Mondays and Thursdays and leaving at one in the morning on the excuse that my old mother needs my help, that she's reached the age when she leaves the front door open and forgets to turn off the gas, that I'm her only child and she has no one but me, when the truth is that commitment frightens me, the idea that you might want children frightens me

(I'm hopeless with children)

and with all those excuses and postponements it was more than likely that you'd get fed up in the end and if it wasn't Carlos it would be someone else, at least Carlos is a nice steady guy, and he loves you, his mother's fifteen years younger than mine and as strong as an ox, and a woman can't waste her life waiting for some man to make up his mind and spending most evenings alone watching videos, a woman needs company and conversation, she needs a man to take care of and I'm no good at all that, Manuela, I spend the evenings here looking at my watch, afraid I'll miss the ferry, I plant a hasty good-bye kiss on your forehead, I give you a quick phone call from the office, then last week you said

—I really need to talk to you

and I realized that you wanted to tell me that Carlos was ready to give you what I've never given you, that it didn't suit your temperament to be all alone, to go to the beach alone, to go to the cinema alone, to have no one to look after you when you get one of your sore throats, I hear my voice

—The rabbit's delicious

knowing full well that this isn't what you want to hear, knowing full well that what you want to hear is

—I'll marry you, forget about Carlos

but I can't, I'm simply incapable, I love you and yet I can't see myself living with you, do you understand, love is such a strange thing, Manuela, I promise you that I do feel love for you, I promise you that I would so like to take your hand and say

—I'll marry you, forget about Carlos

but the words won't come out, there you are waiting and the words won't come out, there you are silently assuring me

—If you stay, Carlos can go to hell

and all I can do, idiot that I am, is to compliment you on the braised rabbit instead of complimenting you, taking your hand and saying

—I love you

because I do love you, I don't know anyone who does macramé as well as you do, or who keeps their house as clean, their clothes as immaculate, not a speck of dust on the furniture, I don't know anyone who would treat me the way you do, I think Carlos is a very lucky man, I think I'm going to feel your absence deeply and yet I'm not such a fool as to break down in front of you, I speak to you as if there were nothing wrong, I put my napkin back in its ring, I get up, I button my coat and you

—I really need to talk to you

and I, because I'm not such a fool as to break down in front of you, with my hand on the door handle

—Tomorrow, tomorrow

knowing perfectly well that I won't come tomorrow, that I will never come back, and that if I did I would find the table laid and Carlos sitting in my place eating my braised rabbit and rice and saying

—We need to go to the Registry Office to sort out the paperwork

knowing perfectly well that in two or three months' time I'll peer over into the garden at the Gulbenkian Museum, and you'll both be there with your witnesses taking photos of you by the statue, by the lake, and you might even see me there, Manuela, you might catch sight of me among the bushes, you might look at me as you're looking at me now

—I really need to talk to you

except that you won't say anything because it's too late, you can't spend the rest of your life going on your own to the beach, to the cinema, with no one to take care of you when you get one of your sore throats, you might wave to me, I might wave back and then immediately catch the bus home because my old mother needs me, she's reached the age when she leaves the front door open and forgets to turn off the gas, when I go in, my mother looks worried

—You look pale, Jorginho

and I quickly

—It's nothing, Ma

and I go and sit in the back garden until it's dark, not crying, of course, I'm not such a fool as to start crying, only wimps cry, and I'm not crying, don't go thinking I'm crying, I'm not, I sit in the garden until it's dark feeding corn to the chickens, feeding corn to the chickens, feeding corn to the chickens.

THEORY AND PRACTICE
OF SUNDAYS

W hy are Sundays so long, Filomena? I don't have to be at
the office by nine, you don't have to be at the nursery by
half past eight, so we get up late, have breakfast at our local café,
buy the Sunday newspapers, and rent two movies from the video
club

(a thriller for me and something romantic for you)

no one is there to give us orders, no one is demanding anything
of us, no one is hassling us, so why is it that Sundays are so long,
Filomena, why is it always the same time by the clock, why is it that
I want anything, although I've no idea what, anything rather than
being here with you? And I love you, really I do, I should feel good,
but I don't, it's not unease that I feel, it's not anxiety, it's just some
vague sensation, a discomfort, a disquiet that I don't understand
and yet I can't imagine myself alone, I can't imagine myself without
you, I love your face, your body, I married you for love, so why are
Sundays so long, Filomena?

It has nothing to do with the area, I like the area, it has nothing to
do with the apartment, three rooms are more than enough, plus we
have the verandah, the view, Queluz, the river, the boats, if we feel
like it we can go to Sintra or to Cascais, to the cinema at Amoreiras, we can go window-shopping, we can go to Cacém to play cards
with your brother and his wife, your brother sprawled on the sofa,
unshaven, his chin propped on his hand, bored stiff, flipping chan-

nels and eating popcorn from a cardboard bucket and his wife in the kitchen shooing the children out and ironing shirts. Do you think they find Sundays long, Filomena? You slip into the kitchen to talk, I eat popcorn and flick through the pictures of their cruise to Tangier in August

(smiling people at supper holding up a glass of wine, a dance aboard ship, your brother wearing a funny hat, arm in arm with a mustachioed Arab)

your brother says to me, pointing at the photographs and switching to the sports channel

—I was bored stiff, Alfredo

you from the kitchen

—Pop in here a moment, will you, sweetheart

to show me the new microwave, to show me some electrical gadget for grinding something or other

—We could buy one of these in November with our Christmas bonus, sweetheart

your brother from the other room, his mouth full of popcorn

—The tennis is on, Alfredo

their apartment is half the size of ours, a basement apartment, opposite a store selling roast chickens, with the chickens on the spit coming in through the living-room window, dripping juice, chickens that resemble fat naked ladies with their knees up, and me thinking how long Sundays are, Filomena, it takes an eternity to reach four o'clock in the afternoon, it's sheer torment, and given that I love you, I don't understand why, I mean, I'm not even unhappy, I'm not unhappy, really I'm not, it's such a strange thing, a feeling of constraint, a nagging anxiety, I don't know what it is that I want, but I don't want this, this tunnel of hours, this armchair that is fine during the week and so uncomfortable on Sunday that I can't sit still, can't settle. And at seven we go to your parents' place in Massamá, your mother bored stiff and flipping channels and eating popcorn, their half-blind dog snapping at my ankles, your father trembling with excitement as he leans on the cane that, since he had his attack, serves as his spinal column, your father in an apron, beaming

—I was the one who made the soup, I was the one who made the soup.

At ten o'clock at night, driving back from Massamá to Queluz takes no time at all. There's always somewhere to park the car on the corner just beyond the butcher's, the trees are growing pretty again now that Monday is approaching, the hands on the clock start to turn, the idea of going back to the office, a thought that will depress me from Tuesday onward, fills me with excitement, the living room suddenly looks terrific, the vases of flowers, the bamboo, the picture of the black woman with a child on her back, I start to want to hold your hand again, to kiss you, I might surprise you by buying that grinder thing, or whatever it was, for your birthday. As I stand in my pajamas brushing my teeth, my bare feet clenched on the cold tiles, I hear you say from the bed

—Alfredo

and I forget about Sundays, about how long Sundays are, about the discomfort, the disquiet, the unease, I get into bed beside you as fast as I can with my toothbrush still in my mouth, Julio Iglesias is singing softly on the radio alarm, I realize more intensely that I love you, I realize that I'll always love you and that we might just survive the popcorn in Cacém, the soup in Massamá, and the motionless clocks, that we'll survive the shops in Amoreiras and the cruises to Tangier. After all, there's only one Sunday a week, isn't there, that's what we have to remember, Filomena, there's only one Sunday a week, one miserable little Sunday a week. I like your lace-trimmed nightgown, I like the smell of your neck, I like your legs as they wrap around mine. Your sister-in-law's microwave isn't that expensive really

—A bargain, sweetheart

one insignificant Sunday a week and six great whole days in which to be happy.

THE GREAT AND
HORRIBLE CRIME

My mother and I aren't rich. We own the hair salon on the square and the small apartment above it, with the new wooden floor we had laid in June and the enclosed balcony that was built when my father was still alive and when the three of us lived here and he worked as a foreman in Cabo Ruivo. Now the only thing he's in charge of are the cypresses growing around the gravestone bearing a small enamel portrait of him in the Alto de São João cemetery, and when we go there on Sundays, it's as if I can see him, in brown overalls, a burned-out cigarette clamped between his gums, gravely making a note of the clouds with a little stub of a pencil.

My mother and I aren't rich: we have the old man's pension and what we earn from the salon, from nine o'clock in the morning until seven o'clock in the evening, perming the hair of the divorcées who adorn their windows with satin curtains and spend all day painting their nails while they watch the latest soap and await the arrival, in a Mercedes and with toothpick in mouth, of the building contractors who pay for the perms, the curtains, and the nails and who, from beneath their Tyrolean hats, whisper promises to them of emerald rings.

We aren't rich: we have Sunday lunch out, go to the movies, buy something for supper at the mall and since I don't have a girlfriend or any intention of getting one, we talk to each other and, in summer, enjoy vanilla ice cream on the esplanade surrounded by a flutter of startled sparrows. And that's how we were, doing all right, and saving up for a holiday in Spain, when Edilson started visiting us.

I don't know where my mother found him because she and I are together all the time, and I'd never seen him in Marvila: you could hardly miss him, a mulatto guy in a bright red jacket and a yellow tie, with a guitar on his knees, singing a samba, and my mother stroking his cheek, which is how I found them when I got back from the doctor's, where I was going for a course of injections for a slipped disk. I stood there petrified, my umbrella in my hand; my mother was wearing a new skirt and saying in the voice of someone either fainting or yawning

—Oh Edilson

and me consumed with jealousy thinking I'm going to die

—Nice meeting you

and thinking I'm going to die, then, noticing that Edilson was twenty at most, young enough to be her grandson, thinking How embarrassing if the neighbors find out, thinking Well, that's the end of our holiday in Spain, and my mother ignoring me

—Would you like a little shot of whisky, Edilson?

Edilson with his great paw on her knee, not in the least embarrassed

—No, I's drunk enough already

and my mother behaving as if I didn't exist, as if the photograph of the foreman wasn't there on the table next to the sofa, next to the bud vase with the artificial flower in it, my mother all smiles

(and me feeling like killing her)

—One ice cube?

my mother all in blue organdy, my mother in her push-up bra, my mother wearing the necklace with the silver fastening that she wears for weddings, my mother sporting long earrings and a fake beauty spot on her cheek, Edilson tuning his guitar

—Two

crisp, gelled curls, striped socks, patent-leather boots, my mother turning to me, in a grating voice like chalk squeaking on slate

—Bring us some ice, Aníbal, don't just stand there gawking

I opened the fridge, and from the kitchen balcony you could see the containerships on the river, you could see the cranes, only I couldn't, you could see the gulls, only I couldn't, you could see Seixal, only I couldn't, I took the knife out of the drawer to loosen the ice cubes which didn't want to come out of the tray, you could see a ship, only I couldn't, the cubes still didn't separate under the faucet, I struck them hard with the handle of the knife

(you could see Seixal, only I couldn't)

and still no luck, I tried with hot water and still no luck, and my mother from the living room, in a grating voice like chalk squeaking on slate

—Are we going to get that ice today, Aníbal?

and I could have killed her, your honor, I could have killed her, we'd been doing all right for forty-one years, we had lunch out on Sundays, went to the movies, enjoyed vanilla ice cream on the esplanade surrounded by a flutter of startled sparrows, you could see the cranes, only I couldn't, I never had a girlfriend, my mother saying

—Put the knife down, don't be so silly

nor any intention of finding one, my mother, her hands covering her face, saying

—Edilson

my mother, in blue organdy, saying

—Edilson

you could see a ship, only I couldn't, and when they took me to the police station, I didn't even protest, you're not telling me that was my mother, it wasn't my mother, my mother was nothing like the local divorcées and she would never ever wear a fake beauty spot on her cheek, my mother, who was a lady, would never ever wear a push-up bra.

THE LONELINESS OF
THE DIVORCÉE

On weekends when I don't go out with my cousin Bé, I stay home and watch TV. Watching TV means watering the plants on the balcony, reading my horoscope in the magazines, undoing my knitting from the previous Sunday, switching channels every twenty seconds, and thinking about killing myself. The problem is that as soon as I get up to take all my sleeping pills, my mother phones from Alcobaça to find out how I am, I can hear her shouting on the answering machine

(my mother, who is terrified of telephones, always shouts)

and since it isn't possible for someone to commit suicide and talk to her mother at the same time, I forget about the pills and assure her that I'm fine, I don't have a fever, I smoke at most three cigarettes a day, I'm eating well and I haven't lost weight

(—Are you sure you haven't lost weight?)

I'll visit her in Alcobaça next week without fail and some day, I promise, I'll find myself a nice young man

(—I can't believe there isn't a nice young man where you work, dear)

I'll even remarry, and by the time I put down the phone, I'm exhausted and my head is splitting and the only thing I want is an aspirin and complete silence, I no longer want to commit suicide because you can't kill yourself if you're not feeling well.

On the weekends when I go out with my cousin Bé, we go to Loja das Meias and to Escada dreaming of cashmere jackets

(—I might be able to afford one with my Christmas bonus)

and long coats, we bore ourselves to death at the movies that got rave reviews in the newspapers, we meet up in a bar with her colleagues from school who discovered a really cheap Italian restaurant in Alcântara last week, and more than once I've awakened on a Sunday morning in an apartment in Campo de Ourique or in Beato beside a math teacher with a fridge full of yoghurts past their sell-by date, an abandoned slipper in the bidet and, next to a broken coffee cup, a tin ashtray with cigarette ends overflowing onto the floor.

Feeling incapable of washing in a shower in which there's no soap and no water and that, besides, is filled with piles of old newspapers, I race back to Lumiar without saying good-bye to the bearded man lying there snoring, his cheek on the pillow

(—I can't believe that Bé doesn't know some nice young man, I can't believe that Bé doesn't know some nice young man)

with one shoulder sticking out of his frayed pajamas and I sleep until the shouts from Alcobaça wake me, my heart thumping, demanding of the answering machine if I've been eating too many french fries.

I don't eat too many french fries, I don't smoke too much, I don't drink too much, I don't have too much sex, I don't have too much of anything, Ma: I listen to the pile on the carpet growing, I switch TV channels every twenty seconds, and I read my horoscope on the next-to-last page of the women's magazines after the fashion notes and an article that explains how a garter belt and a pair of red shoes could change my love life. Would a garter belt make the past-their-sell-by-date yoghurts disappear from the fridge? Wearing red shoes, would I find showers without piles of newspapers in them? My horoscope for this week, divided as always into three parts, Health (watch your liver!), Money (don't be too extravagant!), and Love, which predicts that on Wednesday, regarding matters of the heart, an unexpected encounter will change my life forever. Wednesday was yesterday and the unexpected encounter consisted of spotting my ex-husband on the subway: he's grown a mustache, was accompanied by a mulatto girl half his age, and didn't even see me. Did he ever see me?

There are soaps on all the TV channels. I can hear the October rain on the windows and the couple upstairs moaning in time to their creaking bed. If I get up to take all my sleeping pills my mother will immediately start shouting on the answering machine, so it's best just to sit here quietly on the sofa and look at the plants and at the photo of my little nephew and not think about suicide. What's the point?

For six months I save money on lunches

(an espresso, a croissant and a codfish cake)

eaten standing up in the shopping mall, I buy the Escada blazer and a pair of red shoes, the colleague at work who sells gold promised to reduce the payments on a ring, and I spend the evening alone, in blazer, shoes and ring, looking stunning, switching channels and listening to the pile on the carpet grow.

CONVERSING WITH CAGES

Senhor Rui hasn't been to see me at the hospital for quite some time now. He's a man of sixty, always clean and pressed, in suit and tie, his hair impeccable, with a briefcase in his hand and a pension of 22,300 *escudos*. The briefcase is full of oranges

(—I can't afford restaurants on 22,300 *escudos*, doctor)

Senhor Rui opens it and offers me one, I stand there with the orange in my hand while he sits down opposite me because I'm the doctor and Senhor Rui is the patient, I have just put the orange down among the prescription pads and I ask

—So how are you, Senhor Rui?

Senhor Rui replies

—Fine

and he really is, he looks extremely well, already suntanned from the zoo

—I still go there every day to talk to the animals

because Senhor Rui spends most of his pension on tickets to the zoo, where he talks to the animals and the animals talk to him. The animals in question are tigers. Senhor Rui despises all the other creatures

(—The lions and leopards have absolutely nothing of interest to say, doctor)

he turns right and heads straight for the tigers without so much as a glance at the rhinoceroses and the giraffes, and, neatly pressed

and very clean, he installs himself, with his briefcase, opposite the
cage, ready for dialogue

(I pick up the orange again)

ready for another thrilling exchange with the tigers before going
back to his rented room in Largo do Calvário

(—Five thousand six hundred *escudos*, doctor, and one bath a
week)

where he arrives at six in the evening and waits for the morning
because, alas, the zoo closes

(—I just don't see why they have to close, doctor)

and interrupts Senhor Rui's communion with the animals just at
the point where he and the tigers are about to discuss a matter of
vital importance to the country which Senhor Rui

—Secrecy is the soul of commerce, doctor, but as soon as the animals and I have it all sorted out, you will be the first to know

declines to divulge out of delicacy and friendship and a desire

(I put the orange down)

to spare me disappointment: Senhor Rui hates to disappoint his
friends. When I first met him he had been seeing another doctor

—I had to change doctors, your colleague simply didn't understand animals, whereas I could see at once that you really sympa-
thized with them

and was full of anti-tiger pills, and since I envy a man capable of
conversing with cages, I took him off the anti-tiger pills, which were
also anti–Senhor Rui pills that left him stupefied and drowsy

(I pick up the orange)

and Senhor Rui recovered his vitality and continued exchanging
points of view with the fauna of Sete Rios.

Years ago, entirely by chance, I saw him at the zoo, sitting opposite the animals with his briefcase on his lap taking advice from a
tiger that kept roaring and roaring. I'm too insignificant a creature
for him to have noticed me, and besides he was listening intently to
his friend's important discourse. On his next visit to me, I tell him
that I saw him sitting by the cage, discussing life, and Senhor Rui

(I don't know what to do with the orange)
immediately grabs my arm
—And didn't you think the excellent creature was right, doctor?
(I really don't know what to do with the orange now)
I hesitate
—Don't be afraid of the truth, doctor
I say tentatively
—Possibly
Senhor Rui is most offended
—Possibly?
I hurriedly correct myself
(I start to peel the orange)
—Possibly is just a way of saying, yes, of course, he was
Senhor Rui thinks for a moment, leans over the desk and asks me
softly
—If you had a pension of 22,300 *escudos* wouldn't you talk to the
animals so as not to go mad?
I drop the peel in the wastepaper basket, I share the orange with
Senhor Rui, a segment for him and a segment for me
—If I had a pension of 22,300 *escudos*, Senhor Rui, what else would
I do but talk to the animals?
and as Senhor Rui finishes the orange
—So as not to go mad
Senhor Rui standing up now
—You'd better make an appointment with yourself then, doc-
tor.
Which is what I did. I made an appointment with myself, but
there's such a long waiting list that I can only see myself in October.
Until then, you will find me every weekend at the zoo talking to
the tigers, sitting side by side opposite their cage with a gentleman
carrying a briefcase, wearing a suit and tie, neatly pressed and very
clean, and eating oranges a segment at a time.

THE NIGHT OF THE
BEAUTY CONTEST

The most important thing that happened to me when I was ten years old was my sister Deta's being voted second maid of honor in the Miss Estrela beauty contest. I'd never seen the dance hall looking so pretty, with the portrait of the club's bewhiskered founder adorned with garlands and paper lanterns, the Accomplices of the Night rumba-ing on stage, leaping about in their patent-leather shoes, with a blue spotlight on the drummer, a poor soul who never had a girlfriend because, by the time he'd finished dismantling his equipment at the end of a dance, endlessly unscrewing cymbals and drums, the other Accomplices, who only had to stash their fifes or flutes or whatever in a case, had vanished with the beautiful assistants from the hair salon, then Senhor Porfírio, the owner of the salon, who also organized popular marches, arranged funerals, and consoled widows during matinees at the Eden with romantic whispers and promises of family vaults, called for silence with his hands transformed into gulls, flicked the microphone with one finger to check the sound

—One two three testing

and his voice, above the shouting and whistling of the Final Judgment, summoned the five contestants up onto the stage, all of them dressed like the movie stars who appeared on packs of chewing gum, and my sister Deta, wearing the skirt that my mother and my grandmother had taken nearly a month to make, was the loveliest of them all. To be perfectly honest, I hardly recognized her: at first, with all those frills and necklaces, I thought she was Marília, the master builder's girlfriend who, imperious and alone, drank tea in the Red Pearl Café with her dog on her lap, surrounded by a cloud of perfume that was the mystical incense

(and other less confessable things)

of my youth. Then, when I looked more closely and saw her bitten fingernails, I knew that it must be Deta

(Marília's nails were long and magnificent)

plus the scar on her cheek that had earned her the nickname of Al Capone from her colleagues at the tailor's shop, and I still to this day don't know how she got it because whenever I was stupid enough to ask, she would start chasing me with one hand raised to deliver an avenging slap. But on the night of the beauty contest my mother and my grandmother had applied so much cream to her face that you couldn't see a thing, I said

—With so much cream on your face, Deta, all you need are a few candles on your head and you could be a birthday cake

and Deta started screaming, my grandmother threatened me with the slipper and if my father hadn't had one too many *bagaços* because Oriental had won its match, I would have ended up in the hospital having a nurse put my leg in a cast. Senhor Porfírio introduced the terrified contestants who paraded past and made clumsy twirls and bumped into each other to the sound of a special rumba from the Accomplices of the Night, who devoured the girls with their eyes, all except the drummer who, judging by the way he was wielding those sticks, seemed to really hate his instrument. When the music stopped, Deta and her rivals lined up on stage, the jury, that is the master builder and the nephew of the founder of the Estrela soccer club, swiftly eliminated the one in the middle and the one on the far left, both of whom, coincidentally, had refused to have lunch with them in Caldas da Rainha and who left the stage hurling insults at them, and my mother swelled with pride and relief

—At least we'll get a sash and a bunch of flowers

there were two hairdressers left and my sister, all three of them sashaying about and smiling at the jury, ready to walk to Caldas da Rainha if necessary, as hopefully as pilgrims to Fátima, even if all they got was a toasted sandwich, in fact, the hairdressers must be there right now because one was voted Miss Estrela and the other first maid of honor, both in their crown and sceptre, while Deta, as well as missing out on the toasted sandwiches, had to make do with a few faded roses, a sash that wasn't much bigger than a ribbon, some faint applause from my family, the consoling words of her work colleagues

—You're sure to win next year, Al Capone

and my joy as I danced around her

—Go on, lend me your sash for a moment, lend me your sash for a moment

until I fell asleep on my grandmother's lap rocked by the cradling rhythm of a rumba. The other night, over supper, when we were remembering the contest, my brother-in-law and me

(my brother-in-law gave up playing drums for the Accomplices of the Night and is now a meter reader for the gas company)

he told me, tenderly pinching his wife's bottom

—If Al Capone here hadn't stayed behind weeping with rage, I'd still be single to this day, Armando, given how long it always took me to put away my drum equipment

and I didn't understand, I really didn't understand, why my sister stuck a fork in his fingers, left the table and ran out of the room, slamming the door so hard that their wedding photo fell off the wall, cracking the glass and tearing the happy couple in two and leaving the frame made of clay daisies shattered forever, alas, on the floor.

THE LIEUTENANT COLONEL
AND CHRISTMAS

The only thing I want from Christmas is for it to be over quickly, for it all to be over, the brightly lit avenues, the lights in the trees, the bustle in the shops, all those people out in the streets, the packages, the big bows, the ribbons, the neighbors who leave pine needles on the stairs, the concierge's son who works for a clothing store and sets off wearing a bright red jacket and blowing through his cotton wool beard at me

—Good afternoon, sir

and I unplug the phone so that no one bothers me, I ignore the mailbox to avoid putting up with anyone's Christmas wishes, I sit with the television off too because I hate religious movies, bells that clang, messages from prime ministers and circus performances, and at this point the engineer who lives in the third-floor apartment on the left rings my bell, all smiles

—My wife wants to know if you'd like to spend the evening with us so that we can enjoy a slice of Christmas cake together

the engineer with spit in the corners of his mouth when he speaks, and me gripped by a kind of horrible fascination unable to take my eyes off the spit, watching the little bubbles that shrink and grow, sweet really

—It'll just be my wife, my sister-in-law and me, just the immediate family, you understand, an evening with friends the engineer, it's clear, wants to unload on me his nuisance of a sister-in-law, who's a widow and lives six blocks down, on the corner of Praça Paiva Couceiro, a blonde with stiffly lacquered hair who goes to the market wearing jewels and a fur coat and who isn't in fact bad looking, and me staring in hypnotized horror at the spit

—You know what an unsociable old bear I am

when it might not be so bad sharing the sofa with the sister-in-law and her rings and her necklaces, to have a good ogle at her décolletage, meanwhile holding one hand underneath my slice of cake because of the crumbs, the engineer's wife, leaning solicitously toward me

—Would you like a saucer, lieutenant colonel?

the sister-in-law dabbing at my hand with her napkin and brushing my wrist with her little finger, the sister-in-law with eyelashes as long as cockroach legs that wriggle and wriggle, the sister-in-law pouting her lips coquettishly

—Don't worry, we've got the problem solved, haven't we, lieutenant colonel?

and now that they've put me on the reserve list, I could even go with her to the market, I could even invite her to a matinee, we could even have supper together in the Baixa in some discreet corner, next to the aquarium full of lobsters very slowly colliding with each other, she telling me about her late husband and I thinking

—If I touched her would she get angry?

hesitating, shall I shan't I, shall I shan't I, the engineer's sister-in-law sticking out her chest and spreading butter on a little morsel of bread with all the delicacy of a watchmaker

—Please, call me Ofélia, why so formal?

and me unable to decide, shall I shan't I, shall I shan't I, shall I shan't I, blowing my nose, the better to be able to appreciate her perfume, seeing the tremor of her nostrils, moved by the fact that her eyeliner is smudged

(she's the only woman in the world who could move me with her smudged eyeliner)

and me shall I shan't I, shall I shan't I, the lobsters colliding with each other in slow motion and the wretched waiter breathing an apology

—I'm so sorry but we're about to close

me in the taxi heading for her apartment building and feeling her thigh against mine, shall I shan't I, shall I shan't I, shall I shan't I, a plump thigh, perfumed, round, soft, and she in a whisper so that the driver won't hear

—Does the cat have your tongue?

alarmed or amused or concerned

—Aren't you feeling well?

and me shall I shan't I stammering as I feel for my cigarettes

—No, I'm fine, never better

but I wouldn't be fine, I would be sorry if she left, I would miss her, the apartment would be much better with her here, I imagine place mats, I imagine flowers, I imagine all the nice little touches, and the engineer still there on the landing with the little bubbles of spit growing in the corners of his mouth

—You're not an unsociable old bear, lieutenant colonel, we'll see you at eleven

it's past midnight and I'm here all alone, with the television off, the phone unplugged, I've put on my slippers, my pajamas, my woolen dressing gown, the blanket over my knees because it's freezing cold, down here I continue to imagine the sister-in-law upstairs, her perfume, her blonde hair, her necklaces, her jewels, the smudged eyeliner, and I don't have the courage to go up that one flight of stairs to join them, the fact is I don't like Christmas, I hate Christmas, I hate the brightly lit streets, the lights in the trees, the bustle in the shops, the packages, the big bows, the ribbons, the champagne, I hate Christmas cake, most of all I hate Christmas cake, Christmas cake eaten alone, in a room with no Christmas tree and no hand held underneath to catch the crumbs, next year if the engineer invites me again, I'll say yes, the sister-in-law might still be a widow, she might still go to the market in her fur coat, I might, she might, we might both still be alive, three hundred sixty-five days, well, it's not that long.

THE NEWSPAPER CROSSWORD

It's quite difficult being alone at night. Of course I can read, I can listen to music, I can rent a video, I can phone Esmeralda, I can do an hour's crocheting before I go to bed, but I miss having Renato at home, Renato sitting in the armchair where he always sat, Renato doing the crossword puzzle in the newspaper or staring up at the ceiling because he was never a great one for talking, he would give me kiss and ask

—Did the maid help iron my shirts?

and if I put my arms around his neck

(Renato is tall and I'm rather short)

wanting to stroke his beard

(I love stroking Renato's beard)

he would shrug off my tenderness

—The bath water was almost cold today because the bottle of gas is nearly empty

he would take a pen from his jacket pocket, put on his glasses and start doing the crossword puzzle while I went into the kitchen to heat up the supper. As soon as supper was ready I would call him

—Supper's on the table, sweetheart

and Renato wouldn't hear, bird, four letters, dove, reptile, five letters, snake, and me

—Supper's on the table, sweetheart

Renato from the depths of the paper, not moving

—Coming
the supper is cold, and me
—The supper's cold, Renato
Renato walking over to the table muttering
—Honestly
putting his napkin around his neck and looking at me indignantly, protesting
—I can't eat this, why didn't you heat up the disgusting stuff?
and me in the kitchen reheating the soup and Renato in the living room
—The day we have a decent supper in this house I'll let off some fireworks
and me anxiously
—I did call you twice, sweetheart
Renato with the newspaper on the tablecloth, mammal, three letters, dog
—If you'd called me, I would have come
Renato ignoring me, putting the newspaper down and turning on the TV with the remote control
—Mealtimes are such a drag, we haven't a thing to say to each other
leaving me to clear the table, not even carrying out a single plate, sitting in his armchair changing channels while I put away the crockery in the kitchen
—In fact I spend the evenings alone without speaking to a soul and if that's how it's going to be, I'd rather go back and live with my father
and me running back into the living room, drying my hands on a cloth and Renato
—If you think it's any fun living with a woman who never takes off her apron and never gets dressed up you're wrong
me in the bedroom putting on makeup, changing my dress, slipping on some high heels, brushing my hair, standing in the doorway for Renato to see and Renato

—That skirt's hideous, I've told you a hundred times that skirt's hideous

I start to cry, covering my face with my hand and Renato gets up, looks for the car keys, comes back to pick up the newspaper he forgot, Renato at the front door

—I'm not putting up with neurotic women who burst into tears over nothing

me on the landing

—Renato

Renato one floor down

—You don't need a husband, Cristina, you need a psychiatrist

and so for the last two months it's been quite difficult being alone. Of course I can read, I can listen to music, I can rent a video, I can phone Esmeralda, I can do an hour's crocheting before bed, but I miss having Renato at home, I miss Renato's beard

(I love stroking Renato's beard)

I miss having someone to look after, someone to cook for, someone I can ask the maid to iron shirts for and I can't bring myself to admit that he won't be back and so if the maid should ever say with surprise

—Senhor Renato's drawers are empty

I'll say

—He's been transferred to Coimbra and had to take his clothes with him

because I want to think that he'll come home later tonight, give me a kiss and ask

—Did you change the bottle of gas?

and sit down in his armchair as if nothing had changed and do the crossword in the newspaper.

THAT'S LIFE

D on't worry about me, I knew things couldn't last forever. You weren't made to live in a two-room apartment with a writer who doesn't write, to have to take freezing-cold showers because the gas company won't give me any credit, to put up with the rudeness of the landlord because I fell behind in the rent. Don't worry about me: I understand why you're leaving, I won't make a fuss, I won't beg you to stay. Obviously it's hard for me, I'll miss you at first, during the first few days, when at seven o'clock I hear footsteps on the landing I'll run to the door

—It's Teresa

and it isn't Teresa, it's the neighbor from the opposite apartment carrying a supermarket bag in each hand, the neighbor recoiling from my embrace thinking that I must have gone mad and me retreating in an agony of embarrassment

—Sorry, Senhor Vasconcelos, I thought you were someone else

the neighbor advising me sourly to lay off the liquor and then bolting his front door for fear I should turn up again wanting to kiss him and calling him my love. But don't you worry about me: in six months' time I'll be fine, in six months' time I'll have found someone new and received an advance from the publisher, in six months' time, I promise you, I'll have forgotten all about you, I'm sure. These things always seem so dreadful at first and then, as we get used to them, we feel less like crying, we start taking an interest again in terrorist attacks and royal divorces, which are the two kinds of disaster we most like to read about in the newspaper, we stop boring our friends with late-night phone calls and one day

(that's how life is)

we find ourselves whistling to the mirror as we shave in the morning, and if someone in the café asks us

—What's happened to Teresa?

we have to make an effort to remember which Teresa

—Which Teresa?

—Your wife of course, who do you think?

and we say nonchalantly, genuinely

—Oh, Teresa, I've no idea, I haven't seen her in ages

and we discover without surprise that saying your name no longer hurts, that we can't quite remember your face, that you have definitely ceased to exist. So don't worry about me: it will pass. The desire to die will pass, the desire to write Teresa on the steamed-up window and in the dust on the furniture

(because I won't have anyone to do the dusting)

will pass, as will the stupid habit of spending days lying on the sofa, staring up at the ceiling and remembering that trip to Foz do Arelho, and that blue dress I'll never see again, the adorable way your front teeth stick out ever so slightly, the Sunday when you burned the supper, how you used to get irritated with me because I squeezed the toothpaste tube in the middle and left the faucet dripping in the sink all night

—You're not made of money, you know

or when I used to read the newspaper over your shoulder and you angrily

—I'm sorry but I can't read the newspaper with someone peering over my shoulder

flinging down the paper and shutting yourself in the bedroom yelling

—God, you're annoying

you who would move your leg if I touched yours with mine, and go rigid if I tried to kiss you, you stopped holding my hand in the cinema, and if I asked

—Do you love me?

you'd say nothing or mutter like some climber in the Himalayas, as if the words were as heavy as ton weights and the oxygen was running out

—If I didn't love you, do you think I'd be here?

you had sex without saying a word, your fingers lying limp on my back as if

(imagine me thinking that, how stupid)

as if you wanted it to be over as quickly as possible, as if you wanted to be free of me, and if I asked

—Was it good?

you would say

—I'm tired I have a headache I don't know

and would immediately go and wash yourself as if I'd infected you, splashing about in the bidet for half an hour. I knew it couldn't last forever. You weren't made to live in a two-room apartment with a writer who doesn't write, you weren't made to take freezing-cold showers because the gas company wouldn't give me any credit, you weren't made to put up with the landlord's insults because I fell behind in the rent. Don't worry about me: I understand that you're leaving, I won't make a fuss, I won't beg you to stay, I promise I won't get angry if the male friend you're telling me about and who I don't know comes with you to help take your clothes away, your books away. I won't get angry: as soon as you two are off down the stairs I'll call Mariana or Paula or Raquel, I'll invite them out, I'll start life again. Don't go thinking I'm going to dissolve into tears or that I'll kill myself. I won't. I can assure you I won't. On the other hand, just in case, best leave me the tissues and the box of Valium. We always need something to keep us company, don't we, and I hate having to wipe my nose on the sleeve of my jacket, just as the idea of throwing myself out of the window repels me: I might even fall on top of the two of you, waiting downstairs for a taxi, I might even fall on top of your friend and injure him or break a bone and you'd probably think I was feeling aggressive

   but I'm not

   toward that son of a bitch, sorry, toward that young man who must be, who surely is, who I bet my bottom dollar is an absolute gem of a person.

RANDOM GHOSTS

I live near the station in Alto de São João and since I retired, I've led a very methodical life: I get up at eleven o'clock, have breakfast, shave, wash, straighten the house, get dressed, sit down at the window and watch, from beginning to end, three funerals a day. When the third is over, I cross myself, quickly comb my hair in front of the mirror, grab my umbrella, and set off to Bar Mimosa in Praça Paiva Couceiro to have a few large glasses of wine. By the tenth one, night has fallen. I return to the station with the aid of my umbrella, which serves to fend off any importunate lampposts and trees that insist on bumping into me, I have another breakfast which I call supper, talk to the photo of my wife, sit down at the window again, this time in my pajamas, feeling rather miffed that the cemetery gates are now closed, and I fall asleep listening to the dogs in Rua Morais Soares barking at the dark as if they were anxious orphans.

My apartment is on the ground floor, the concierge's apartment. If the concierge was married to the concierge's husband, a supervisor at the local high school who went from class to class with the register, noting down any absentees, noting the absence, recording the emptiness, I am married to no one. I am the concierge's widower, and the only absence I note down, the only emptiness I record is the silence in the cellar when the dogs stop barking. Fortunately, I bring back from the Bar Mimosa in Praça Paiva Couceiro a good ballast of booze to help me combat the silence, for silence, like drunken sailors, must be beaten back with a bottle because if you try to wrestle with it bare-handed you're sure to end up in the sawdust on the floor. And so when silence threatens me, I brandish a bottle to frighten it off, an imperious sceptre of a bottle, and I begin to list out loud—a tic of the profession—the names of my brothers, my friends, my colleagues, the people I knew when Lisbon and I were both young. Since no one answers, I'm forced to conclude that they have died of absence and that, unlike at school, it is not the teachers who have put them in detention but the undertakers when they placed their ashes in urns. And there is something of the embarrassment of a flunked exam about the family's grief.

My wife doesn't respond to this reading of the register, but she's there, smiling at me from the sideboard. It's a smile that's at least thirty years old, a smile that, with time or the lack of glass in the frame, has grown yellow, the inevitable fate of smiles and of wallpaper. In addition, smiles lose their teeth and wallpaper loses its color and people lose all these things along with their hair and their interest in things, so that anyone coming into this apartment while I'm here would take a while to tell me apart from the other gray objects. Age is the perfect camouflage, and if I were the general of an army of old people, I wouldn't lose a single battle, because they could invade an enemy city unnoticed, they could occupy a whole country with their insidious rheumatism, their all-conquering diabetes, and their rampaging asthmatic bronchitis. And the enemies would be condemned to spend their time playing cards in the park, wearing slippers on their left feet and shoes on their right and spearing the butt-ends in the flower beds with their canes.

My wife doesn't respond to the register or to my questions, but she's there, gliding on her crocheted doily like a swan on a lake, accepting me without recriminations. When it's time for the TV soap, I remove her from the crochet lake and place her beside me on the sofa, at suppertime I again remove her from the crochet lake and take her with me to the table, where I enjoy the company of that girl young enough now to be my daughter, framed in tiny ceramic nuptial roses as if we had only just arrived back from the wedding buffet at the Bar Mimosa in Praça Paiva Couceiro, awkward and anxious, not knowing what to do, avoiding each other with shy delicacy, so ignorant of what to do that when we went into the bedroom, I started whistling. That, I think, is what is known as chamber music. A couple of propitiatory drinks ensured that I didn't whistle too out of tune.

My wife doesn't answer to the register, but she doesn't tell me off for having spent the whole day out. If I can put it like this, we enjoy a happy widowhood and there's rarely a disagreement or an argument to bring disharmony to her absence. We have, I believe, each found our place in life: she on the crochet doily watching the stillness of the living room and I at the window watching the funerals in the hope of seeing a familiar face, a companion or two from the Mimosa, for example, following behind a coffin without a priest, one or two of my fellow drinkers accompanying a funeral that must be mine. It'll only be a matter of months: sooner or later, I'll watch my own death from here. I know how it will be: a wreath from the school executive committee, and a cortège of absentees, a cortège of random ghosts staggering along on crutches, unseen by anyone. Then someone will place a second photograph on the crocheted doily and two yellow smiles will light up the gloom like the tremulous flames of oil lamps while the dogs bark at the dark as if they were anxious orphans.

THE LAST KING
OF PORTUGAL

—And why exactly don't you want the child, may I ask? said the woman sitting on the edge of the bed brushing her hair, the man was standing with his collar turned up, tying the knot in his tie and he caught her reflection in the mirror.

—I've always said that I'd like to have a child, but not right now.

The woman in the mirror and the woman outside the mirror seemed different. Only one of them was left-handed, but both looked as if they hated him and he found it difficult talking with two creatures with only one voice, a voice that was still pursuing him

—And why not now?

The man closed his eyes: he thought that if he closed his eyes, the women would disappear and the voice too. But they didn't disappear: they continued to brush their hair as they sat on the edge of their beds, brushing their hair with the same slow movement, thoughtful, repetitive, interminable.

My God, what I'd give not to be here, thought the man who was now turning down his collar and taking a tiny step back to observe the effect, trying to gain time to come up with a cast-iron excuse. A cast-iron excuse, a cast-iron excuse. He couldn't think of any cast-iron excuse.

—We would need a bigger apartment and we still haven't finished paying for this one. There's no way we could live in a three-room apartment if we had children.

He turned around and the woman became one again: I'm afraid of her, how odd, thought the man. A nightgown, a fair head, a brush following the whole length of her hair, the soft fair down on her arms

—But will you at least come with me to the midwife when I have the abortion?

asked the woman in the same casual tone she would use to ask if they were eating out on Saturday

(they ate out every Saturday)

or if they were going to see the movie they had circled in the newspaper. That week they had earmarked three films and a play: he was the one who chose and they rarely disagreed about his choice. They tended to agree about most things, thought the man, about almost everything. Until today, with that thing between them, that stupid mistake separating them. And what midwife, and where, and what did they do? And what if there was some, oh, I don't know, some complication, some problem?

—Yes, I'll come with you to the midwife

said the man

—I wouldn't want you to have to come home alone.

He found the address of a midwife in Campo de Ourique, she wouldn't let him in. He waited outside in the car, double-parked, thinking She must be furious with me, thinking She's sure to go on and on about it, thinking In a day or two I'll give her a bunch of flowers, in a month or two she'll have forgotten about it, I mean she's bound to, just think of the number of bad things he, a man, had forgotten, his mother's death, his brother's death, a former girl-friend who had dropped him for someone else and left him contemplating suicide. By the time the woman got back into the car, the man was thinking that it really was amazing how we do forget everything. She didn't even look very pale

—So?

he said. The woman said nothing. She was holding a little package of pills, she took one pill as soon as they got home, she took a second pill half an hour later and then went to bed, the man sat for a while in the sitting room, not listening to music, not watching television, not reading. When he went into the bedroom, the woman was sleeping and continued to sleep when he lay down beside her and when he switched off the light. He left for work in the morning and she was still sleeping. He phoned before lunch, he phoned after lunch and there was no answer, he was worried, he asked his manager if he could leave early and arrived at the apartment at twenty past three. The woman was out on the landing with her suitcases

—I'm going to spend a week with my parents and then I'll be back. Don't worry, I've already called a cab.

He wanted to help with her luggage, but she wouldn't let him. The suitcases bumped down the stairs as she went, bumped really hard on the stairs and yet still nothing had changed in the apartment, apart from the fact that there was no one in the mirror

—It's only for a week

the man reassured himself as if he actually believed it

—She'll be back in a week.

MISSING IRENEIA

Do you still have fair hair, Ireneia? Do you still live in the same street as the school? Do you still wear that very short green skirt and the white skates, do you still spin round and round and round at the ice rink at the Académico, with your arms above your head, not looking at me, not looking at anyone? Do you still make a deep curtsy when the music ends even if no one is there to applaud?

I remember seeing you walking out into the street with your skates slung over your shoulder and being surprised that you walked just like other people, that you walked like me because I found it hard to imagine you outside of the rink, spinning round and round and round, with your arms above your head, because it was hard for me to imagine you leading a life like ours, work, home, supper, toothache, colds, gas bills, it was hard for me to imagine you surrounded by dripping faucets, by roofs that leaked in winter, by arguments, pimples, blackheads, dogs we forgot to take for a walk and that relieved themselves on the rug.

Do you still wear that short green skirt, Ireneia, do you still look very serious when the music stops, head bowed in a deep curtsy, not looking at anyone?

Your father worked on the trams, he clipped my ticket many a time, his name was Senhor Geraldo and he was bald, your mother gave up her stall in the marketplace because of her arteries, I can still remember her saying to my aunt

—My weak points are my arteries, Dona Lúcia

and I thought it very odd, I thought it impossible that you could be their daughter and live on the same street as the school in a basement apartment with two rooms at most, with windows level with the sidewalk and with a yappy little dog that always wore a woolen coat, I thought it odd that you should live with Senhor Geraldo and the lady with the arteries

—The doctor just can't seem to get my medication right, Dona Lúcia

who heaved her body along with the help of a stick and complained that Senhor Geraldo got violent when he'd had one too many beers

—He even kicked our little dog, Dona Lúcia, and she didn't stop whining all night

I thought it so odd, so impossible that, as far as I was concerned, Ireneia, you didn't live in that street, you lived at the ice rink in the Académico spinning round and round and round in that very short green skirt and your white skates, untouched by arteries, dogs, and beer and acknowledging the applause that no one gave you, you existed alone, above us, ethereal, unreachable, different, untouched by our problems and our lack of money, sailing by with your hair tied back with a ribbon

your fair hair, Ireneia

in an area where there were no pawnshops or road construction or unemployed men sitting in the square playing cards, on the bricks left there from some never-completed building job, which the laborers had abandoned halfway through, leaving the dust and the sacks and the scaffolding to block the path to the church and forcing us to go the long way around via the gypsy encampment or past the circus, which consisted of one clown and a mangy lion waiting outside a caravan for a public that never arrived.

What has become of you, Ireneia? They tell me you've put on weight, but I don't believe it, that Senhor Geraldo died, that your mother died, that you still live in that basement apartment on the same street as the school and are married to a man who works for the phone company and that you, too, have problems with your arteries, that you never again skated at the Académico, but it can't be true. Tomorrow afternoon I'll go to the rink to see you because I'm sure that even after thirty years your hair is still fair, Ireneia, that you still have that little short green skirt, that you still spin round and round and round with your arms above your head, and that when the music stops, you take a low curtsy without looking at anyone, and if you happen to notice a boy sitting on the benches applauding, it will be me. I haven't changed much. Obviously I'm older, but I'm still me. That boy with a stutter and a slight cleft lip, who never had the courage to say hello to you. Dona Lúcia's nephew, the one Dona Lúcia was sure would never get anywhere in life because of his club foot and his speech impediment. And it's true I never did get anywhere in life, but I still go to the ice rink on Sundays hoping to see you spinning round and round and round and to feel happy again. It would be great if you were to go there one of these days, Ireneia: it's a bit sad sometimes applauding an empty rink.

WILL YOU TEACH ME
HOW TO FLY?

I don't know what my life would be like if it wasn't for my collection of butterflies. Especially in winter, you understand, with the short days, the rain, the sad trees, the fading wallpaper leaching into my mother, into me, the apartment suddenly much smaller, a desire for something that isn't there, especially on winter Sundays when we have to turn the lights on at four o'clock and I feel like dying. Not actually dying, of course, of a disease or something, but simply ceasing to exist

poof!

like a lightbulb blowing, disappearing completely, without a trace, never having been born, never having inhabited an uncomfortable body with too many arms and too many legs and too many painful teeth

(speaking of which, I must, without fail, make an appointment for next week)

a body moreover that is cold, wearing two sweaters and with knees pressed up against the heater, and my hair that is starting to go thin on top despite the treatments I read about in the paper, incredibly expensive glass vials that I buy at the drugstore and that don't do a thing, yes, just ceasing to exist

poof!

like a lightbulb blowing, without my mother realizing, poor thing, my mother who came home with the collection of butterflies after my godfather died

—Your Uncle Fernando left you this

five glass cases with the insects, wings open, pinned to bits of cardboard, their names in Latin underneath, five glass cases of colored insects, blue, yellow, scarlet, green, with spots and stripes and circles and symmetrical marks that made my mother feel sad and that I thought were lovely. And so in winter when I feel like dying, I fetch the butterfly collection from the closet in my room, I place them side by side on the dining table and I spend hours gazing at these creatures so utterly indifferent to the rain and to the sad trees. From her crochet work, as she counts the stitches with one fingernail, my mother protests

—I still don't see why you like them

but since she hates me to go out because I might fall into bad company and catch a disease from some woman, she says nothing more in case I might put away the butterflies and go down the stairs

(we live on the fourth floor)

to the pool hall on the avenue, full of men who grow the nail on their little finger long and full of women who smoke

(in my mother's eyes a woman who smokes is clearly no better than she should be)

and come sweeping back into the living room with a girlfriend who would inherit all her jewels, decide what we have to eat and put her in a home for the elderly. Not that she has many jewels: my father wasn't rich, no one in our family was rich, and all she has, apart from her wedding ring, is a ring with a stone that is not only tiny but also, I think, fake, as well as a pearl necklace that you can see from a mile away is also fake—too perfect, like false teeth. The butterfly collection has the advantage of keeping us both in the apartment, I because I don't have time to find a girlfriend and get married and my mother because, in her view, I would never voluntarily put her in a cellar for the old

(my mother imagines that old people are always put in bug-ridden cellars to starve to death)

and she's quite right about that because I'm very fond of her and we get along well. We rarely disagree, we rarely argue, I have no complaints about the food and there's never any dust lurking in the corners, and if, in winter, I didn't have such a desire to die, I'd be happy. Not that I'm particularly unhappy: I've always, thank goodness, enjoyed excellent health

(apart from my hair falling out, God, what a drag)

I don't earn a lot, but with my father's pension, and if we keep a sharp eye on the electric bills, it's perfectly adequate for the life we lead, plus we own the apartment, and next spring we're going to have the kitchen balcony enclosed to make a utility room that will be ideal for doing the ironing

(I like the smell of the clothes, that smell of hot dampness when you iron)

and as soon as I feel the fading wallpaper starting to leach into me, I hurry to my room and bring out the butterfly collection that belonged to my Uncle Fernando, my mother's brother who died of an aneurysm three years ago in January. He was a bachelor like me, but he lived alone and, on occasional Saturdays, since we live near the soccer stadium, he would come and have lunch with us before the game. After lunch, while my mother was pouring him a coffee, he would ask me with a smile I never quite understood

—Will you teach me how to fly?

and I'd look at him like an idiot, thinking he must be crazy, and my mother, warily

(my mother is wary of everything)

—What on earth do you mean, Fernando?

And my Uncle Fernando, very earnestly, his lips cautiously pursed so as not to burn them on the coffee, his hand pressed to his chest so as not to dirty his tie

(my mother says coffee stains are impossible to get out)

—All children know how to fly, Madalena

and I would cling on to the furniture, afraid that I might suddenly fly off down the corridor. It was, I think, that longing to fly that made my Uncle Fernando

(my Uncle Fernando worked in a bank, in the currency exchange office) without a word to anyone, start collecting butterflies. Perhaps he found the winters hard too

(the short days, the rain, a desire for something that isn't there)

perhaps on Sundays, when there was no soccer, he too felt like dying. He lived in a very dark two-room apartment with a lot of coffinlike furniture and he ate alone reading the newspaper or, rather, with the newspaper positioned between his plate and the water pitcher

(his doctor had told him he mustn't drink wine because of his arteries)

and I'm not surprised he felt like dying. There are times, I think, when everyone

(even if they collect butterflies)

feels like dying, and if they taught us how to fly, we would all disappear off to some other country, to those countries that don't have winter Sundays

(there must be countries that don't have winter Sundays)

where you don't have to spend all evening crocheting or looking at glass cases full of insects—because you're happy.

ON WIDOWHOOD

Discretion was always my husband's strong point, and he died without bothering anyone. We didn't have to call the doctor because there was no illness: halfway through supper he calmly put down his knife and fork on his fish fillets, rice, and greens, looked at me as tenderly as he always did, and said

—Alice

which surprised me a little because my name is Felicidade, he smiled at me, then stopped smiling and headed chin first for the bread basket, he was dead by the time he had reached the rolls, slightly stale ones because what with its being my day for doing the housework I hadn't had time to go shopping. There was no unnecessary expenditure on doctors or on medicine, the fish fillets went back in the freezer and as for the rolls I toasted them later, spread a little raspberry jam on them and ate them with a cup of tea on the night of the wake. Given my fragile state, they were just what I needed.

We didn't have to call the doctor, the undertaker didn't have to struggle taking off the dead man's pajamas and putting his brown suit on him because my husband, who was never a rigid man, bent his arms and legs with exemplary submissiveness and by four o'clock in the afternoon he was in room B-2 of the Church of the Angels, with his shoes polished and his hair combed, looking very dignified, with a cross in his hands, with me and my sister Alice perched on red velvet chairs, catching up on our news, because we both lead such busy lives, full of work and complications, we don't even have time to phone and only see each other once in a blue moon. She thought I looked well, I complimented her on the silk scarf she was wearing, my husband listened without saying a word

(he always listened without saying a word when we were talking, as if he wasn't there)

and for the first time ever he didn't start ogling Alice's legs thinking I wouldn't notice and he didn't try to run his hand over her bottom when I turned to say hello to the widow in room B-3, whose dear departed only agreed to climb into the coffin after months and months at a private clinic notching up enormous bills for IV drips, X-rays and catheters, one of those extravagant people incapable of understanding that their time has come and who don't care if they leave those left behind without two cents to rub together, not even enough for a bus trip for single ladies to Spain, where there are, so they say, some very generous young men, with a highly developed sense of solidarity, who for a handful of pesetas will offer you consolation in discotheques and other places of worship I wouldn't mind visiting.

Apart from my sister and me, there was no one else: I don't have brothers- or sisters-in-law or cousins, my husband was never very sociable and only went out for two hours each afternoon, with a bag of corn in his pocket, for a solitary walk in the Baixa and a visit to the pigeons in Praça Luís de Camões, and so my sister and I, when we'd run out of things to say, sat silently before the coffin until I recalled his death over the fish fillets, and I said to my sister

—Did I mention that before he collapsed on top of the rolls he said the name Alice?

Clutching her silk scarf, a really nice scarf with a leaf pattern, I wish I had one like it, she turned beet red

—Alice?

and I

—Yes, Alice, imagine that, heaven knows why

my sister standing up, a strange look on her face

—Wait here a moment while I go outside for a breath of air

that was three months ago now and I haven't seen her in the flesh since, but I came across her yesterday when I happened to open the drawer of my husband's desk, looking for a pair of nail scissors, and found an envelope full of photos of the two of them with their arms about each other, my husband holding the bag of corn for the pigeons in one hand and my sister wearing the silk scarf around her neck, the two of them standing smiling by the statue of Camões. Perhaps they were just friends. Yes, of course they were just friends and the letters accompanying the photographs, one of them thanking him for the scarf and promising I'll wear nothing else next time you come and see me, my beloved lion, and another that ended Love and bites from Alice, were clearly just a joke between brother- and sister-in-law, despite her legs and his hand on her bottom. My sister is a very warm, open person

(at twenty-six everyone is warm and open)

and without a malicious bone in her body, and my husband was a very proper man. Perhaps that's why I'm sure to feel a touch guilty when I go to Spain this summer on a bus trip for single ladies and walk into a discotheque with a charming young man whispering in my ear, in between loud kisses, asking me to lend him the money for the bill because, what a nuisance, he's left his wallet at his parents' house.

A DROP OF RAIN
ON THE FACE

If I didn't have a stutter, it would be easy for me to talk to her. She lives three blocks away, we catch the same bus every day, I get on at the fourth stop and she at the fifth, we exchange long looks during the twenty minutes

(half an hour if the traffic's bad)

that it takes to travel from where we live to the ministry, she works two floors above me, we go up in the same elevator, still looking at each other, sometimes she seems to be smiling at me

(I'm almost certain she is)

we see each other in the distance in the canteen, each of us with our tray, I could almost swear she beckons to me sometimes to sit at her table, but I don't because I can't be sure she did

(I think I'm sure that she did)

we look at each other in the elevator afterward too, she smiles again when I get out, she looks at me in the bus on the way home and I can't speak to her because of my stutter. Or rather my stutter isn't the real reason: the reason is that because I can't get the words out, because I want to express myself and can't, my face goes purple and my eyes bulge

(I watched myself in a mirror and it's true)

with my mouth open, full of teeth, stumbling over some interminable consonant, filling the air around me with a storm of anxious spit, and I don't want her to see how ridiculous I look, how ugly, how I'm transformed physically into a gargoyle on a fountain, spitting and sobbing and moaning incoherently. With my work colleagues it's easy: I just nod or shake my head, I sum up my responses with a vague gesture, I reduce a speech to a lift of the eyebrows, my opinions on life to a shrug of the shoulders

(even if I didn't have a stutter I would still reduce my opinions on life to a shrug of the shoulders)

whereas with her I would be obliged to speak at length, to converse, to whisper in her ear

(if I ever dared whisper in her ear I bet she would immediately get her handkerchief out of her handbag to dry her cheek before fleeing in terror)

to whisper sweet nothings into her neck, to entangle her in a web of words

(women, I think, love to be entangled in a web of words)

while I took her hand, she would close her eyes, proffer her lips in the infinitely stupid expression all lovers have when waiting to be kissed, and now put yourself in her place and imagine a wild-eyed stutterer leaning toward you, scarlet with effort, opening and closing his mouth, a mouth that cannot get past the first consonant, his whole body trying to squeeze out an

—I love you

which will not come out, which cannot come out, which will never come out, an

—I love you

that remains trapped on my tongue behind a great stopper of spit, with me waving my arms up and down, loosening my tie, undoing the top button of my shirt, but no

—I love you

emerges, or, worse still, is replaced by a caveman bellow, and she pushing me away, arms outstretched, getting up, disappearing through the door, horrified, leaving me alone in the café bent, still panting, over my hot water and lemon and the custard tart of my definitive defeat. I must not make the stupid mistake of trying to talk to her, I simply have to make do with the exchange of glances on the bus, with the smile in the elevator, with the silent invitation in the canteen until the day when she appears hand in hand with some other man, possibly older than me, but at least capable of whispering effortlessly into her ear

(there are people who can whisper effortlessly)

what I would love to say to her but can't until the day she stops looking at me and smiling and inviting me to sit opposite her at lunch

(soup, a choice from two main dishes, dessert or fruit, a roll and a small carafe of wine, all for 440 *escudos*, is pretty good value for money)

and when I see her at the far end of the bus, her head resting on the shoulder of some other man, unaware of me, as unaware of me as if I had never existed, I will understand that if I have ceased to exist that means I never existed, and later that night when I look at myself in the mirror I will see no one or at most a pair of eyes

(mine)

staring disapprovingly back at me, a pair of eyes with what I would swear was a tear trembling on the eyelashes and rolling slowly down one cheek, or perhaps it isn't a tear but only

(it will, after all, be winter)

a drop of rain, you know how it is, running down the window-pane.

THE PERSON WHO WAS
DULCE IS NO MORE

I don't exist. Ever since yesterday, when the doctor spoke of cancer, I've been trying to get used to the idea that I don't exist. In the last few years, every now and then, I've been told about various people's deaths. Young people who vanished from the world in a matter of months. I was told that they'd departed, but not how. I'm going to find out how, sooner than I thought.

I'm not at home to anyone today. I've unplugged the phone, if someone rings the doorbell I won't answer, if someone throws stones at my window and calls up to me from the street, I'll sit here quietly on the sofa with an unopened pack of cigarettes and a magazine beside me. When night comes I won't turn on the lights. I close the blinds so that people will think I've gone out, I don't turn on the television, I don't listen to music. I don't even move. I don't exist. Ever since yesterday, when the doctor spoke of cancer, I've been trying to get used to the idea that I don't exist. In the last few years, every now and then, I've been told about various people's deaths. Young people who vanished from the world in a matter of months. I was told that they'd departed, but not how. I'm going to find out how, sooner than I thought.

At the moment it doesn't seem so very difficult, but this is just the beginning. I don't even have any pain, just a lump in my breast and other lumps in my neck, in my armpit, along my shoulder blade. The doctor was astonished that I hadn't noticed. When you took a shower for example, he said, didn't you notice anything unusual, these bumps on your body? When I say nothing, his eyes scream at me You're doomed. The pocket of his white coat full of pens. His spidery hands that measured the cancer, from top to bottom, meticulously. Now and again, as he examined me, he nodded. The nurse behind him kept absolutely still. In the hospital courtyard the patients walked to and fro. A species of gaunt bird in pajamas, their eyes different from healthy people's eyes. What has always impressed me about sick people is that light in their eyes. I looked at myself in the mirror and found nothing like that in my face. Just my usual face. No thinner or paler, no more anxious. Just my usual serious face, the left eyelid slightly drooping. Like my mother. It seems we inherited this from her father. I didn't know my grandfather except in photos. There are loads of people in my family I only know from photos. I don't look like any of them. Since I'm not at home to anyone, I'm not at home to any of those dead aunts and uncles either.

With no phone, no music, no light, the apartment seems strange. I notice the furniture, I notice the door, I notice the rug, like a dark stain. I notice my legs too. Another hour or two and all of this will disappear into total darkness, the furniture, the door, the rug and me. I'm not hungry. I'm not thirsty. There are tangerines in the fridge. I like the cold taste of tangerines, the small hardness of the pits. I used to squeeze those little teeth, baby teeth, between my tongue and the roof of my mouth, and then line them up on my plate with my finger. I've done that for as long as I can remember. One after the other. Or in a circle. Or in a cross. Not white teeth, but yellowing teeth. It seems so strange that trees can grow from those seeds, that there should be whole microscopic trees inside, ready to grow. While the doctor was examining me, that was what came into my mind, not death or cancer, but the disproportionate difference in size between the seeds and the trees. It seems so strange that this should be happening to me.

Anyway, I'm not at home to anyone today. I don't want pity. I don't want to be consoled. I don't want hopeful smiles. I want to imagine the future knowing that there is a wall interrupting my days on earth. The others walk through that wall. I stay on this side. The doctor told me that they would send me a postcard giving me dates for my admission to the hospital next week or the week after. I probably won't be coming back to this apartment. Not that it worries me much. It doesn't matter. When I think about it, I never was particularly happy here.

BETTER THE LIGHT
THAN THE DARK NIGHT

There's a bottle of nail polish on top of the microwave, where she usually leaves the notebook with any messages for the maid. I always find two sorts of handwriting on the same page, her message at the top and the maid's reply below. Some loose change left over from the shopping. And the words of an American song going round and round in my head

Better the light than the dark night.

My son woke in the middle of the night, crying. He's only three. I thought he might have a fever or be teething or something so I picked him up and carried him into the kitchen to look out the window at the street. I like the kitchen at night, with its granite countertop and its large square appliances that seem to grow more useful in the dark. I like their capable appearance and their mysterious innards full of screws and fans. White machines, like round spectacles where the clothes spin and froth. I thought of turning on one of the machines to entertain my son. To entertain myself. I do sometimes sit on a chair and watch. They click, change speed, change sound. Like living organisms. My son smells of sleep and tears. The street is quiet. Cars lined up along the sidewalk. I can see mine between a dusty gray van and a car covered with a cloth. I know the owner. On Sundays, in shorts, he removes the cloth cover and spends hours cleaning the car with a sponge. He never smiles. Cleaning the car is the most important activity in the world. When he finishes he goes back into the house and returns half an hour later followed by his family. They drive around until suppertime, proud of their gleaming marvel. There is a song that says better the light than the dark night. A husky American voice. Better the light than the dark night.

Weary of crying, my son falls silent. I put him back to bed. He lies very still, hands clenched, sleeping with a haughty look on his face. I go back into the kitchen. My wife left a bottle of nail polish on the counter. She is sleeping too, but face down, clutching her pillow. She sometimes mutters things in her sleep that I can't understand. The bottle of nail polish on top of the microwave, where she usually leaves the notebook with any messages for the maid. I always find two sorts of handwriting on the same page, her message at the top and the maid's reply below. Some loose change left over from the shopping. And the words of an American song going round and round in my head

Better the light than the dark night.

Why do I stay here? There's my son, there's my wife. Is that all? Questions and more questions without any answers. My head is full of questions. Not doubts. Not anxieties. Questions. My mother used to tell me When you're older you'll understand. I'm obviously still not yet old enough because I don't understand anything.

I concentrate on the street while scraps of ideas and memories rush in on me and move off. For example, my grandmother covering the mirrors with sheets when someone in the family died. She swore that if death saw itself in the mirror it would never leave. She wouldn't let us throw bread away either: she kept endless plastic bags full of stale bread. When there were too many bags and my mother complained, my grandmother would disappear downstairs with them and come back empty-handed. No one ever knew where she hid the bread. She died at seventy-six and after her departure, death was free to look at itself in the mirrors.

I'll go back to bed soon. The warm sheets. The phosphorescent numbers on the alarm clock turning the room blue. The engraving of a child and a bear. All real things. Pleasant. Authentic. I stare at the engraving and the questions gradually leave me. As does the memory of my grandmother. Where did she hide the bread? I'm not thinking about that now. I'm not thinking about anything. I feel myself sliding very slowly down and down, with the song repeating in my ears, better the light than the dark night. Better the light than the dark night. Even if some very pretty young woman should appear, I won't abandon my life.

DON'T DIE NOW,
PEOPLE ARE LOOKING AT US

Antero. Antero. Antero. Don't go to sleep here on the esplanade, Antero, don't close your eyes, don't sit slumped in your chair like that, look at the little boats on the Tejo, look at the gulls, you've always liked gulls so much, Antero, drink your beer before it gets warm, sit up straight, don't make that face, if you didn't want to come to Algés for the day you should have told me so this morning, why didn't you tell me

—I don't feel like going to Algés this Sunday

and fine, we would have just stayed home watching the plant in the living room grow as we have done every day since we retired, I never argue with you, do I, I never complain, you bought that hideous sofa and I didn't say a word, you removed the photo of my sister from the sideboard and not a peep from me, I don't know what it is you have against my sister, whenever she visits, you start pursing your lips, sighing, moving things around, don't lean forward like that or you'll knock your beer over, watch your elbow in the plate of lupine seeds, don't be silly, Antero, you're always so serious nowadays, I haven't heard a good belly laugh from you in ages, I hope you're not going to decide to play the fool now, with all these people around, sit up, Antero, wipe the drool off your chin, and keep your teeth in, don't make me have to put them back in for you, such straight, white teeth they are, when you take them out at night to clean them, you seem somehow shorter, when you put them back in, though, you look a real treat, you remind me of a king with his crown and everything, be careful with those dentures because they cost a fortune, Antero, don't lean so far over toward the woman at the next table, her husband might notice, honestly, Antero, all these gulls and you're not even interested, Antero, ships, the Lisbon train whistling and everything, we can see to the other side of the river from here, it's a lovely day, and if it wasn't for that child in the stroller screaming its head off, it would be really peaceful, Antero, if it's because of that child you've gone all funny, we can change tables, we'll pick up the beer, the lupine seeds, the juice, the custard tart and we'll go over there, Antero, don't look so pale, stop sobbing like that, stop shaking, speak to me, I'll put your dentures in my bag, all right, but speak to me, Antero, I don't mind seeing you without your teeth if you'll only talk to me, people are looking at us, that woman over there is nudging her husband and pointing at us with her toast, Antero, you've never liked drawing attention to yourself. What's wrong, Antero, why, if I ever wore a slightly low-cut blouse, you'd tell me to put on my sweater

—Don't be so shameless, Maria Emília

if I crossed my legs and showed my knees, you'd tell me to pull my skirt down to cover them

—We're not at the circus, Maria Emília

if I dyed my hair to hide the bits of gray showing through, you'd tell me to go back to the salon the very next day

—What do you think this is, Maria Emília, Carnival time?

and here you are attracting everyone's attention, sliding down in your chair the way kids do, with those little pink bubbles frothing at your mouth, how would you like it if I told you off, how would you like it if I got angry and said

—We're not at the circus, Antero

but I'm not angry, I'm behaving perfectly correctly, I'm not causing a scene, I'm just asking you to sit up straight, that's all, I'm just asking you to speak to me, to lick your lips and get rid of all that saliva, don't drag your fingers in the dust, it's dirty, full of cigarette butts, peels, pigeon poop, bits of paper, Antero, you don't feel ill, do you, you're not going to die, are you, don't die now, people are looking at us and it's embarrassing, I can't say to the waiter

—I'm terribly sorry, but my husband has just died

wait until we get home and die then if you want to, but not here, Antero, it looks bad, it's embarrassing, if you really want to die, do it properly, like other people do, moaning in hospital, with X-rays and blood tests and doctors, imagine what the neighbor upstairs will say

—Antero died in a sidewalk café with his nose in the lupine seeds, imagine that

I mean how would you like people to say that about me, with my nose in my custard tart, imagine that

it's not very nice, is it, Antero, a former department head with his nose in the lupine seeds, get up, get up, will you please get up and wait until we get home, there's a bus every ten minutes, it's not that hard, and then you can take off your jacket, unbutton your collar, make yourself comfortable, and no one will say a word, while I heat up the supper.

ALVERCA, 1970

I had only recently finished my medical degree when my grandmother fell ill. I mean that one day she was fine and the next she went into a coma: a thrombosis, some malfunction of the brain, not to mention her age, of course, and there was very little that could be done. My father wanted to call in a specialist, but I persuaded him to allow me to resolve the matter or, rather, to take care of her in a way that would prove cheaper for us and save her any unnecessary suffering. Although I still have no idea how on earth you're supposed to know if a person in a coma is suffering. My father hesitated

(after all, she was his mother)

but the prospect of saving money won out. I went to fetch my stethoscope from the drawer in the sideboard, a secondhand stethoscope with the rubber earpieces slightly worn that was stolen from my car the following year, and I began my scientific maneuvers. A drip

(a drip always looks impressive)

injections, moving the body every two hours to avoid bedsores, a catheter, a bedpan, the smell of medicines stinking up the house, my family looking at me with respect for the first time ever. I took her blood pressure and asked one of my cousins to record her pulse morning and night, first on one page of a diary and then on the back of a leaf from the calendar that I tore off along the dotted line.

It gives me such pleasure tearing along a dotted line and hearing all those teeny tiny noises one after the other. I also like stapling and that device you have to squeeze to make holes in sheets of paper to be filed away in a ring binder. My grandmother was sleeping peacefully, apart from the damp wheeze of her lungs and the occasional low moan she let out when she pulled up or stretched her legs.

To compensate, the peach tree in the garden waved its branches wildly all night, its leaves glossy one moment and dark the next, and the river in the distance looked like a huge, silvery flame serenely and peacefully raising and lowering the boats. My grandmother's friends came to stand at her bedroom door and shake their heads. Their false teeth clicked. Whenever my father asked

—How is she?

I would show him the record of her pulse rate on the calendar and we would both stand studying it for ages, grave and silent, certain that therein lay the secret of life. Perhaps because it was May, small fluffy white seeds kept flying in through the window. When I was little, I was assured that these were the souls of angels and I think that for quite a few years I believed it to be true. Angels adrift alighting on the mirror, on vases and on the clothes brush. I would blow on them and they would wobble away up to the tops of the closets.

I treated my grandmother for a week. At the end of that week, in the afternoon, she turned purple. Her entire face was purple, she gave a kind of sob, and then nothing. Her head, it seemed to me, was pressed into the pillow, her bones completely soft. My father picked up the record of her pulse rate, carefully folded it and put it away in his pocket. I assume he thought of it as a kind of souvenir. I turned off the drip and put the stethoscope and the catheter in the drawer. There was the noise of tinkling: perhaps the leaves of the peach tree, perhaps the false teeth of her friends whispering behind my back. I put on my tie, went downstairs to the bar and ordered a glass of beer and a hot dog. I was always fascinated by the capable gestures of the man drawing the beer, he had a part just above one ear and each thread of what remained of his hair was combed carefully across his bald pate. He probably took ages each morning engaged in this extraordinary operation. Among the bottles on the shelf stood a highly varnished caravel model that he himself had made out of matchsticks. I once suggested that he sell it to me so that I could give it to my girlfriend and the man looked at me as if I were a murderer and shoved the plate of lupine seeds toward my chest. When I returned home, they had dressed my grandmother and there she lay on the silk bedspread, her rosary wrapped around her wrists. She was still sleeping, but she no longer pulled up or stretched out her legs. Her shoes were so new that we could almost see ourselves reflected in their soles. They placed candles on the sideboard on top of lids from cans of shoe polish so as not to mark the varnish. Out here in the garden reigned the kind of vast peace that comes about when everything is finally in order. Such a vast peace that I didn't even bother to remove the laundry basket that had been abandoned near the washbasin. When everything is finally in order, it's best to touch nothing.

THE TWO OF US HERE
LISTENING TO THE RAIN

Noveber is a difficult month: it was the month when your mother died and we lost the dog. With your mother we more or less expected it, given her age and her diabetes. The doctor told us
—Be sure to keep her warm
and we piled on more blankets, you crocheted her a nice thick shawl, we bought an oil heater that we put right next to the bed
—There you go
gave her more chicken soup, but, of course, eighty-three is eighty-three, your mother's eyesight wasn't good, she tripped on the heater, broke a bone in her leg, and the people in the emergency room told us straight out
—That broken bone is going to be a problem
she came home, we gave her more blankets and shawls, and at least we have the consolation of knowing that she died warm. Odd though it may seem, without her the living room seemed much bigger.

The following week it was the dog. He was neither old nor diabetic. I took him out to do his business on Mondays, Wednesdays, and Fridays, you took care of his bladder needs on Tuesdays, Thursdays, and Saturdays, and on Sundays we went out together, arm in arm, to do a bit of window-shopping in the local stores, you holding the lead and me whistling to him

—Here, Benfica

we got distracted looking in the store selling lamps, trying to see the price of a chandelier

—Not the one on the right, Henrique, the one on the left

on a ticket that swayed about among the prisms, we forgot about Benfica for a second, he was sniffing the tires of a parked car

he loved to sniff tires

and his passion for tires was his downfall: despite the instructions we always gave him before going out

—Now you be careful, Benfica

he tried to sniff the tires of a car that happened to be still in motion, we heard a dull thud and that was it. In death, your mother and the dog shared a certain family resemblance, as I pointed out to you when we bent down over the dog in the street

—Don't you think he looks a bit like your mother, Irene?

and you agreed with me, sadly blowing your nose, the owner of the car said

—It wasn't my fault, really it wasn't

you pointed at the dog

—It's just that he looks a bit like my mother, you see?

the driver stared at her openmouthed, and the very next morning, the garbage truck took the dog away. The living room grew still bigger, and now that we had no one to take for a walk, we stopped looking in the windows of the local stores.

So here we are alone. There's a photograph of your mother on the sideboard and the dog's leash is in the drawer, sometimes we look at the photo or open the drawer to touch the leash, but we're still alone. We sit in our usual places, you in the rocking chair doing your crocheting, me on the sofa pretending to read the newspaper, a huge silence between us and, with a little luck, the rain outside. When we hear the rain falling you look up from your crochet work

—Listen to that rain, Henrique

I look up from the newspaper and nod, and we sit staring at the window, at the drops running down, lit from behind by the street-lights. At least we're talking. At least you said

—Listen to that rain, Henrique

at least I nodded from behind my newspaper, at least, for a moment, we weren't alone. We're quiet people, incapable of making a fuss, incapable of empty chatter and futile emotions. I think that's what brought us together, shyness and an absence of tears. Luckily. Luckily for us I mean. We married thirty-seven years ago and we've never had a single argument. Why would we argue? And then there are moments like this, after supper, when it starts to rain and we're inside, at peace, almost happy. And I say almost happy because for me to say we were happy, the rain would have to be so strong that it would uproot the whole building and sweep it away down to the Tejo, something, of course, that will never happen. Perhaps it's just as well: the summer, thank God, is gone in a flash, and before you know it, November is back. We'll lose your mother again, once again we'll lose the dog. It doesn't matter. As you said, there are always compensations and we have the rain to console us. You'll say to me

—Listen to that rain, Henrique

I'll nod, and for a moment there we are the two of us, and I could say on behalf of us both, and leaving out the almost, that, for a moment, we feel happy.

GOODNIGHT, EVERYONE

No need to wave good-bye when the train leaves because you're still here on the platform. It was merely your past leaving, in the third or fourth of the second-class cars, the one that has just disappeared into the tunnel. It was merely your past leaving: your present stayed behind. Your present consists of going into the station bar, without even having taken your handkerchief out of your pocket, no regrets, no remorse, no sadness, and looking through the glass pane of the door at the empty platform, with the clock indicating a time that is no longer yours. Don't think about the luggage that no one will collect at the station of a city you will never go to: what you packed inside has ceased to belong to you. This Lisbon evening, perhaps the odd pigeon, the odd statue, the river, these belong to you. Put your hand in your pocket and throw away your house key, your identity card, your address book, the photo of your children, the overdue electric bill you ought to have paid: your past has left, your wife has left, your job has left, you have ceased to exist in the day before, you have ceased to think about tomorrow. In the station bar you watch to see the next train leave, it's at nine o'clock. Will they be waiting for you to begin supper? Will they have laid a place for you at the table, your plate, your glass, your knife and fork? Your eyedrops, those drops that sting? Don't worry about the supper or about the drops: it isn't you they're waiting for. You have no name, you have left, neither gulls nor peo-

ple notice you, nor do beggars, no dog sniffs you. If someone should
greet you, say nothing, if they ask you something say

—I don't know

or invent a language to say

—I don't know

for example

—Vlkab

or

—Tjmp

and point at the river. Then start walking toward the water,
where you will no longer be able to hear the trains, or the cars, or
the people behind you, too far away now, or the bats pursuing you
beneath the streetlights. It's the time when the last bus came down
the street where you lived, the street where the person with your
name used to live. Number forty, first floor on the right, a camphorwood chest in the hallway and, above it, a mirror that belonged to
your mother. The carved wooden frame is chipped, but that is the
mirror in which ancient faces look at themselves from time to time,
surprised to find that they're dead. Lean over the wall and look
out at the river and you'll see no one: the train took you away. Perhaps a phone call, perhaps a colleague wondering where you are,
perhaps your eldest son downstairs, on the corner, because a cab
might appear, you might appear working late in the office perhaps, a
friend from military-service days, a doctor's appointment that took
longer than expected, your wife standing between the landing and
the window, something resembling a tear, a sob: don't listen. Listen to the water in the Tejo without seeing the water in its carved
wooden frame with that chip in it shaped like a basket or a stray
boot, someone's reflection, but whose? Say

—Vlkab

say

—Tjmp

it's the only language you really know. Do you remember your
father in the garden? His slightly crooked thumb, the scar on his

wrist? Do you remember furtively smoking a cigarette behind the chicken coop? Stealing eggs and selling them to the shop? The ceramic cat? The real cat, all eyes and tail? Your past has left, you remember nothing, none of that exists and it is night. Say

—Goodnight, everyone

say

—Fednqr

the Tejo understands. And then, very slowly, go down to the river. Notice the camphorwood chest, the mirror above. In the chest the sheets from the wedding trousseau, in the mirror the ancient faces waiting for you. You are one of them, you were always one of them. When your wife or your children walk through the hallway, they will find you there, between a basket and a stray boot, and they will know you have come back. And because they know you have come back, your mouth, beneath the water, begins to smile.

I'LL WAIT FOR YOU IN
THE MIDDLE OF THE GULLS

W hy is it that the only time you ever come close to me is when you want to make love? The rest of the time you arrive home from the bank and you're just a newspaper and a pair of pants on the sofa, if I try to speak to you, the newspaper trembles with rage, if I try again, your legs cross themselves impatiently the other way, your shoe tapping furiously in space, I touch you and you cringe, I stroke your hair and your head shrinks away, horrified, and a snarl of protest emerges from behind the news

—What is it with you?

—Can't a person even read in peace?

—Will you leave my hair alone?

you eat supper sighing and making little balls out of breadcrumbs, and disappear before I've finished, not a word about my new skirt, not a question about what kind of day I had at work, not a kiss, you sit with your hands in your pockets staring at the building opposite, you switch to the sports channel when the TV soap is just about to begin, you get bored with the sport, and flip back to the soap

—There you are, you can watch this junk to your heart's content, if you want

everything annoys you, bores you, wearies you, and once a week, just as I'm dropping off to sleep, there's your arm tugging at me, your shoulder digging into me, a brief frenzy, a truck outside in the street making the building shake, me staring at the luminous numbers on the alarm clock on the other side of your indifferent back, what happened, my love, to make you change so much

(—I haven't changed, don't be stupid)

when we met, ten years ago,

no, I lie

eleven years ago, you came to me all shy, rubbing your hands, a smile fluttering about your lips but never daring to settle

—One of these days I'll invite you out for coffee, Miss Clara

so attentive, so sweet, so considerate, noticing when I changed my earrings, my hair, my ring

—Those bangs really suit you, Miss Clara

My father took to you at once because whenever I came into the room you always got up with that same flickering smile on your lips, what happened, my love, to make you change so much

(—Oh, God, there she goes again)

we would walk along by the river wall, in November, with all the gulls on the beach, we would run along hand in hand to shoo the birds away, you thought I was elegant, you thought I was pretty, you said I was even lovelier when I ran

—You look just like a gull

you said that one day I'd fly away, flap my wings and fly off after a Turkish cargo ship, you would whisper in my ear, asking anxiously, fearfully

—You won't ever leave me, will you?

(—Dear God, the stories you come up with)

you would hold me so tight around the waist I could barely breathe, please tell me what I did to make you change so much, if we were to go back to the beach in November, I can still run the way I always did, what happened to your smile, to that way you had of rubbing your hands together, I put on a different color of lipstick, a low-cut blouse, a pair of shoes I've never dared to wear because I don't want men coming up to me in the street

—Some men still find me attractive, you know

(—Good luck to them)

I go down to the river wall and stand in the middle of the gulls
waiting for you to arrive

(—Have you gone mad or what?)

with no newspaper, no pens, no little balls of breadcrumbs, inviting me nervously for coffee on the esplanade, saying breathlessly
through the smile that doesn't stop, that doesn't stop

—I so want to kiss you, Clarinha

(—Lord, the stupid things people say when they're young)

and just then, I don't know if you noticed, the gulls all vanished
and we were left alone, my love, just the beach and the waves and
me so happy, so certain

I'm still certain

(—Well, everyone's certain about something)

that we would be happy forever, that we would be happy if one
day you let me

please, let me

(—Christ, you do rattle on, you're obsessed, you are)

put my arms around you.

SUGGESTIONS FOR THE HOME

G ray Sundays leach into us: the sickly light of the lamp, the sickly rain, noises tiptoeing by as if they were at a wake. The soul drenched and downcast as a dog. A desire for old magazines, secondhand books, last week's newspapers. The most obvious smells: the carpet, the clothes in the drawers, the neighbors' lunch wafting out onto the landing. The grocer's oranges try in vain to inaugurate the morning. A desire for lap throws on knees, a game of patience, Chopin played on a 78 record, in which the jumps made by the needle are now part of the music: with each turn, a cracked sigh increases the melancholy of the piano. A memory of Chinese teapots, old sugar bowls in the glass-fronted cabinet. The photographs so upright, so stiff, a girl wearing a big bow, an ancient uncle as a child, wearing a smock and holding the handlebars of a bicycle. Against each fold of the curtain a startled head. Satin cushions embroidered with treble clefs. Recipes pasted into notebooks. Herb teas that taste vaguely of the names of distant female cousins: *macela, lúcia-lima.*[*] Dying didn't make much difference because we simply became sonnets in an almanac, dried leaves in albums. The rusty water in the bud vase. Dying wouldn't make much difference. Would it?

The water in the bud vase that the flower rusts, a suitcase forgot-

---

[*]*Macela* is camomile, *lúcia-lima* is lemon verbena.

ten on the bed: labels from French hotels, a set of brushes bound together with elastic bands. Crossword puzzles completed in pencil, seven across

Tributary of the Amazon

left blank. A nostalgia for sponge cake, toast, cookies that crumble between your fingers. Burned-out matches in the ashtray. Candy wrappers on the history textbook, lilac, silver, blue. The ironing board open in the laundry room, with a basket of washing on top. Plastic clothespins on the line. The bentwood chairs around the table, waiting. Inherited from the girl with the big bow, from the uncle with the bicycle? Stamps in plastic envelopes, the remains of a philatelic past. Congo, Uruguay, Sudan, strange animals, queens in profile. Bottles whose contents are unidentifiable and that it's best not to touch. Jars of jelly lined up in the pantry. Tributary of the Amazon, five letters. No one knows. Now and again the rain lets up, people shake their umbrellas. The pizza delivery boy gets off his motorbike, approaches with a cardboard box, we see his helmet, the arm reaching out for the doorbell. The concierge's son goes to meet him in envious admiration. He's usually playing hopscotch just outside the front door. The concierge tells him off for pissing in the plant pots in the hallway. Now and then he changes legs and continues hopping. The plants stink of ammonia. One of the eyes of the admirer of motorbikes swivels to look inside, despite the patch over the left lens of his glasses. When his mother tells him off, he chews his thumb, the stray eye becomes pensive and adult. It must have been born earlier and had to wait for the rest of the face to appear. It wandered about between eyebrows and nose until it found a place. The concierge's son is called Artur, a name that is older than he is, contemporary with the eye. Artur for some reason reminds me of *cavacas*, those cookies you can buy in Caldas da Rainha. In the dental clinic in the building across the way, a chair sits in the shadows, as isolated and majestic as the electric chair. The size of the dentist's Jeep gets bigger every year: he must thank God for tooth decay. He has a dog that shares Artur's clandestine taste for flowerpots, raising its leg as delicately as if it were a little finger while the dentist pokes and probes, wearing a mask so that he can't be recognized by his victims:

—Was it you who drilled through my tooth?

And the dentist, hand on heart, all innocence

—Me?

I think I'll go out into the street to play hopscotch. Tributary of the Amazon, five letters. I try not to read the solution, upside down in one corner of the page, I cover it with my sleeve, think for a bit, then uncover it: it's hard to decipher the tiny characters. A child's footsteps in the apartment upstairs, a man shouting

—Shut up

an enormous stool topples over in the silence. My horoscope recommends: Pay attention to your liver. I pay attention to my liver, I try to listen to it. Should I take it by the arm, show an interest in its life? Sulky and stubborn, my liver says nothing. Perhaps it's gone, perhaps it's outside with the concierge's son, coveting that motorbike. Or prowling around the plants, waiting. There's no point in worrying: it usually turns up at mealtimes. I have become a sonnet in an almanac, a dried leaf in an album, the rusty water in a bud vase. Dying wouldn't make much difference. It wouldn't. Would it?

NO, THAT'S NOT QUITE IT

She had to do the dishes herself after lunch because the dishwasher broke down and the repairman said

—It will have to wait until Monday, Senhora, half my staff are on vacation

and put the phone down on her, having first made a note of her address, muttering something or other about people always choosing Saturdays to call him. She washed the dishes, lined them up on the drainboard, cleaned the aluminum sink with a sponge to remove any trace of foam, put the sponge back in its usual place behind the faucet, took off her Snoopy apron

was it Snoopy, the dog whose name she could never remember and that spent all its time lying on the roof of its kennel

hung it on the hook for dish towels, pressed the pedal on the pail lined with a plastic bag from the supermarket, tied the handles of the bag together, put it on the stool by the kitchen door, looked around to make sure that everything was in order and it was, apart perhaps from the bronze ashtray shaped like a shoe that could be just a tad farther over to the left, it had burnt matches in it as usual, she picked up the matches

five matches

and slipped them into the bag through a little gap that revealed a few discarded peels. She looked around the kitchen again and

this time turned off the ceiling light using the switch that always
sparked and was the despair of the electrician

—I just can't understand what's wrong with those wires.

She thought she'd sit down for a while in the living room, but she
didn't like the living room, so she turned left into her son's room

the stickers on the window, the surfing posters, a photo of his
father that had fallen over ages ago, and that neither of them had
picked up. A forgotten tennis shoe beside the computer seemed to
mock her

—Go on, pick me up, I dare you.

She ignored the tennis shoe, she peered out at the street from the
balcony in the study without actually seeing the street, she went
into the bathroom where her son's toothbrush wasn't in its mug

of course

but in the sink by the drain along with the toothpaste tube without its top and the razor with which he shaved off the one bristle on
his chin. She came to and found herself sitting on the edge of her
bed, in front of the mirror, examining her hands. She could see the
place where her wedding ring had been, the ring she had stopped
wearing long after the divorce, two months ago at most, the paler
mark still clearly there on her finger. She looked for the ring that
had belonged to her grandmother in the little jewel box and smiled
to herself at the word jewel, an old lady's ring with a purple stone

—I'm forty-one

set in engraved silver that had grown dark over time. She tried on
the ring and her grandmother's voice immediately said

—You've become thinner, Susana

she took off the ring, and her grandmother, thank God, fell silent,
she decided

—No, I can't wear that

turned on the bedside lamp, with the little pleated shade that she
had liked at first but didn't like at all anymore. She moved her face
closer to the other face in the mirror, wetted her little finger on her

tongue and smoothed her eyebrows, if she could have, she would
have smoothed her nose, her cheeks, she said

—Hello, Susana

and the reflection said hello at the same time and with the same
smile. She studied the skin on her neck, studied her shoulders,
her breasts, she sat up straight to make her bust look bigger, but it
seemed to her that it looked just the same. She smiled again

—You look just the same

although her smile, it seemed to her, was angry

not angry exactly, but how else could she explain it?

she searched for an adjective to describe her smile but found
none

disappointed? resigned?

no, not disappointed or resigned, and neither disappointed nor
resigned, she gave up, left her place on the edge of the bed, walked
around to the table on her husband's side, opened the top drawer
and found a diary from eight years ago which announced for the
ninth of April

Dentist at five o'clock, meeting at seven, supper with Susana at
her parents' house.

In the second drawer, expired car insurance documents, the bill
from a restaurant in Bicesse

—Why did he keep that?

and a starter pistol without a trigger that was of no use to anyone.
On the back of the bill for the restaurant in Bicesse was a telephone
number in pencil. She dialed the number, which rang once, twice,
three times, four times, after the eighth ring someone said in her
ear

—Hello?

she stopped breathing so as to listen more closely

—Hello?

and someone said

—Hello?

and then

—Shit

and then hung up, while she sat staring at the phone, a faint tinkle and that someone in her ear, intrigued

—Hello?

and before they said

—Shit

again, she picked up the starter pistol, pressed the plastic barrel to her temple, squeezed the nonexistent trigger, sighed

—Bang

and was dead for part of the afternoon until her son came home.

NOT JUST NOW,
BE PATIENT

H e felt something odd, not exactly dizziness, not exactly a
headache, not exactly a discomfort in his stomach, but a
mixture of all those things without its being precisely any of them,
so he sat up on the sofa listening to his own body, hoping that it
would tell him what was wrong. All his life he had believed that
the body has its own ways of speaking to us and that to understand
you have only to listen.

—What's wrong, Carlos?

asked his wife interrupting the news from his intestines, which led
him to place one finger vertically over his lips so that his body could
discourse freely on what was happening inside. But his wife, ignoring the finger, was already by his side clutching his arm, asking

—What's wrong, Carlos?

and placing the palm of her hand on his forehead to see if he had
a temperature. It irritated him that at the slightest sign of indisposi-
tion his wife always placed her palm on his forehead, as if sickness
and health were merely a matter of having or not having a fever. He
thought of pushing her away with his elbow, but he didn't have the
courage. Besides the dizziness

was it dizziness?

was getting worse, the TV set in front of him started to shake,
and it was always useful to have someone close by. The headache
seemed to him more diffuse, although the discomfort in his stomach had now taken the form of a ball pressing in on him or that

might start to press in on him, he wasn't sure. Whatever it was, he
began to feel frightened and he knew he had started to feel frightened because the palms of his hands became damp, sliding against
each other like bars of soap, independent of him. They ended up
on his lap and stayed there, together, while he looked at them in
the certain knowledge that they did not belong to him. His wife
touched his chin and he turned to her. Her eyes were bigger than
he had thought and her anxious face was almost pretty. It occurred
to him that as soon as people grew serious their features improved
and he remembered his mother, after supper, doing the dishes in
the kitchen. All his gestures were suddenly harmonious, and for the
space of a second he envied his father who had died eleven months
earlier from throat cancer. Despite his illness his father had continued to smoke like a chimney and spent all day coughing. But he had
been a good father.

—Perhaps it was the dizziness that made me think of that

he thought while the TV set spun round and round and the ball
in his belly divided up into an infinite number of smaller balls that
spread throughout his stomach. After his father's death, his mother
used to leave the dirty dishes to accumulate for weeks on end and she
spent a vast amount of time at the window staring out at the street.
Perhaps, after he died, his wife would also spend a vast amount of
time at the window staring out at the street. There were thirteen
years between them and from time to time he felt guilty that he
was so much older. His hair was getting thin on top, the doctor had
recommended taking some drops for his blood pressure. He kept
the prescription for the drops in his wallet as if it were a badge for
the disabled. He had never had the prescription filled and had never
taken the drops: he preferred simply to keep that bit of paper with
the doctor's name printed on it, to put on his glasses and read: XV
drops before each meal. He thought it odd that the number of drops
should be in Roman numerals: it reminded him of his grandfather's
clock on the sideboard, a relic without any hands and with a rust
stain on its face. He couldn't think of any other way of putting it,

but it pleased him to have a paper clock with the number XV on it. The real clock stopped at XII.

—Carlos

said his wife again, and her voice sounded as if it came from far away even though her mouth was close to his ear. There was a time

how long ago now?

when he had liked that mouth. And that nose. And the sway of her hips when she walked. Over the years his wife had grown slightly fatter, she had changed, and yet her eyes were the same: large, watchful, not solid exactly, two small spheres of dark water, which now, it seemed to him, were shadowed by fear.

—Are you all right now, Carlos?

and the question sounded so anxious that he said yes. He leaned back on the sofa again and tried to pick up the newspaper. The words made no sense. He looked up and the furniture in the room made no sense. The paintings made no sense either, especially those two on the wall above the table, a wedding gift from a friend, although he could no longer remember which friend it was. His wife, relieved, picked up her needles and resumed her knitting. She was like his mother doing the dishes in the kitchen after supper. A good mother, a good father. He folded the newspaper and put it down on the cushion to his left. Those little balls continued to divide and multiply and were now filling his chest. He consoled himself by repeating over and over that he didn't have a fever. At least, thank God, he didn't have a fever. The telephone in the bedroom rang and his wife got up to answer it. Contrary to his expectations, he felt very alone. He settled himself more comfortably on the sofa. His wife laughed into the phone. He smiled at his wife's laughter and leaned his head against the back of the sofa. Nothing made sense and yet he didn't mind. He didn't mind about anything. If his wife were to ask

—What are you thinking about?

he wouldn't know what to say. He was thinking about nothing, he was thinking about the void.

VACATION

I look out of the window and see houses. Nothing but stillness and houses, the cars parked right on the sidewalk, the newsstand closed. On some of the balconies there are creepers, flowers, a woman who looks at me for a moment, then looks away. At night there are brightly lit dining rooms, lamps, paintings, a child smoothing a sticker onto a windowpane with the flat of his hand, a man with a white mustache down below, talking to someone I can't see, the gypsies' van parked in the little square. My husband turns the page of his newspaper.

I stop looking out of the window and sit down on the sofa, in my place. My husband's place is in the armchair, which is starting to take the shape of his body. I can't remember who gave it to us: my in-laws, his godfather, his friend at the furniture factory? My son mumbles into the phone, his back to us. In ten minutes or so he'll ask us to let him borrow the Jeep or, rather, he won't ask us anything, he'll just wave the key at us and announce

—See you guys later

with his baseball cap on backward, I'm sick to death of telling him that he looks stupid wearing his baseball cap that way, and he looks at me stupidly, silently telling me that I'm the one who looks stupid. He may be right: my usual hairdresser is sick and her replacement has given me the kind of haircut a librarian might choose. If I wore glasses and lace-up shoes, people in the street

would start stopping me to borrow books. I asked my husband
what he thought: he looked at me for a second and then turned
another page of his newspaper.

I suppose we must be happy: we have this apartment and the
apartment in the Algarve,* next year we're going to be buying a
slightly bigger boat, with two berths instead of one and a kitchen
the size of a matchbox. My husband has promised me that he's
going to have my name painted on the hull. He often has to go to
London and he always brings back two bottles of perfume. He gives
me one. The other is for his partner as a surprise gift for his wife.
My husband helps his partner to surprise his wife every month, but
I've never noticed his wife wearing the perfume. The person who
smells like me is the junior secretary at the office. When I said this
to my husband, he said I was paranoid and asked me to pass him a
pen so that he could do the bridge problem in the newspaper. Coincidentally, at office parties, the junior secretary wears clothes like
mine and a ring like the one I was given for my birthday. But as far
as I know she doesn't have her name painted on a boat. Perhaps
when we have one with four berths and a kitchen the size of three
matchboxes. My husband said I was being paranoid again and told
me it was my fault he hadn't managed to solve the bridge problem
in the newspaper.

We must be happy, mustn't we: we are happy: we don't argue, my
son hasn't so far killed himself in the Jeep, my mother-in-law swears
that she adores me, my father-in-law has put the country house in
our name. It has a chapel with a bell. You pull a string and the bell
starts ringing. My father-in-law adores that bell: whenever we go
there he says to me

—Look, Luísa

and he grabs the string and starts clanging that bell so loudly I
feel like strangling him. I wouldn't strangle him suddenly, I'd say

—Look, Pa

*The Algarve. Portugal's southernmost province. Its capital is Faro.

and place my hands around his throat, squeezing slowly until the old guy finally lets go of the string, his face purple and his tongue dangling. We could use the chapel for the funeral mass. Everyone could sleep here and after the funeral we could have a picnic in Santarém. I'm sure the junior secretary is wearing a bracelet the same as mine.

So, yes, we're happy: in the summer we spend two weeks in the country and two weeks in the Algarve with our friends, my husband's partner and his wife, the other junior secretary who wears the same watch and necklace as the partner's wife, my son wearing his baseball cap backward and splashing about in the water and drenching us all, my husband who's always tired at night

—I'm tired, Luísa

I have the distinct impression that the partner's leg and the leg of the other junior secretary are talking to each other under the bridge table, but of course if I were to say anything about this, my husband would say

—You're paranoid

and of course if I said anything to his partner's wife she would say

—Are you talking about me or about you?

Which is silly because we're happy, yes, my husband and I are happy, no one can be tired every night for two whole months, one of these days

—Come here, Luísa

one of these days

—We need to have a little chat, Luísa

one of these days there'll be only one bottle of perfume when he comes back from London, only one pair of earrings, only one ring, my hairdresser will get better, my son will wear his baseball cap the right way, the Jeep will stay in the garage, my husband will get up from his armchair and come and sit on the sofa next to me

—We need a second honeymoon, Luísa

and we'll have one, of course we will, shopping in Paris, a week-end in Madrid, a dressmaker where no one copies my clothes, the junior secretary dispatched to the Milan branch, I love you, Luísa, you're as pretty as you were when I first met you, Luísa, you excite me so much, Luísa, and I might let my father-in-law ring the chapel bell as often as he likes and resist the desire to put my hands around his throat, I might agree with him and say approvingly

—Yes, it really is a lovely bell, Pa

and stop looking out of the window at the houses, nothing but stillness and houses, the cars parked right on the sidewalk, the news-stand closed, on some of the balconies there are creepers, flowers, a woman who looks at me for a moment, then looks away, while my husband, indifferent, distant, so very distant that I can't even reach him, turns the page of his newspaper.

I'M NOT LYING, HONEST

It's not so much when it rains. It's more when there's a rainless, gray sky, with the chimneys and the trees, legs in the air, pressed against it, when the cellophane-wrapped sun seems ashamed of us

(so many identical suns, beneath the sign saying ORANGES, in the crates in the grocery store)

it's more when we look up and hesitate for a moment, shall I take my raincoat or shan't I, when we've already closed the door and it opens again and our wives stand poised on the doormat

—Take your raincoat

and we with the raincoat weighing on our arm like a dead weight and then out we go into the street and glance angrily back up at the balcony of our apartment

—It's not going to rain

because it's not so much when it rains, it's when we look back at the balcony of our apartment and then at the rainless, gray sky with the chimneys and the trees, legs in the air, pressed against it, and the orange that escaped from the grocery store and grew in size, that we see the gentlemen in bowler hats strolling about in the air. A dozen gentlemen in bowler hats, dressed like those relatives in the album relegated to the highest shelf in the pantry, smiling and solemn, behind the jars of jelly and the broken heater, whom we only ever knew motionless at picnics in the small faded squares of photos

(Uncle Narciso, Lieutenant Santos)

a dozen or so slow, dapper gentlemen strolling about in the air, greeting each other

—How are you, Uncle Narciso?

—How are you, Lieutenant Santos?

walking back and forth, hanging in midair, in their small, gleaming patent-leather shoes. It's odd that only I see them. No one stops to look at them, no one is interested, no one notices these relatives, and I stock still, all alone, watching their bows, their waves, the hurried frown with which they appear and then disappear from the rooftops

—How are you, Lieutenant Santos?

sometimes rolling a cigarette, asking the others for a light, talking in grave whispers about illnesses and retirement, leaning against a television aerial to examine the square, one of them, in dark glasses, stumbles on a bird as if on a pebble, rights himself and walks on, I ask my wife

—Can't you see?

my wife, pretending she doesn't understand

—See what?

very patiently I show her

—That gentleman there, stumbling over a bird

my wife presses the back of her hand to my forehead to see if I have a fever, then she looks again

—What gentleman, Armando?

she eyes me, strangely distrustful, she shakes her head, she glances up one last time, checks again to see if I have a fever, then asks

—Did you sleep all right, Armando?

in the morning she smells of soap and warm sheets, she smells of the remains of sleep, her makeup from the night before gives her a passing resemblance to a wall from which the Town Hall has not entirely removed some party political propaganda, still written on her right eyelid is the remnant of a message

DOWN WITH PA

a scrap of a poster showing an earnest politician is peeling off her cheek

VOTE FOR EDUA

and only I and the gentlemen in the bowler hats notice, the man with the dark glasses offers me his handkerchief so that I can wipe the earnest politician from her face, my wife immediately grabs the handkerchief, imagining lovers

—Where did you get this, Armando?

a handkerchief with an N embroidered on it

Uncle Narciso

smelling of old-fashioned cologne, the man in the dark glasses is worried

(my mother, poor thing, used to say that Uncle Narciso always worried about the family)

my wife sniffing the eau de cologne

—Who is she, Armando?

suspecting the widow who spends her afternoons reading magazines in the café, I explain that one of the bowler-hatted gentlemen gave me the handkerchief, I climb up onto the stool intending to show her the album on the pantry shelf, looking for Uncle Narciso among the birthdays, foolish pranks and gaiters

—There isn't a she, it's my Uncle Narciso

but there's no photograph of Uncle Narciso, someone must have taken him out because you can still see the mark left by the glue and one torn corner of the photograph, I ask

—What's happened to Uncle Narciso?

my wife examining every inch of the handkerchief

—Don't change the subject, Armando

stopping at a trace of lipstick the same color as the lipstick the widow wears

(my mother, poor thing, would stroke the photo with her little finger and say that Uncle Narciso's only fault was that he was a bit of a womanizer)

—A heart of gold, but a bit of a womanizer
I even tried to tell my wife this
—Uncle Narciso had a heart of gold, but he was a bit of a womanizer
while she was packing her suitcase in the bedroom, while she was wiping away a tear with the flat of her hand, while she was standing on the landing about to disappear down the stairs, and she threw the handkerchief at me so that it draped itself over my shoulder, the house without my wife has grown in size, the living room, the bedroom, the kitchen, the verandah, especially the verandah with the pot of geraniums on the balustrade, beyond the balustrade the rainless, gray sky, with the chimneys and the trees, legs in the air, pressed against it, the cellophane-wrapped sun, and Uncle Narciso, in his bowler hat, asking me for his handkerchief back and then going off with it, stumbling over the sparrows.

AS IF THE DEW
HAD KISSED YOU

I don't know quite what it is I'm waiting for. For you to come home, for me to hear the door open and then close, to see you look in through the living-room door

—Hi

to hear your steps heading off down the corridor to the kitchen or to the bedroom, a blind being lowered, a faucet being turned on, a closet door opened, you coming back and coming over to me, sitting down in the living room with a sigh

—So what's new?

then forgetting about me, turning on the TV, picking up a fashion magazine from the basket beside the armchair, your profile, wearing glasses now, leafing past horoscopes, clothes, makeup, then turning around, one finger keeping your place between the pages

—Are you hungry?

your mouth serious, your eyes serious, your Mexican necklace was it Mexican?

the same color as your blouse, you taking off one earring to answer your cell phone with a

—Hi

different from the

—Hi

you gave me, slower, warmer, tied up with the ribbon of a smile,

I recognize that way of speaking from years ago, that body leaning slightly back, those fingers smoothing your hair as if the voice I
can't hear could see you

 —No, not tomorrow, the day after, Wednesday

 I'm sure it's a man whose identity I don't know or prefer not to
know, you cross your legs the other way

 —I'll call you later, OK?

you put your cell phone back in your bag, your smile dissolves
into the serious mouth, into the Mexican necklace

 —You didn't say whether or not you were hungry

 how long ago was it exactly that you stopped loving me, how long
ago that you started going to bed earlier than me, waking up for a
second when I get into bed

 —Would you mind turning out the light?

your head buried in the pillow, your back turned to me, I get
undressed by the glow of the numbers on the alarm clock, the mattress dips and wakes you up again

 —Oh, for God's sake

in the morning I find my cereal in a bowl on a tray and the apartment empty, a few drops on the shower curtain, your still-damp
toothbrush beside my dry toothbrush, your absence all too present
in the fashion magazine abandoned on the sofa, your cereal bowl in
the dishwasher with the spoon still in it, half full of whitish water,
the frayed edge of the rug where one of your high heels caught it,
the Mexican necklace

 was it Mexican?

on the sideboard, I wonder what clothes you have on today, how
you're wearing your hair, which shoes you've chosen, who you're
going to have lunch with, if I ask my secretary to ring yours, you're
out or if you're not

 —Be quick, will you, I'm really busy

so I don't know quite what it is I'm waiting for. I stand with my
car keys in my hand outside the bathroom looking at the drops
of water on the shower curtain and imagining you coming out of

the shower with the bath towel around your waist and the smaller towel wrapped around your head, dripping little tears of steam as if the dew had kissed you. I imagine your feet on the tiles, your back, your shoulders, I get into the car with you naked beside me and, gradually, as we approach the company parking lot, I'm filled with a feeling of peace and contentment, the excitement of someone in love. I have your photo here on the bookshelf, alongside the medal I won in the tennis tournament and the framed letter from the minister, a photograph taken five years ago at most, you're on the beach, wearing dark glasses, waving at me. We used to have supper on the balcony shooing away the mosquitoes, and out at sea, dozens of lights appeared on the fishing boats. Perhaps we were happy then. We must have been happy because the walls of our hearts were so thin you could hear them beating from the other side.

A NICE LITTLE CHRISTMAS

Our Christmas consisted of just the two of us here at home with a tree and lights that blinked on and off all night. We'd throw the tree out the next day

(at first, it leaned by the door alongside the trash and then stood upside down in the garbage can out in the street, along with the empty bottles and the wrapping paper, with its other fellow Christmas trees, equally bereft of stars and silvery balls)

but the lights, linked together by an electric wire, we kept in a cardboard box, formerly a shoebox, which in turn we placed on the highest shelf in the pantry, home to the things we use least often

(a broken heater, a crutch from when I sprained my foot, the photo of my father-in-law, medicines past their sell-by date)

and there the lights stay, not blinking at all, until next Christmas. To retrieve them, my wife goes out onto the verandah and brings in the ladder

(which I hold steady because of treacherous tendencies that they manifest through various wobbles and tremors)

fearfully climbs the three metal rungs saying

—Don't let go

rummages around behind the heater, the crutch, the photo and the medicine bottles

(somehow or other, the lights always migrate right to the back of the shelf, the abode of cockroaches, old slippers and dust) manages to reach the box after endless maneuverings—accompanied by a vocabulary worthy of a taxi driver after someone has just plowed into him from the left side, and whose energy and variety never ceases to surprise me in this otherwise placid, silent person—attempts to hand me the Christmas lights, demanding that I take them from her but without loosening my grip on the ladder, which is not an easy thing to do, utters a few more choice taxi-driver phrases, feeling for the next step with her foot as she descends, testing each one. Disheveled and exhausted, with her back still turned to me and with the Happy Christmas in her arms, she regards the ladder and utters one final profanity, swearing that next year she'll keep the decorations in the silver drawer, which doesn't require any mountaineering skills. I take the ladder back out to the verandah, bumping into the furniture and scratching the paint, and since we've already put the new tree in its pot

(not letting it suspect its imminent fate in the trash can)

all we have to do is arrange the garland of different-colored bulbs on the branches, hang up the silvery balls, put the star on top, and plug in the lights so that Christmas can start winking out its pulsatory joy. Normally, as soon as I place the two little metal cylinders of the plug in the socket, one of the bulbs explodes, the fuses all blow and we are left scrambling in the dark and bumping into each other

(me and the taxi driver whose expressive talents are greatly enhanced by the darkness)

in search of the fuse box. Once we've found it, having burned our fingers on matches and burned a hole in the carpet

(the taxi driver always goes ballistic when she notices the hole)

we flick the switch, study the bulbs one by one, tighten any fittings that seem loose, fearfully pick up the plug, push back the sofa

(at this point, the sofa, which is usually very light, decides to weigh a ton)

to try the apparently more benign socket in the wall behind, we look at each other to pluck up courage, push the two little metal cylinders into the socket, and the whole building disappears with a bang. The men from the municipal office, summoned by a neighbor who is beginning to hate us, speak of a systems overload, which seems rather a grand term when applied to something that can be stored in a shoebox, and they suggest, through a spokesperson in a beret who understands the mysteries of resistors and amps, that if we want to have "a nice little Christmas" the best thing would be to turn off all machines, light some romantic candles for supper instead of switching on the chandelier, and swathe ourselves in blankets to reduce the likelihood of catching what he, with great conviction, called a "stonking case of pneumonia." And so we stick two or three candles on two or three saucers, with drops of wax that choose not to fall on the saucers and that, when scraped at with a knife, ruin our sideboards, we scatter these funereal little flames about the room

(the holes in the carpet are now complemented by black stains on the ceiling)

my wife gets her shawl, I put on my overcoat, we eat our traditional salt-cod supper and we exchange gifts, with the tree appearing and disappearing to the rhythm of the lights and with us appearing and disappearing too, one moment blue the next nothing, one moment green the next nothing, one moment yellow the next nothing, and whenever we're blue or green or yellow, we're ghostly and enormous, projecting vast shadows on the walls. My ghost receives a pair of woolen gloves and a key ring, my wife's ghost an almost-authentic pearl necklace and a little copper dustpan and brush for removing crumbs from the table. After half an hour of icy silence, one of us suggests that we turn off the tree, the other, intermittently invisible, comments that we can't do that out of consideration for the other people on the block. And we end up going to bed making gestures that the tree paints in rainbow colors, unable to sleep because of that luminous fury that transforms the whole block into a misshapen ventricle of electrical systoles and diastoles, while the candle flames dissolve in the saucers in a cloud of pestilential smoke. We wake not in an apartment but in a Turkish prison after a riot over which Christmas continues indifferently to blink, unalterably content, and we use the little copper dustpan and brush to sweep up the corpses. When Amnesty International comes to investigate our crimes against humanity they will be received by a lady in an almost-authentic pearl necklace and a gentleman in an overcoat—both intermittently blue, green, and yellow—clutching an innocent little tree in one hand.

BETWEEN MARQUÊS DE POMBAL
AND LARANJEIRAS

If I were to tell you that I'm offering you this smile because I have no flowers to give you, would you understand? I wasn't expecting to find you sitting there opposite me in the subway, with that blue skirt and that white blouse, with those eyes that meet mine in the reflection in the window but immediately look away, surprised at first, then angry, leaving me orphaned, your knees avoid mine, it seems to me that you shrug your shoulders, open and close the zipper on your neat little handbag, perhaps angry with me, perhaps impatient, I get the impression that you're shaking your head in irritation or scorn, I widen my smile and no one receives it, I try to catch it in my hand, but it escapes in your direction, it's not my fault it escapes, if it wasn't for that skirt, if it wasn't for that blouse, for the curve of your right earlobe just visible beneath your hair, I wouldn't even have noticed you, I was thinking about work, about my wife, about supper, I got promoted this week, my wife loves me, we're having meat loaf tonight

would you like some?

we've just finished paying off our apartment, we're happy, or, rather, I was sure we were happy until you sat down opposite me in the subway, it's odd, isn't it, how unexpected life is, I've forgotten all about my promotion, I've forgotten all about food, how can I possibly think of promotions and food when I can see your right earlobe just visible beneath your hair, the four-leaf clover of your silver earring, the little beauty spot above your eyebrow that

   don't deny it

   calls to me, you can avoid my knees if you like, but that beauty spot is calling to me, you accept my smile, will you accept my flowers, I'm thirty-six years old, my name is Fernando, I love you, look at my mouth silently telling you

   —I love you

   how come it isn't you, but the creature sitting on the aisle seat who smiles at me, with no blue skirt, no white blouse, no beauty spot above her eyebrow, her eyes in the reflection in the window fixed on mine, her knees brushing mine, the tip of her shoe bruising my toes, no glimpsed earlobe, no silver clover, the neat little handbag replaced by a plastic shopping bag out of which vegetables are sprouting and so I shrug my shoulders, shake my head, think of my job, my wife, supper, I was promoted this week and want nothing to do with her, I love my wife, you know, and would never fall in love with someone I happened to meet at seven o'clock on the subway, I bet your meat loaf is bland and crumbly, don't make me avoid your knees, get up, run away, don't go imagining that this smile represents the flowers I don't have with me, don't get up as well, don't follow me, leave me alone, please leave me alone, don't take my hand, don't ask me where I live, and don't tell me you're a widow either, nor that you'll defrost the salt cod in the microwave, don't lock the door, don't slip the key down your décolletage, leave my shirt buttons alone, don't throttle me with my tie, by now the meat loaf will have gotten cold, by now my wife will be worried to death, in tears, phoning all the hospitals, I've never missed supper without warning her first, I've never been this late, how am I going to explain this mark on my arm, the love bite on my neck, but now that I'm lying here, let me at least bury my face in my arms and imagine a four-leaf clover and a beauty spot above the eyebrow falling asleep on my shoulder in happy ecstasy.

IT'S JUST A MATTER OF TIME

Senhor Peres never told me he liked me and I never told Senhor Peres that I liked him, perhaps because of the twenty-three-year age difference, perhaps because he was my boss, perhaps because he was shorter than I and the idea of seeing the two of us together in a photo, with me so much taller, made me feel a little awkward. It wasn't noticeable in the shop because I was always sitting at the checkout and Senhor Peres was standing up, attending to customers, always so polite, always in black, always wearing both wedding rings, his own and his late wife's, always so respectful toward everyone and never a great one for talking, apart from when young men came into the shop with their earrings and their long hair, and when they left, Senhor Peres would say: what is this country coming to, where will it end. At five minutes to seven, I would get up, fix my hair in the mirror, and say

—Goodnight, Senhor Peres, see you tomorrow

Senhor Peres, eight inches closer to the floor than me

—Good night, Miss Noélia, see you tomorrow

and in the next block, number 33, second floor on the left, my mother waiting with the soup on the table and the soap on the TV. It's not a bad life: we have my father's pension, we own our apartment and with what I earn and my mother's pension we can afford a trip to Spain every July. There's a photo of me in the living room standing in front of the Prado Museum, wearing a white dress I really loved, but which, unfortunately, I scorched with the iron, and now and again I get a letter from my cousin in Canada. He never mentions marriage, but my mother is convinced that one day he'll take the plunge, men always settle down eventually, it's just a matter of time. The only thing she makes me promise is that I won't go and live in Toronto, especially since I have my own place in Lisbon

(this spring we had a new utility room put in)

a reasonable job, a pretty nice climate, the TV soap and the family doctor who helped me when I had that problem with my kidneys and my bladder. As my mother says, and she's quite right, a good doctor is harder to find than a good husband, and he doesn't pull all the blankets over to his side of the bed during the night. And so in our bathroom there are only two toothbrushes, and my mother thinks we're fine as we are. There are times when I feel tempted to disagree with her, but I say nothing, of course, to avoid giving her palpitations: the doctor told us that my mother has the heart of a sparrow and so, no excitement, Dona Celina, when it gets to the point in the TV soap where the actress kills the brother-in-law to get his share of the inheritance money, turn off the TV and ask your daughter to read the summary in the newspaper, skipping over any mention of guns and blood.

Senhor Peres never told me he liked me and I never told Senhor Peres that I liked him, so I was surprised last week, as I was fixing my hair in the mirror, having already left the register, when he asked me, his mouth more or less level with the fifth button on my blouse, if I would like to go to an open-air café by the river on Sunday, as he used to do when his wife was alive, before the awful month of diabetes and the funeral. My mother was of the view that my cousin wouldn't mind

(—He's a gentleman, Noélia)

and Senhor Peres came to pick me up in his ancient car, pumping out smoke and every bit of it rattling. I wore a woolen jacket, well, with the treacherous weather we've been having, you never know when it's going to turn cold, my mother waved to Senhor Peres from the window, or rather to what she could see of Senhor Peres in the midst of the coal-black smoke from the exhaust, and shouted down to me to keep an eye on my handbag because there was no shortage of pickpockets. The café was in Belém and my shoes were pinching me. Senhor bought me an apple juice and asked my permission

—If you don't mind, Miss Noélia

to drink a beer. His hands seemed to me even smaller than in the store, he was wearing a tie with a pearl tie pin and we spent two hours staring at the boats, in between shelled prawns and embarrassed silences. The people around us were blowing children's noses and an old man was going from table to table selling plaster miniatures of the Venus de Milo, with those amputated arms of hers, like the men who sell lottery tickets. I wasn't thinking about Toronto, I wasn't thinking about my cousin, I wasn't thinking about anything. Senhor Peres was grappling with his prawns, and I could tell by the way he kept avoiding my eyes that he was getting up the courage to inform me of some decision he had reached. He opened his mouth and shut it again. He opened his mouth once more and shut it. After a very long time, he opened it again, hesitated, and stuck an unshelled prawn in it. A stray dog sniffed our legs and then wandered off. Senhor Peres gave up, took his comb out of his pants pocket and fixed his part. Perhaps I could have helped him to speak, squeezed his fingers, smiled. Perhaps my life wasn't really that much fun, despite the trips to Spain. Perhaps I and Senhor Peres. Perhaps Senhor Peres and I despite the age difference. Perhaps my mother would approve. Perhaps I should have shelled a prawn for Senhor Peres so that he didn't choke. Perhaps the idea of the two of us together in a photo wouldn't make me feel so very uncomfortable. I would have to walk on the lower part of the sidewalk, to wear flat shoes, to stoop very slightly. Perhaps if it wasn't time to go home

—Good night, Miss Noélia, see you tomorrow

—Good night, Senhor Peres, see you tomorrow

and he wasn't disappearing in his ancient car, pumping out smoke and every bit of it rattling. But it doesn't matter: any month now I'll get a letter from Toronto mentioning marriage. Men always settle down eventually, it's just a matter of time, my cousin is almost a foot taller than me and in October we're going to have parquet flooring put down in the living room. When I think about it, I really have nothing to complain about.

ON THE HOUSE

I t's not the buildings on the other side of the street that are
the problem, the chimneys, the rooftops, the verandah where
a woman beats her rugs with a carpet beater made of willow
switches, the stuffed weasel on the windowsill of a basement apartment and its small, furious, blind, lacquer eyes: the problem is the
absence of clouds and pigeons, the sky rising vertically just above
the houses, absolutely smooth, with no steps and no shutters, and
where it seems that the air withers, the trees wither, the sounds
   of cars, of people, of radios
   wither too, petals of shadow drooping on their stems, for example, my mother at the front door calling
   —Lurdes
   her feather duster in her hand, stepping slowly and resignedly
out of her clothes, the halo of her hair faded by time, her face still
grubby with sleep
   —Lurdes
   and behind her, in the living room, on the sideboard, the photograph of my father saying
   —Lurdes
   as well, his mouth
   —Lurdes
   his eyebrows fluttering like wings
   —Lurdes

something furrowing his anxious brow, you died so long ago, Pa,
leave me alone, I hardly remember you and he, unperturbed

—Lurdes

beneath a gravestone in the cemetery, in suit and tie

—Lurdes

the new suit, the French tie, the crucifix between his fingers,
while he was alive he never called to me

—Lurdes

he walked past me in silence, obliquely, rapidly, he sat down at
the dining-room table to play a game of solitaire, he kept a collection of jigsaw puzzles under the couch, little bits of cardboard that
you fitted together and now, all this time later, he remembers me

—Lurdes

when I had already forgotten him, very erect in the photograph

—Lurdes

my mother at the front door

—Can't you hear your father?

my mother calling too

—Lurdes

and not a single cloud, not a single pigeon, the sky rising vertically just above the houses where it seems that the air withers, the
trees wither, the sounds

of cars, people, radios

wither too, apart from the syllables of my name, apart from my
mother's question

—Why don't you talk to us, Lurdes

feeling hurt or else concerned, distressed, but why is she concerned, why is she distressed, I'm not ill, I don't feel bad, I just wish
they would forget about me, ignore me, pretend I don't exist, that I
never existed, when it's lunchtime, I have lunch, when it's time to
go to bed, I go to bed, so let me be, like the stuffed weasel on the
windowsill in that basement apartment, staring at the vertical sky
with no steps and no shutters, the withered air, the withered voices,
withered me, perhaps my father isn't the only one who's dead, per-

haps we all are, yes, I'm sure we're all dead in this fourth-floor apartment overlooking the rhombus of the little square below

rhombus?

overlooking the square, if the phone rings, I'm not in, if Aunt Alice's aneurysm gets worse, I don't want to know, I'm a stuffed weasel, Ma, I'm a forty-three-year-old woman looking for steps in the sky or for a shutter where I can peer through to the other side of things just as, when I was a child, I used to peer at the lighted balconies and beyond the balconies at the furniture, paintings, perhaps at myself inside there waving at me, with a different mother and father, younger, taller, my name wouldn't be Lurdes, it would be Teresa

or Isabel

or Fernanda

looking back at me from those balconies as if filled with curiosity as I busily open the box of a jigsaw puzzle that depicts an already elderly woman, standing at the front door, calling for someone or other, calling for someone

I presume

—Lurdes

anxiously calling for someone, her feather duster in her hand.

SATURDAY NIGHT IS THE SADDEST
NIGHT OF THE WEEK

ortunately, I have loads of friends who, ever since the separation, worry about me, phone me, invite me out to the movies, to supper, to concerts, knock on my door if they think I'm lonely, fill my living room with laughter and smoke so that afterward, when they leave, all I have to do is empty ashtrays, take the glasses into the kitchen, open the window to get rid of the cigarette smell, straighten the rugs, turn out the lights, and sit on the mattress staring at the buildings opposite, my chin on my knees, while the morning, what I presume to be the morning, helps me make out on the rug the black circle of a stain and in the Moroccan mirror something on my face that I would like to call a smile, something on my face that I do call a smile. Since I'm fortunate enough to have loads of friends, of course it's a smile. Besides, I'm a happy person, I enjoy life, I've never needed antidepressants or anything, and if no one can come over, I have my music, my books, letters I should have answered ages ago, envelopes full of photographs waiting for me to put them in the album, in the spaces left when I removed all the photos of my husband, the two of us on the beach, the two of us in Madrid, the two of us silent as we were during the last few months, he bored with me, indifferent, distant, I left the house earlier than usual so that he could pack his bags in peace, when I came back in the evening there wasn't a single shirt left in the drawers, not even the smell of him, not even a note, nothing. I walked up and down the corridor for a while, opening cupboards, I thought that he'd be back soon, I missed him, I felt like crying, but fortunately I have loads of friends, I'm a happy person, I've never needed antidepressants, and so I put a record on the record player and ate supper in the kitchen, and the apartment was so still, with no one changing the TV channel I was watching, no one leaving the toilet seat up, taking half the sheets, no shaving foam in the sink, everything clean, tidy, as quiet as a morgue, the two bedside tables all to myself, plenty of room for my summer clothes, the hollow in the sofa left by his body and me wanting to stroke that hollow and then, fortunately, the doorbell and two friends of mine and laughter and smoke, a—how can I describe it—melancholy that passes quickly, immediately after the second glass of whisky, carried off by an anecdote or the tickets for a concert on Saturday that I'm really looking forward to, some topclass Brazilian musicians, after the concert a discotheque, a bar, the attentions of a friend of a friend who treats me the way my husband never did, lighting my cigarettes, finding my opinions fascinating, bringing me home, me explaining that I'm tired, that I'm sleepy, perhaps another day, delicately removing his hand from my knee, turning my cheek just enough so that when we say goodnight he doesn't kiss me on the mouth, wiping my cheek with the back of my hand when he isn't looking, taking off my shoes in the elevator because my feet hurt, sitting in the larger hollow in the sofa beside the smaller hollow left by me, remembering that tomorrow is Sunday, lunch in Tróia, other people's children asking for ice cream, husbands like mine with their noses in their newspapers, going over to the balcony and the silence of the street, a line of parked cars, a line of trees, a dog sniffing the tires and vanishing around a corner, I like this neighborhood, with everything so close, even the beauty parlor, the butcher has known me since I was a child

—Good morning, Miss

my aunt, who's about my age, lives in the square over there, we talk a lot, we get along wonderfully, she's separated as well and still pretty, a married gentleman visits her in the afternoons, look-

ing all around before going into the building, I like this neighborhood, with everything so close, the supermarket, the stores, the
post office, the tax office, the police station, everything so close,
apart, that is, from my husband, not that I miss him, not that I need
him, I'm happy like this, I empty the ashtrays, take the glasses into
the kitchen, open the window to let out the cigarette smell, rest my
chin on my knees and I sit here waiting for the friend of a friend, for
the telephone, for the door, wishing I could sniff the tires of cars and
vanish around a corner.

THE SOUND OF MY BONES

Sometimes, when I'm alone at home, I hear singing far off. I mean: it seems to me that someone far off is singing to me, the voice of a woman I don't know or who got lost somewhere in the past. I get up from the sofa, go over to the window, and there's no one, just as there's no one in the bedroom, in the corridor, on the verandah. No one, and yet the voice continues to sing, not somewhere beyond the balcony, not in the square, inside the apartment, so where, perhaps in my head, but why? I find a dead butterfly on the windowsill, the plates sitting so still on the sideboard, the photo of my son on the shelf, all the lights out in the apartments across the street. How odd that I should be me, how strange that I should live here. Then I think: what's odd is thinking that me being me is odd, what's strange is thinking it strange that I should live here. I chose the apartment, I rented it, I bought the furniture. For years I liked it. Now there are times when it bores me: I wish that, just once, when I put the key in the door, I would find, for example, that the living room looked different. I don't know how, but different, in a way that would make me feel like I never wanted to leave it: the voice would come closer and I would meet the woman singing. My mother? I don't remember my mother singing, she was always standing at the stove looking serious and sighing. That's how I remember her: a serious person standing at the stove sighing. I have even fewer memories of my father: only an umbrella in the umbrella stand in the hallway, which I never dared touch. One of the ribs drooped in just the same way as the wing of a dead bat I saw once. I didn't have time to say

—Papa

and I don't miss him. Who can miss an umbrella in the umbrella stand in the hallway? I miss the voice if I don't hear it when I'm alone at home, the voice of the woman who got lost somewhere in the past. On Tuesday, in the little square below, I noticed a woman hanging out washing and whose gestures resembled the melody of the person who sings. A fairly young woman on a third-floor balcony. As soon as she disappeared, I felt like shouting

—We can't lose each other before we've even met

and instead I leaned against the wall and there I stayed, waiting. I made a decision: after the third red car, I'll get up, and after the third red car, I did. Since then I've avoided that square.

Now I'm alone in the apartment and I can hear the voice. I open a magazine at random, I cross my legs the other way, I put the magazine down. They're calling me from the past, even if my past is only a few sighs uttered over a stove and an umbrella in the hat stand in the hallway. In the upper part of that hat stand was an oval mirror, and in the mirror my mouth would smile at me from beneath a pair of grave eyes. I would rub my eyes with my right hand, they rubbed themselves with their left hand, which means that perhaps they weren't my eyes. I didn't like the idea of having eyes like that, the same eyes that look at me when I shave in the morning. They rummage around inside me, they change my features all the time. Fortunately, they're not watching me now that I've undone the catch on the verandah windows. From here to the sidewalk it's about twenty feet, twenty-five maximum. If I bring the bench in from the kitchen and stand on it, that's almost thirty feet. There are clouds over near the river, gray against the black sky, the silhouettes of rooftops, the lights along the bridge, the streetlights one after the other on the road to Almada. Nothing could be simpler: open the verandah windows, stand on top of the kitchen bench, and it's a drop of thirty feet. The voice has fallen silent, waiting. A few dogs run a few steps and stop to watch us, waiting for us to join them. Clouds over near the river, gray against the black sky. I lean out from the verandah, I open my arms. Tomorrow morning, will the woman hanging out her clothes read about it in the newspaper?

WILL YOU PLEASE STOP
BUGGING ME?

Alfredo said that he wasn't, but I have my doubts. It's not that I don't believe Alfredo: we were born on the same street, his mother treated us both the same, by which I mean that if she slapped him, she would slap me too, we went to the same school, did our military service in the same barracks, joined the same company, had a few girlfriends in common, shared a passion for billiards, got married within a week of each other, and then there are the lunches for four on Saturdays at my cousin's restaurant in Ginjal, where my cousin almost always comes over to the table to talk to us, but not only does he never knock a cent off the bill, he nearly always makes a mistake by adding to the bill a rice pudding that none of us ate. He'll get rich on those rice puddings one day. In fact, he's already starting to get rich: he gave his daughter a Jeep and intends opening a second restaurant in Almada. The restaurant hasn't gotten beyond the planning stage. His daughter, a fully fledged project, turned nineteen in March. The Jeep is brand new and, for a while now, I've noticed it hanging around Alfredo's building. In my role as my cousin's cousin and therefore as cousin, albeit once removed, of his daughter, I asked Alfredo if he was seeing the girl. Alfred said he wasn't, but I have my doubts.

I find this whole business irritating. I don't want to lose our lunches on Saturday in Ginjal, Alfredo's like a brother to me and I wouldn't want to put a stop, just like that, to forty years of friendship. Forty years, as our boss assures us, is a lifetime, especially forty years without a single argument, problem, suspicion or disagreement. The only thing that separates us is soccer: Alfredo never misses a game, and I take the opportunity to go for a little drive, my wife understands that we men need to go out, get some air, spend a little time at the café while they do the housework, well, during the week there's their job and the TV soap, and in my wife's case

and it's true

it has the advantage of my not getting in the way of the vacuum cleaner. So apart from three hours of soccer

an hour and a half of play, an hour and a half traveling

we're inseparable, until, that is, about a month or two ago, this business started with the Jeep, a hot-blooded young girl, and Alfredo

I can see him now

hesitating, giving in, thinking of me, hesitating again, giving in a little more, thinking of his wife, hesitating some more, looking at the girl and giving in entirely. And if the girl is as I imagine her to be, in no time at all he'll be getting divorced, and if he gets divorced, he'll be the one adding a rice pudding to our bill and running all my cousin's restaurants.

It worries me. Not that he might cheat me over a rice pudding nor that he might become a relative

it's difficult being a brother, being a relative is easy

it's the prospect of a divorce that worries me. Our wives, thank heavens, get along really well, phone each other, go shopping together, and if he does leave his wife, I really don't think it will be the same with the girl, given the difference in ages and tastes, and I can't imagine Amélia going out in the Jeep, not with her back. And then there's Alfredo's wife. And that, quite frankly, is where the problems begin. As long as Alfredo is married, it's fine: we have the three hours that the soccer lasts, we listen to the broadcast, and when the game finishes

—Right, sweetheart, I'd better leave before he comes back and catches me here

and Eunice, knowing that her husband and I are like brothers and that I would hate to hurt him, understands. But if he leaves her, that will change the picture entirely. She'll start asking me for things, pleading with me, making scenes, wanting me to leave Amélia, I want you to come and live here with me, I want this, I want that, in short, my whole life will be ruined. I'll tell her I can't, I'll say

—Will you please stop bugging me?

I'll have to tell lies right, left, and center, invent excuses, endure sleepless nights, lose my appetite. And I just won't put up with that. And so, to safeguard my friendship with Alfredo, I went to see my cousin and told him everything. My cousin packed his daughter off to stay with his brother-in-law in Venezuela, set her up in a dress shop, and she, from Caracas, declared on Tuesday that she's going out with the godson of a garage owner and has no intention of coming back. I bought the Jeep. My wife, poor thing, can't drive it

still that trouble with her back

so I go out in it while the soccer's on. Alfredo's wife has an excellent back, I pick her up and drop her off in a quiet road near here where no one will see us, and Alfredo and I remain inseparable. Our boss is right: although it may not seem it, forty years of friendship is a lifetime.

TAKE NO NOTICE OF ME
AND MY SUSPICIONS

I don't know how long I've been sitting here waiting for you. A quarter of an hour? Half an hour? I think: if ten red cars pass and she doesn't come, I'll leave. I think: I'll count from one to three hundred and if, when I reach three hundred, she still hasn't come, I'll ask for the bill. Twelve red cars pass and I'm still here. I reach four hundred twenty-three and continue to wait. I count backward from four hundred twenty-three to zero, certain that by the time I get to one hundred fifty, I'll see you arrive, waving to me as you walk between the tables of this sidewalk café, some problem at work, a phone call from your mother, the difficulty of finding a space for the Jeep in the parking lot. But given that your lipstick has slid from your mouth onto your cheek and that, as well as your own perfume, I'm pretty sure I can smell shaving lotion, I have some difficulty believing you. I say

—You have lipstick on your cheek

your eyes change but keep looking at me, then you get out your compact to look at your cheek, you ask me for a tissue, remove the lipstick, rummage around for the silver tube in the jumble of keys and diaries, redo your lips more slowly than usual as you search for an excuse, put everything back in your bag, and smile because you've come up with a lie, your eyes change again, your hand rests on mine, you order something or other from the waiter, your hand moves from my hand to my chin, you explain that it was all the fault of the Jeep's suspension that your lipstick missed the mark, you started applying your lipstick at a red light, the light changed to green, a van behind you honked, and it's hard for a woman to drive and make herself look sexy at the same time, it's difficult, you say, to pay attention simultaneously to your face in the rearview mirror and to the sobs of the traffic. Your hand leaves my chin, pinches my ear and when you pinch my ear, I almost believe you. The part of me that remains unconvinced goes on

—You smell of someone else's shaving lotion

the hand stroking my earlobe

(no one strokes my earlobe as you do)

hesitates, grows offended, your chair moves away indignantly, I notice that you sniff as if you had a runny nose, pick up the smell of the shaving lotion and move a little farther away so that I'll be less aware of it, I notice that you attempt a joke

—I was shaving my mustache

that, as usual, you defend yourself by attacking me

—It's impossible to live with a man who's suspicious all the time

that you try to resolve the matter by taking offense

—I find your lack of trust really hurtful

that you light a cigarette in the hope that the cigarette will cancel out the smell

it doesn't

you look prettier when you sulk, tempted by your beauty, it's my turn to stroke your earlobe, you push me away

—Stop it

consolidating your victory by demanding apologies, I say tentatively, afraid you might get up and leave

—Maybe I was wrong

and then I remember that the shaving lotion is the same one your cousin's husband uses, the guy who takes your Jeep to be serviced

—Carlos is so sweet, poor love

and who last summer drove you down to the Algarve because

you had some work commitment or other in Lisbon, while I went down two days earlier with the kids. I remember, too, that I phoned you in the evening and you didn't answer

—I must have slept like a log

that you had a dark mark on your arm, like a love bite. Carlos is taller than I am and has the voice of a radio announcer. He knows how to make people laugh. He calls me

—Shorty

and slaps me so hard on the back he nearly dislocates my vertebrae. You usually go out with him on the Jet Ski, and it seems to me that there's really no need for you to hold on to him quite so tightly when he performs those turns near the beach. Judging by the look on your cousin's face, I would say she agrees with me. I might be wrong. I must be wrong. Your sulky face is so lovely that I'm sure I'm wrong. After all, I don't take your Jeep to be serviced, when people are tired from working, they do sleep like logs, and you have to hold on tight because you never know with Jet Skis, your cousin exaggerates, why shouldn't you love a short guy like me with fragile vertebrae who pays too much attention to unimportant things like lipstick and shaving lotion. I drag my chair closer to yours and ask you to forgive me. Later, if you're in the mood

you rarely are in the mood

—We'll do it tomorrow, OK?

but we might . . . you know . . . except when we do, you just lie there staring at the ceiling with a kind of grimace on your face

no, it's not a grimace, of course it's not

and I, not noticing the love bite on your arm

you never let me give you a love bite on your arm

I, despite the love bite on your arm, settle myself more comfortably on the pillow, feeling

how can I put it?

satisfied, Fernanda, satisfied.

MY FATHER'S ROBUST HEALTH

Last week my mother went off with my father's best friend, Senhor Bentes. My sister and I can't understand why: Senhor Bentes is at least sixty, probably more, he has one front tooth missing, he wears glasses, and now and then he gets up
—Will you excuse me a moment
Senhor Bentes is at least polite
and goes inside, looking very pale, to give himself his diabetes injection. My father, on the other hand, has all his teeth and is in robust health. Robust health is my mother's expression
—You and your robust health, Agostinho
always said with a snarl, followed by various muttered angry comments that my sister and I try to wrap up in an apologetic smile, intended to indicate to Senhor Bentes that my mother's anger is just her way of showing affection. Senhor Bentes smiles back, thin and gaunt, perched on the end of the sofa, thoroughly approving of that robust health and that affection, he takes from his pocket a little box of sweeteners—I tried one once, it made the coffee taste sad—gives an ineffectual shrug of his narrow shoulders
—What I'd give to have your energy, Agostinho
and sits there stirring his coffee with the spoon, defeated by the sheer vitality of my father, who empties half the sugar bowl into his malt drink with a triumphant smile, thus emphasizing the size of his teeth and underlining his victory, while my mother

—Look at him, the pig

sits down grumpily on the sofa next to Senhor Bentes, in a way that gives me the impression that their fingers intertwine. When I mentioned this idea to my sister, she assured me I was exaggerating. I probably was. One, because my father weighs nearly two hundred pounds, and two, because Senhor Bentes's fingers are so thin that you'd hear them crack if my mother took hold of them. I didn't say anything to my father about all this: not only does he enjoy robust health, he's a very impulsive man and very free with his hands. My mother, who calls a spade a spade, says that he's always itching to whip someone, whereas Senhor Bentes, because he's so gentle, reminds her of the white mouse with pink eyes that my grandfather gave her when she was a child, only to step on it by accident two weeks later. This clearly upset her greatly because my grandfather had the mouse stuffed. It's still there, slightly lopsided and glassy-eyed, on the doily on the sideboard, next to the china St. Sebastian in which every arrow is a toothpick. After supper, my father pokes around in his mouth with the arrows, then puts them back in their place. The white mouse serves no good purpose apart from making my mother sigh each time she looks at it.

My sister thinks my mother will come back: if she had left for good, she would have taken the mouse. Maybe. But I have a feeling I heard her call Senhor Bentes

—My little white mouse

when she opened the door to him last month, just as I had a feeling that she passed one cautious hand over his small, fragile features. I could swear that Senhor Bentes squeaked. My sister suggested that maybe Senhor Bentes had asthma. Diabetics

according to the *Family Medical Encyclopedia*

tire very easily. Anyway, last week my mother disappeared, and Senhor Bentes's godmother, with whom Senhor Bentes lives, told us that her godson also had disappeared. Add to this the fact that the woman in the basement apartment swore that a cousin of hers saw them in a boardinghouse in Torres Vedras and that my mother assured him she was going to Spain to live

—With a little white mouse I happen to know
meanwhile telling Senhor Bentes
—It's time for your insulin, snookums
to which Senhor Bentes replied
—Will you excuse me a moment
and went inside looking very pale. My sister doesn't believe any
of this. In her opinion, people love inventing stories, and other people's happiness makes them feel uncomfortable. By happiness my
sister means the conjugal life

the *Family Medical Encyclopedia* is always talking about conjugal
life

of my parents. But I'm not so sure. I keep going over and over it in
my head and I'm not at all sure. Before Senhor Bentes there was Senhor Cosme, before Senhor Cosme there was Senhor Osvaldo. All of
them thin and gaunt. All of them very polite. All of them small. Not as
small, thin and gaunt as Senhor Bentes, but still very small. I'm trying
to summon the courage to talk about this with my father, to sound
him out, to ask him what he thinks. Maybe he doesn't think anything.
Since my mother vanished, he has barely left the garden. He carried
the bench from the kitchen out into the middle of the cabbage patch
along with the china St. Sebastian and he spends the nights cleaning
his teeth with a toothpick and counting the stars above the loquat
tree. When my sister calls him for supper he replies
—Two hundred thirty-two
or
—Three hundred seventy-four
and waves her away with his hand. None of us has ever known
him to cry: it's harder to see the sky if you cry. For my part, I don't
think my father is the type to shed tears. Enjoying robust health is
enough to make anyone happy. I don't know how many stars he's
gotten to now
eight hundred?
nine hundred?
but scattered around the trunk of the loquat tree are about twenty
of St. Sebastian's arrows.

THE THING THAT I'VE BECOME

Some days I just feel so tired. It isn't the job, it isn't the kids, it isn't everything I have to do when I get home, it isn't even my husband. I start feeling tired when I park the car in the garage, when I press the elevator button, when I open the door to the apartment, and at the precise moment when the kids and my husband, as one, look up from the TV and smile at me, I realize just how exhausted I am and I don't know why. They've set the table already and all I have to do is heat up the supper that the maid has left in the microwave. Next to the microwave is the change from the shopping and a note on the pad that ends See you tomorrow. Her slippers are out on the verandah next to the mop, and they look so lonely that I almost feel like screaming. Why? Questions, questions. In blue lettering on the ballpoint pen we use to write to each other are the words Hotel Palmenhof, Frankfurt. I don't know who brought it. Who did bring it? More questions. Has it always been like this? I just hope to God no one asks me how my day went, I just hope to God they let me put away the dishes in peace and shake the crumbs off the tablecloth over the balcony feeling as if I were shaking my life. My oldest son is playing hopscotch in the corridor, my husband is playing backgammon on the computer, there's that dry twig in the vase with something about it that resembles me, that resembles the thing I've become. I just hope my sister doesn't phone to invite us to Ericeira on Sunday. My youngest son must have fallen asleep on the sofa. We undress him, put on his pajamas and as soon as we lay him down in his bed, he wakes up. We turn off the light and he lies there in the dark, his eyes obstinately open. My husband kisses me on the neck as we go back into the living room and the smell of him pleases and displeases me. A damp feeling on the back of my neck as if a snail had left its slime there. I hang back to wipe away the slime without his noticing. Or wait until the backgammon starts again. The small mud stain on his shoes suddenly seems enormous. Despite the armchair and the magazine my eyes keep wandering off to fix on that stain. My oldest son says goodnight to us with his mouth full of toothpaste and wearing his favorite slippers, which are two stupidly radiant Mickey Mouses. The Mickey Mouses disappear in silence and after a few minutes, as soon as the computer is turned off and my husband comes and sits on the arm of my armchair, I get up on the pretext of going to check to see if the eyes of our youngest son are still obstinately open in the dark. Through the curtains at the window, in the spaces between the streetlights, the trees in the park wave slowly. I turn on the light in the bathroom, put on a headband, and take off my makeup. Even after twelve years, the sight of my wedding ring in the mirror still surprises me. I hear my husband sorting out things in his briefcase for the next day, the TV screen becomes a tiny vanishing incandescent dot. Without makeup my face has emptied, I no longer have eyelashes, eyebrows or mouth, I have the feeling that a child, wearing my clothes, is staring at me in horror. In the morning I change her as quickly as I can into a grown-up so that my husband won't see her, and now I lie down with my back to him afraid that he might find her. A knee between my legs, a chest brushing against me, a finger rolling and unrolling a lock of my hair, stroking my ear, tracing my profile, a foot tickling my foot, the unbearable little heartbeat of a wristwatch, the smell that both pleases and displeases me. I ask him to turn off the bedside lamp, an elbow reaches across my cheek, finds the switch, is transformed into more fingers, which, amid incomprehensible whispers, hurriedly, urgently unbutton me. When I get up for a drink of water, the trees in the park wave in the spaces between the streetlights. I lean against the tiled wall and see the slippers on the verandah, beside the mop. They're just as lonely as before, but now I feel not the slightest desire to scream.

A FEELING OF
OH, WHAT'S THE POINT

I don't need you to say or do anything, it's good that you're here, that's quite enough. I haven't changed the color of the sofas, the curtains are the same, the painting you brought with you when you were single and that I never liked

(my mother gave it to me, you said, and I never contradicted you, though I didn't believe it)

is still there opposite me above the bar cart, the photo of us in Foz has a place of honor on the shelf, the homes and gardens magazine you left open when you left

("Ten ideas from ten Portuguese interior designers to enliven those dead areas in your home")

waits on the armchair where you always used to sit, assuring me that with a little imagination and taste we could change our life for the better. I was probably the one who lacked imagination and taste: weekends just leave me feeling helpless, all those empty hours I don't know how to fill, a movie perhaps, a trip to the beach, a museum

but which movie, which beach, which museum?

your bored face going back and forth between the bedroom and the living room, your reluctant feet, with nothing to do, the angry silence, the perpetual

—You choose

waiting for the salvation of a phone call from one of your girl-

friends inviting us out to one of those couples' evenings where I
shrivel up and say nothing, with a glass of whisky or a vodka far
away at the end of my arm, listening to the pointless, fascinating
rhetoric of others

politics, work, a week in Madrid, things like that

conversations that seem to me

(because I lack imagination and taste)

of no interest, immensely long, expendable, me nodding, eyes
drooping, until someone says

—Your husband's dozed off, Liliana

and then the burst of indulgent mockery around me, the whisky
or the vodka, which they take from me before I drop it, the glassy
cascade of a guffaw whose sharp edges wound me, you on the other
side of the room, fenced round by gestures, smiles, discussions
about jazz

—The big surprise would be if he didn't

surrounded by women and men positively bursting with imagination and taste, and so happy, dear God, so capable of amusing
you, so skilled at talking about everything while I fidget in a chair
that doesn't fit me, wishing I were home looking at the painting you
brought with you when you were single and that I never liked

(I know your mother gave it to you, well, let's pretend that she
did, there's no harm in pretending your mother gave it to you)

a painting that seems suddenly pleasant, restful, pretty, wishing
I could read the paper in peace and feel your presence behind and
in front of the homes and gardens magazine even if I can't actually
see you

(Enliven those dead areas in your home)

thinking about how to enliven the dead areas in your life, which
is to say, your marriage to me, which is to say, me, which is to say,
the endless lethargic yawn that, and it's entirely my fault

(of course it's my fault, what did you do wrong?)

the endless lethargic yawn, as I was saying, which you, through
no fault of your own, have become. What could I possibly do to

charm you? Being a salesman for a company selling agricultural machinery doesn't thrill anyone, especially when the size of the salary is in inverse proportion to that of the tractors, I enjoy silence, a lot of noise and fuss unsettles me, having to be friendly and ready to be amused wears me out, I always laugh at the wrong moment and it always rings false, I don't understand jazz, I don't keep up with which princesses have just gotten divorced

(it's my lack of taste, I'm a hopeless case)

nor with which top models have found passion with tiny, plump Egyptian millionaires and claim that the money gets in the way of their love, I don't need an apartment in the Algarve

(we rent one each summer)

nor do I need to travel down there in the Renault towing a Jet Ski, and when you tell me yet again that my problem

(I have various problems)

that one of my problems is that I have no dreams, and when you gaze at me sadly, I would, I think, look up at you, from the safety of the newspaper, with a face empty of everything except genuine incomprehension, because I feel comfortable with you, I feel comfortable with you now when you've just rung the doorbell and come into the apartment with a young man

—This is Carlos

whom I recollect meeting at one of those evenings of mutual self-celebration, you sat down for a moment in the armchair, glanced around shaking your head with a look on your face as if you missed the place even though you felt irritated, even though you were bored, and said that you'd come to pick up the rest of your clothes, although I don't need you to say or do anything, it's good that you're here

even if you are here with Carlos

and that's quite enough. I haven't changed the color of the sofas, the curtains are still the same, the photo of us in Foz has a place of honor on the shelf. Perhaps one of these days I'll read those ten suggestions for enlivening the dead areas in my home from those ten Portuguese interior designers with imagination and good taste. And perhaps because, at moments like this, even with Carlos here, even if you have only come to pick up the rest of your clothes, I feel that the apartment is complete. And when you close the door, when you leave, I can pick up the paper and sit reading it for hours, trembling and blinking every time an ambulance drives down the street.

NIGHT FALLING ON
THE GERANIUMS

My old man died yesterday. Alone. My sister and I used to drop by in the evening, after work. My sister, who is married, would cook him his supper and then go home to get supper for her son, I'd stay on, and we'd talk about this and that in the kitchen, by the door that opens onto the garden, watching the night fall on the geraniums. If I ever have to spend a week without going to my old man's house, the first memory that comes to mind is of night falling on the geraniums, the way the dark starts from below and creeps up the walls until it reaches the top of the acacia tree and from the top of the acacia tree takes a little leap up into the sky. That's the moment when the streetlights come on and we notice the first star. Then my old man and I would bring our chairs indoors and stop talking.

I don't know what will happen now. I suppose my sister will want to sell the house, buy somewhere better for her family and no longer have to sleep out on the closed-in verandah with her husband. With my half I can find something for myself as well, two rooms will be enough, I've never put much emphasis on furniture or luxuries and the company of the cat doesn't take up any space. But I'm really going to miss watching the night falling on the geraniums. My old man would have been seventy in March and apart from a problem with bladder stones, he'd never been ill. He brought me and my sister up

(I never knew my mother)

he worked as a motorbike mechanic and on Sundays played French billiards at the Académico. However hard he tried, he was never much good with a cue in his hand, and I think my old man considered that lack of talent to be worse than a physical defect. In contrast, I like books

(which he also thought was worse than a physical defect)

especially novels about war and books about animals and, in my old man's opinion, I ruined my eyesight with my mania for reading, which is why I have to wear glasses. He may have been right. But on Sundays, a man with no one beside him is bound to get bored, the cat only comes to see me if there's no food in its bowl and since I don't like movies or going for walks, I entertain myself by turning pages. The last story I read

(I finished it last week)

was about lions, that is, about the friendship between a lion and a man. It takes place in a circus, the man's a lion tamer, the lion dies in the end and the man is so heartbroken that he stops being a lion tamer and starts begging in the streets instead. I very nearly cried. In fact, I did cry, I didn't sob or anything, but I did shed a tear or two. If my old man knew about it, he'd be furious. I can say this now because he can't get furious with anyone. When I arrived at his house, I found that my sister, instead of making the old man's supper, was busy shaving and dressing him with the help of a cousin of ours. She didn't have to explain. I left her pressing the suit and the shirt that my old man had been keeping for a special occasion he'd never had the chance to enjoy and I went to the undertaker's two blocks from where I work. It was late and the assistant was putting up the shutters. He didn't seem too happy about having to come with me with his tape measure and the catalogue of coffins for us to choose from:

—I assume you'll want this one

he said, showing us the cheapest model. My sister, who was putting shoes on my old man and polishing them with a brush, nodded. The assistant made a note of the measurements and left almost at the same time as my sister, who was anxious to get back and make her son's supper. At first, I stayed in the bedroom staring at the gleaming tips of my father's shoes and at his hands, which lay so naturally on his belly. Then I thought about the night falling on the geraniums, took a chair out into the garden and sat there. The darkness had crept up the walls and reached the top of the acacia tree, the streetlights were lit, and I saw the first star in its usual place, between the chimney pots. It seemed a shame not to sit and watch the night, so I brought out a second chair and sat on in the garden. I thought perhaps my old man would get up from the damask bedspread and come and keep me company, neither of us saying anything, with him thinking about French billiards and me about lions.

MY DEATH

I don't talk much. No, I don't talk much, indeed, I talk less and less. In the first place because I get distracted during conversations and lose the thread, and in the second place because people don't expect me to respond, but to listen, which is easy enough if I just nod occasionally and say

—Of course

when they look at me with raised eyebrows waiting for agreement and applause. I have become a specialist in the

—Of course

which I can say in twenty-three different ways depending on the angry or urgent look

(or lack of either)

on my interlocutor's face, and if they ask in surprise

—Of course what?

I merely give an enigmatic, subtly approving smile so that they, reassured, throw aside their doubts, smugly clap me on the back, and say with a relieved sigh

—I knew you'd agree with me

and if they launch into some tortuous story in which I lose myself on the first bend, I continue to murmur while thinking of something else entirely

—Of course

in the pauses they leave for me now and then, pauses intended to be filled by my admiration or my applause. Because even if I don't speak

(and I don't)

I'm on their side, I'm always on their side, and I'm on their side because I've heard nothing and because I loathe arguing and being right, I loathe opinions, convictions, motives. That's why I stick to

—Of course

and to the silent nod. Earnest. Frowning. Fraternal. Sometimes I replace that form of applause with a sigh that means

—I know, I've been there

or by the adverb

—Exactly

which, contrary to what you might think, is the vaguest, most innocuous and stimulating of comments, the one that allows my companion to explore the many different variations of his theme, to confront them, to select them, to refute them, to bat them around, to assess their density and weight

—Exactly

which I usually follow up with

—That's exactly right

which up until now has always met with success. That's why I can't understand what happened last week, when Pedro called me to arrange to meet at the café next to his house. I ordered hot water and lemon while he ordered coffee and began to talk. It was three o'clock in the afternoon, and the only other people present were an elderly gentleman sitting doing a crossword at a table by the window and the waiter behind the counter polishing glasses. And the reason I can't understand what happened is that I behaved as I always do. I said

—Of course

I nodded, I smiled in an enigmatic, encouraging fashion, and, on four or five occasions, murmured

—That's exactly right

I sighed in solidarity

—I know, I've been there

Pedro clapped me smugly on the back

—I knew you'd agree with me

and I added, thinking of Ana, of Ana's body, of Ana's kisses

—If I were you, I'd do just the same

and I don't know what it was that made him take out a gun and shoot me twice in the chest.

What worries me most is the thought of Ana being left alone with the children now that her husband's in prison. The other thing that worries me is that I can't go and visit her because I'm stuck here in the hospital connected up to this machine. It's unlikely I'll ever see her again: the doctor has agreed to wait until my youngest sister arrives from Fundão to say good-bye to me before they pull the plug.

SOMETHING LIKE THAT

We live here, in this little house right by the station, with a bed of geraniums growing out back. Since our parents died, we've often thought, my sister and I, about selling out and buying an apartment in the center, even if it's only small

(we'd never get much money for the house and our pensions aren't exactly generous)

yes, buying an apartment in the center to escape the trains.

The railroad station is fifty yards at most from the little living room where, after lunch, my sister does her crochet work and I pass the time with my stamp collection

(apart from the living room we have two bedrooms, the kitchen and a sink in the yard, beneath a porch with a fragment of mirror hanging from a nail and our two toothbrushes on a little cast-iron shelf)

and every five minutes or so the whole house shakes as a train passes, we put the plaster cat in the very middle of the table so that it doesn't fall off and break, we push the glasses and the bottles right to the back of the sideboard, and we've taken to laying any photographs flat since last month, when the glass in one frame broke and tore in two our father's smile in a picture taken thirty or forty years ago, in the days when he was the age I am now and worked in the notary's office in Queluz.

I can remember so clearly what he looked like then, small and thin, with a dozen or so sparse hairs dragged across his bald pate from his left ear to his right, the hairs shiny with gel, stuck to the skin of his skull with such energy that they didn't even vibrate with the clatter of the passing trains.

The problem for my sister and me isn't the fact that the house shakes, or that we can't sleep because of the bells at the grade crossing and the whistles from the trains. It isn't just the cracks in the ceiling and the walls or the smoke that blackens the curtains, the sheets, and the petals from the geraniums that my sister usually picks and places in the living room in a little glass vase underneath the calendar frozen at March 1972, the month our mother died. The real problem is the passengers.

For anyone leaving the station, ours is the first house on the way to the stop for the buses into town. Otherwise, there's only a bit of scrubby wasteland that serves as the local garbage dump, full of leftover food, trash, broken pots and pans and even a lion-footed bathtub in which the mice have made a nest, as well as a shortcut that leads to the school and to the place where the circus with its threadbare tigers pitches its tent at Christmas and at Easter. It isn't a circus full of international performers, caravans with strange number plates and Russian trapeze artists: it's just two trucks that drive down from the North, with the tent, the tent pegs, the benches for the audience, and the sentry-box-cum-ticket-booth stolen from some derelict barracks.

The clowns arrive later, by train, and they invade our house. That's why my sister and I are thinking of selling out and buying an apartment in the center, even if it's only small, even if it's a basement apartment, even, if it's all we can afford, a superintendent's apartment. My sister has already said that she wouldn't mind cleaning the stairs and carrying the trash down from the landings to the street, and it wouldn't bother me in the least running errands for the tenants, buying cigarettes or paying their gas or phone bills. I don't care, as long as we can rid ourselves of the clowns.

The business with the passengers started seven months ago, if that. I remember it perfectly because it was my sister's birthday and it was a Sunday. I had bought her some earrings at the craft shop and a cake with one candle on it, one of those cream sponge cakes she likes. I was just about to light the candle when they knocked at the door.

At first I thought it was a cousin of ours, then I realized it couldn't be because she's in the hospital with a kidney stone and then it occurred to me that, apart from my cousin, we don't have any close friends. More knocking, I peered out of the window and outside, carrying a suitcase and wearing a red nose, huge shoes and a saxophone, stood a poor clown, crying.

My sister's birthday was ruined of course. The clown ate the lighted candle from the cake, deposited himself on my father's wicker chair and sat there staring at us from beneath his furry orange eyebrows and blowing one long interminable note on his saxophone while the tears streamed down his painted face.

My sister and I are by nature discreet, and we didn't dare ask him anything, and he didn't say anything either. He didn't even open his mouth when there was another knock at the door and in walked two more clowns. They must have been twins because they were dressed identically, in striped T-shirts and purple suspenders, and in their hatbands they had sunflowers that occasionally sent out a jet of water that stained our sofa. That night we had to sleep in the kitchen, and the fridge kept shuddering and whirring.

Ever since, even when the circus doesn't have its tent pitched on the square, we've been afraid of the trains. We hear the passengers taking the shortcut to the school and we sit waiting for one of them to knock on the door. We're afraid. Afraid of the clowns who cry and the ones who wear sunflowers in their hats. My sister stopped doing her crochet work and I abandoned my stamp collection. That was when we decided to take the bus into Lisbon.

For four days now we've been drinking milky coffees and eating cupcakes in the cafés in Praça do Chile, four days ago we put an advertisement in the newspaper to sell the house. The only thing that pains us is the thought that the clowns will forget to put the plaster cat right in the middle of the table. We would never forgive them if, as the railroad cars come shuddering past, it fell to the floor and was broken. Our mother adored the creature. But, as I tell my sister, we have to sell the house. We might find a buyer who, having approved of the living room, the bedrooms, the kitchen and the outside sink, won't mind if he finds a man with a saxophone and orange eyebrows quietly weeping among the geraniums.

CONJUGAL LOVE

I've been married for twenty-four years and I don't know whether I like being married or whether I've simply gotten used to it. I don't get excited at the thought of my husband coming home from work every day at half past six or seven, but it's not unpleasant either. I'm not crazy about the fact that I have to spend the whole month of August with him and the kids, but I don't hate it either. Making love isn't the most wonderful thing in the world, but I couldn't say it was a total drag either. Zé Tó has a sense of humor, he's not ugly, he's not stupid, he still doesn't have much of a belly, he's not bad for his age at all, he brings me flowers now and then, he buys me perfume from the duty-free shop when he comes back from meetings in London. I started going out with him when I was seventeen, I've never slept with anyone else, and I can't honestly imagine ever sleeping with anyone else and yet, you see, I don't know whether I love him or whether I've just gotten used to him. I think I love him when I compare him with other men, with my friends' husbands, for example, with my brothers-in-law, but when I see a film starring Robert de Niro, I think that I've just gotten used to him. It's not that Robert de Niro is handsome or anything: it's his smile, it's something about his eyes, it's the emptiness I feel inside me when the lights go up and instead of Robert de Niro, Zé Tó is sitting in the next seat, Zé Tó is beside me in the car, Zé Tó is asking me in Portuguese whether the maid has pressed his gray pants, the faucet in the bathroom is running, and I'm already in bed, and it's Zé Tó in his pajamas who lies down at my left side with those magazines about Jeeps and SUVs that he loves to read, it's Zé Tó who gives me a kiss and turns out the light, it's Zé Tó's heel touching my leg, it's Zé Tó who falls asleep with such irritating speed and leaves me alone in the darkness staring up at the ceiling waiting for the sleep that doesn't come, which won't come, which takes ages to arrive. Obviously if Robert de Niro were actually here, I wouldn't even want him. He probably has all kinds of irritating habits, he's bound to be self-centered, he might be into making model planes or something equally stupid, he would probably cheat on me right, left, and center with Hollywood actresses

(and here I am pushing forty-six and, although I may not be ugly, I'm not exactly Jessica Lange)

and my life would become a hell of jealousy and silly marital spats.

Sometimes, you see, I wonder what it is that makes me wonder whether I still love Zé Tó or whether I've just gotten used to him, sometimes I ask myself if it matters whether or not I love him, if love really matters, if the most important thing isn't, in fact, friendship, companionship

(that's an awful word, a Boy Scout word, isn't it, a dreadful word, I think, but I can't come up with another)

the kids are great, no trouble at all, they're not into drugs, they're both in college, they've never totaled the car, they worry about us a lot, especially Diogo, because Bernardo was always the more independent of the two, but that's not to say he's not a real sweetie too, sometimes I ask myself if the most important thing isn't, in fact, complicity

(I don't like that word either, it makes me think of armed robberies)

the absence of arguments, Zé Tó's good nature, the way he puts up with my moods, with the slightly prickly temperament I inherited from my father, with my desire to have a boob job, a face-lift, to

look like the person I was even if, when I smile, I end up feeling like
the corners of my mouth are going to tear with a sound like splitting fabric. I'm so glad you agree with me, that takes such a load off
my mind, I'm so glad you think friendship is more important than
love, friendship and companionship

(that word again, dammit)

the kids, complicity

(that other word)

the absence of arguments, Zé Tó's good nature, I'm so glad that
you don't think I should worry about whether I love him or whether
I've just gotten used to him, I'm so glad you've invited me out to
supper, but I can't possibly meet you for supper, doctor, what would
I tell Zé Tó, but we could perhaps make it lunch on Friday in a restaurant that's not too near your office or my apartment, and preferably where we won't meet anyone we know, there's even something
about you that reminds me of Robert de Niro, your smile, something about your eyes, as soon as I came in I thought

—This psychiatrist reminds me of Robert de Niro, I'm sure we're
going to get along really well

and now I'm convinced we're going to get along well, I'm convinced that after lunch we're going to get along like a house afire.

ABOUT THE PHOTOGRAPHY

The author wishes to thank Antonio Pedro Ferreira, Augusto Brazio, and Pedro Loureiro for graciously allowing a selection of photographs to be used in this book. Antonio Pedro Ferreira's work is on pages 62, 76, 90, 170, 256, 262, 296, 310, 316, and 354. Pedro Loureiro's work is on pages 108 and 152. Augusto Brazio's work can be found on pages 4, 23, 38, 103, 164, 204, 227, 228, and 384.

ABOUT THE TRANSLATOR

Margaret Jull Costa has worked as a translator of Portuguese, Spanish, and Latin-American writers for over twenty years. In 1992 she was joint recipient of the Portuguese Translation Prize for Fernando Pessoa's *The Book of Disquiet*, and in 1997 she won the translator's portion of the International IMPAC Dublin Literary Award for *A Heart So White* by Javier Marías. In 2000 she was awarded the Oxford-Weidenfeld Translation Prize for Nobel Laureate José Saramago's *All the Names*, and in 2006 her translation of Javier Marías's *Your Face Tomorrow: Fever and Spear* won the Premio Valle-Inclán. Most recently, in 2008, her version of Eça de Queirós's masterpiece *The Maias* brought her both the PEN/Book-of-the-Month Club Translation Prize and, for the second time, the Oxford-Weidenfeld Translation Prize. Other authors whose work she has translated include Bernardo Atxaga, Ramón del Valle-Inclán, Mário de Sá-Carneiro, Luis Fernando Verissimo, and Lídia Jorge.

ABOUT THE AUTHOR

Born in Lisbon on September 1, 1942, António Lobo Antunes grew up during the repressive years of the Salazar dictatorship. He was 31 when the Carnation Revolution transformed Portugal from a virtual police state into a liberal democracy, but the political repression he experienced during his youth greatly influenced his adult consciousness and would inform much of his fiction.

At the urging of his father, Lobo Antunes opted as a young man to go to medical school, where he specialized in psychiatry. Required to serve in the Army, he became a military doctor in Portugal's doomed colonial war in Angola, an experience that influenced many of his novels. After his return to Lisbon in 1973, he began working as a clinical psychiatrist before devoting himself primarily to literature.

António Lobo Antunes has written 18 novels that have been translated into more than 20 languages. His first novel, *Elephant Memory,* was published in 1979. In the same year, his second novel, *South of Nowhere,* a frantic monologue by a former soldier in Angola delivered to a lonely woman he meets in a bar, was published to international acclaim. His more recent novels, *The Inquisitors' Manual,* about life during the Salazar dictatorship, and *The Return of the Caravels,* about the breakup of Portugal's colonial dominion in the 1970s, have both been named *New York Times* Notable Books of the Year.

António Lobo Antunes is considered by many the greatest novelist on the Iberian Peninsula. For George Steiner he is the "heir to Conrad and Faulkner." In fact, the *Los Angeles Times Book Review* commented that Antunes writes "with the insight of Faulkner, of a man who knows the scent and taste of the dust from which his characters are begotten."

António Lobo Antunes has received numerous literary awards, including the Jerusalem Prize for the Freedom of the Individual in Society (2005) and the Camões Prize, the most important literary prize for the Portuguese language (2007). He lives in Lisbon.